Basic Skills
of
Horse Riding
A Manual of Self-Instruction

Tris Roberts

J. A. Allen : London

British Library Cataloguing in Publication Data

Roberts, Tristan D. M.
  The basic skills of horseriding
  I. Horsemanship
  I. Title
  798.2'3   SF309

ISBN 0-85131-391-4

Published in Great Britain in 1985 by
J. A. Allen & Company Limited,
1, Lower Grosvenor Place, Buckingham Palace Road,
London, SW1 0EL

Book production Bill Ireson

Filmset by
Fakenham Photosetting Limited, Fakenham, Norfolk

Printed and bound by
Biddles Limited, Guildford, Surrey

Preface

After many years both as pupil and as teacher, I have come to the conclusion that the pupil's most effective instructor is himself. The teacher can, however, manipulate the conditions so as to enable the pupil to acquire desirable rather than undesirable habits.

How this can best be done is, of course, a matter of opinion, as the many books of instruction will show. I have tried out the advice given by the various classical masters of equitation, from Xenophon to the present day, and have worked out what I believe the pupil needs to know at each stage. I have set this out as a manual of self-instruction since this seems to me a sensible and practical way to help the pupil to learn the basic skills of horse riding.

I have adopted a step-by-step approach, starting with catching the horse and proceeding up to competition standard of horse riding, illustrating the text with my own line drawings, all created from photographs. Almost inevitably, when a photograph is taken, either horse or rider is not quite in the position one would regard as ideal. Sometimes the deviations from the ideal are instructive and I have occasionally drawn attention to these in the annotations and captions.

It is my hope that, in putting into practice the ideas presented in this book, the reader will get as much pleasure as I myself have had from writing it.

Tris Roberts

Contents

List of Illustrations

Acknowledgements

I am grateful to the many pupils, both riders and horses, who have unwittingly helped in the preparation of this book. There are others, however, who have helped more directly.

It gives me particular pleasure to acknowledge my indebtedness to Mr. Charles Harris, F.I.H., F.B.H.S., who encouraged me to go ahead when I first outlined to him my plan for this book. He has also commented on a late draft in detailed correspondence, leading me to a number of useful clarifications. I regard his advice as especially authoritative in view of his long experience of classical equitation, which has included a number of years at the Spanish Riding School in Vienna. Nevertheless, he should not be taken as necessarily agreeing with everything in the book.

At all stages in the preparation of the book I have greatly appreciated the benefit of frequent and helpful discussions with Mr. John D. Christie, who has also checked the proofs.

My thanks are due too to my publisher and his staff for advice and encouragement, and for contributing many valuable suggestions for improving the text itself.

Introduction

The teaching of the art of horsemanship has for centuries been primarily by oral tradition. The various related skills were at one time as commonplace as those involved in the wearing of clothes. The coming of the motor-car changed all that. Riding became virtually restricted to racing and to those who rode to hounds. More recently, however, with the extensive television coverage of show-jumping, there has been a great revival of interest. As a result, effective instructors are in rather short supply and their services have correspondingly become more expensive. Many people are buying horses for themselves and ponies for their children and they are finding that the management of a horse of one's own is a very different matter from just sitting on a well-schooled horse in a riding school. They also find themselves acting as impromptu instructors to visitors and friends who will inevitably be invited to "have a go".

There are many books about horses and about various aspects of riding. To get the best out of them, however, the reader generally needs to be familiar with the oral tradition of riding instruction as presented at a riding school or at meetings of the Pony Club.

Much of what has been written is concerned with what the instructor sees when he looks at his mounted pupil from the side. Meanwhile the movements of the horse are presenting problems to the rider of which the instructor may well be unaware. In effect, the rider learns to sit his horse in much the same way as one learns to ride a bicycle. That is to say, one learns for oneself from direct experience in a prepared situation, rather than from the remarks of the instructor.

The horse is a pupil, just as much as the rider. He signals his doubts, as well as his understanding, by the movements he makes in response to the rider's commands. If the rider will pay attention to what the horse is telling him he will have, I believe, a greatly increased chance of developing a harmonious relationship with his horse. This should lead to greater enjoyment, as well as to improved performance.

My purpose in writing this book has been to help the reader to organise his own self-instruction in equestrianism. The effectiveness of any instruction depends greatly upon the context in which it is given. I have attempted to provide a context by guiding the reader's curiosity, indicating where he should direct his attention, and hoping to build up relevant expectations so that he can see the point of each piece of advice as it is presented.

I have tried to indicate what sensations the rider can expect to encounter and what sorts of things he should feel for in order to establish a rapport and keep up a "conversation" with his horse. I have also tried to explain some of the moves that the experienced rider carries out without thinking. (Often such subconscious moves are essential for the successful execution of a particular manoeuvre but the beginner is usually faced with a long series of awkward failures before he accidentally discovers the moves for himself.) Naturally, as each topic is introduced in turn, the reader will find in this book much that can also be found in many other texts, but in each topic I have tried to add something to explain the way in which horse and rider interact.

It is not uncommon to find that the instructions given to a pupil telling him how to execute a specific manoeuvre, such as starting the canter or making a turn on the forehand, differ widely according to who is doing the instructing. Different books on riding and different riding schools all propound their own preferred systems, often contradicting one another with some scorn. I have tried out the various alternatives known to me and have selected for presentation in this book those routines that I have found to work best.

The basic problem in getting your horse to do what you want is one of communication. He needs to understand you and you need to be aware of his doubts and problems. There should be a continual exchange of signals. Once you know what to look for you will come to realise that the horse is all the time "talking" to you with little signs and gestures. Keep up the conversation by talking back, not only with your voice, but with every part of you, your attitude, your mood, your tone of voice and, particularly, your contact with his body.

My intention, then, is to reinforce and guide your own observations of your interaction with the horse. Read a little, try something out, read about it again, and so on. In this way you will be able to make progress, and perhaps avoid developing bad habits, without having to rely too much on the personal attendance of an instructor. I have concentrated on those aspects of riding that you can undertake on your own, but I have included all the manoeuvres needed for even quite advanced dressage tests. When you enter competitions you will meet many people prepared to offer friendly advice. Test out each suggestion for yourself and make up your own mind which ideas suit the particular combination of yourself and your horse. What works for one rider may not work for another.

The importance of the hard hat cannot be overemphasised. Don't ride without it! I always wear mine. Several times it has saved me from injury. On one occasion, although my hat was smashed in a fall, I myself suffered no ill effects.

An enthusiastic youngster may wish to proceed quickly through the stages of walk, trot, canter and jump without pausing to examine the niceties of any of these. However, since all the refinements of skilled execution depend upon a secure groundwork in the basic essentials, it is convenient to treat each topic in depth as it arises. We shall start with the needs and problems of the beginner and develop each topic in enough detail to be of interest to the experienced rider before passing on to the next topic.

1 Preliminaries

When you go to buy your first horse, take with you someone who knows about such matters and who can advise you. You will also probably have helpers around when the horse arrives home. Learn from all these people but do not be distracted and watch carefully how the horse behaves when he is let out into the field in which he will live.

Greetings and threats between horses

If there are other horses in the field, keep his halter on for a while and take him round to meet the others. They will probably come thundering up to investigate anyway. Keep talking to the horse throughout this encounter. It will relieve tension and establish a placid atmosphere.

Notice how the horses greet one another, tentatively advancing their noses and blowing at one another with heads raised and ears pricked forward (*Figure 1.1*). Sometimes they will snort a little, or squeal and do a little shuffle or dance with the forelegs. By these "greeting ceremonies" the newcomer is helped to find his place in the social structure of the herd. You will need to imitate some of the greetings when you come for your horse on the following day.

When horses are free and in a group they use many signals to one another. Friendliness is indicated by nuzzling. You will see a pair of horses each nuzzling the other at the base of the neck (*Figure 1.2*). On a hot day they stand side by side, head to tail, so that each benefits from the other's tail-swishing to keep away flies. A more active friendly game, with a hint of rivalry

Figure 1.1
First greeting. A tentative approach of noses.

Figure 1.2
Nuzzling caresses. Favoured places are the sides and root of the neck and the region just behind the elbow.

in it, is for each member of a pair to nibble at the sides of the other's face, using only his lips. To do this he has to lift his head, and if the other is also trying to do the same, he will lift his head too. The pair then seem to be fencing with one another (*Figure 1.3*). They may stand together in this play for

Figure 1.3
Horses "fencing". Each tries to nibble the other near the angle of the mouth, using only the lips. As each tries to reach higher, they may both rear up momentarily.

15

Figure 1.4
Mutual grooming. Here the upper front teeth are being used as a scraper.

several minutes at a time, nibbling and parrying in turn, first on one side and then on the other.

Friendly horses will also nibble one another on the neck (*Figure 1.4*), on the shoulder, and on the side of the belly, in each case using only the lips. Occasionally they will give a little nip with the teeth, or will lick the fur, or they will scratch one another's back with the upper teeth.

A less friendly disposition toward another horse is signalled by threats. The most common is the lowered head with ears held back (*Figure 1.5*). The weight is moved forward over the feet so that the head lunges in the direction of the threat. Usually the threatened horse lifts his head and turns away. If

Figure 1.5
Threat posture with lowered head and ears laid back. Used here by a pony stallion to round up his harem.

he does not move away fast enough, the threatener will bare his teeth and charge, aiming to take a bite out of the flank of the offender.

Another common threat is the defensive one of swinging the hindquarters. A horse can turn on the spot very quickly and thus bring his hindlegs into an attacking position. In many cases the swinging of the hindquarters serves as an adequate warning and the aggressor turns away. If he does not, the defender will throw up his heels and kick out. He can reach quite a long way and can do a lot of damage, so it is well to keep out of range.

A horse can execute defensive threats even when travelling at speed. One should keep this in mind when cantering among other horses. You need to keep at least one horse's length clear between the nose of your own mount and the tail of any horse in front. If you spot a horse making even a half step sideways to swing his hindquarters toward you, get clear at once before the threat develops into a full-blooded kick. Remember, this is a defensive threat which can be made very quickly should the horse feel it is being threatened. The moral is: do not approach a horse from behind.

Figure 1.6
Prancing display by "boss" horse. Neck arched, head up, nostrils flaring, and high springy steps.

Another threat is the display put on by the boss horse of a group at the approach of a stranger. This is also used to keep other horses away from their favourite mare. The neck is arched, the head raised with nostrils flaring, the ears are cocked forward and the horse advances with a very high springing step (*Figure 1.6*). Intruders usually keep well away 17 unless they themselves are in a very dominant mood. If an intruder persists, the two will greet one another with snorts, then one will put his ears back, bare his teeth and prepare to charge, whereupon the other will usually turn away. Actual fights are rare, except between stallions, though chases are common enough and displays such as this are used even by geldings.

It is by a succession of encounters, with threats received and delivered, that each horse in a group comes to find his place in the social order. From time to time new challenges are issued and responded to but on the whole a group of horses soon settle down to live peaceably together. Rivalries flare up, however, when food is brought to a group of hungry horses. Hay should accordingly be divided into a number of well-separated portions so that each horse can feed undisturbed without feeling threatened by others.

When your horse has been accepted into his new family, you can relax and go home. Your helpers will also begin to lose interest and drift away. When next you come to him you may be on your own. You may be eager to take him out for a ride. But first you must catch him.

Before setting out, give a moment's thought to your clothes. There will inevitably be a certain amount of mess, particularly in a muddy field, and if the horse has been actively grazing he will probably be slavering and he can cover you with slobber unless you are careful. The smart clothes of the show-ring are not therefore appropriate. If you wear glasses you will find that a peaked riding cap can be a valuable protection.

Catching your horse in a field

If your horse is free in a field, and particularly if he is at all shy, catching him may present some problems. Feeding helps, but sudden movements, especially those made near to the horse's head, can be disastrous. The horse will throw his head up sharply if you make any sudden movement within his field of vision, so it is no use your trying to make a grab at him. If you happen to have a hand or a rope on him when he sees a sudden movement, he will feel the jerk as he throws his head up and this will make him even more shy than before. Gentleness and patience are essential when dealing with a shy horse. The routine described below works with fairly difficult cases. You will soon discover shortcuts that you can get away with when dealing with horses that are used to being handled.

There is a lot to be said for just standing about a few times near to the horse while he is quietly grazing. Watch him carefully as you approach to see if he reacts. As soon as you see any sign of reaction, in head, ears, or feet, stop moving and wait for him to carry on grazing. You can talk to him at this stage, quite quietly. It doesn't matter what you say so long as it is not too urgent. A gentle burble of sound is what is needed. Then as the horse moves on during his normal placid grazing, you move on also, keeping your distance and moving without haste, just as if you were grazing also. A few minutes of this every so often will get him accustomed to your company.

There are several factors as well as his senses of sight, hearing and smell, that play a part in the way the horse recognises you. It is not certain that he can recognise your face and indeed, even for humans, this is a very sophisticated process. He may recognise you from the way you move, or from the sound of your feed-bucket. If you appear one day in different clothes, such as a shiny new macintosh, remember to use your voice repeatedly to establish your new identity. Again, do not be surprised if the horse turns away from you after you have been fondling a dog he has not met and whose smell is unfamiliar to him. He will soon come to recognise your voice, presumably by the pitch and rhythm rather than by the things you say. You may find that one of the high-pitched whistles used for training dogs is a useful accessory with which to extend the carrying power of your voice when you call to him.

Remember to approach the horse from the side. If you approach head-on he will turn aside and walk away. If you approach from behind, he will probably just walk on, keeping his distance. If you do manage to come up close behind him he may kick you. Aim your approach at a point behind the shoulder near where the girth goes. This avoids threatening either his head or his tail. If he walks on, just walk on with him, keeping alongside and gradually converging with him.

The next stage is to tempt him to approach you. Bring a bucket with a handful of feed in it. This time approach from up wind. When he lifts his head, put the bucket down and back off three or four paces, calling to him and using his name. If the horse moves off, pick up the bucket, rattle it, and try again. When he has decided that there is no trap, he will come to investigate the bucket. He is naturally inquisitive, and he will recognise the appetising smell. After a number of repetitions he will come to associate the distinctive sound of his name as a 19 signal that there is food to be had and he will come to your call.

Let your horse feed undisturbed from the bucket for a few minutes, then very cautiously move close, a little at a time. If he shows any reaction, freeze. The aim is to approach his shoulder so that you can "nuzzle" him behind the elbow with the back of your hand. The feel of your hand against his side corresponds to a natural caress that will already be familiar to him (*Figure 1.2*). On no account approach his head directly until he makes his own move toward you. If you are patient, he will let you rub his side behind the elbow without moving off. As mentioned earlier, if he swings his hindquarters toward you, back off at once. This is a warning that he is not ready for your approach. If you persist, he will kick you; and this is no way to build up a beautiful friendship.

When a horse has begun to accept your nearness and is not too scared of you he will lift his head and cautiously approach you with his nose. When standing near a horse remember always to have your weight on your toes and to lean slightly in toward him. If you do this he is less likely to step on your foot. It is very important not to be sudden at this point. You may stand quite still and let him smell you. If you slowly lift the back of your hand he will sniff this and you may even get him to take a little feed from your hand. When offering food, hold your fingers out flat and close together, so that he has no chance to nip your fingers with his teeth. Don't be in too much of a hurry to stroke his face. Keep stroking his shoulder and particularly the root of the neck where it joins the chest (*Figure 1.7*). Here you are imitating the goodwill gesture with which horses greet their friends, two horses nuzzling one another, each with his nose against the neck of the other.

Another way to get a hand on your horse is to move the bucket slowly while he is feeding. He will try to keep his nose in the bucket so that, as you carry it along in front of you, he comes to walk alongside, shoulder to shoulder with you. Put the bucket down again and carry on rubbing his shoulder and chest. Gradually move your hand up onto the middle of the neck and onto the top of the withers. Also work up the further side of the neck until he lets you put your arms around his neck. All through these manoeuvres you are avoiding the "confrontation situation" of looking him in the eye and you are concentrating on giving him the sensations he associates with friendly companionship. The light contact on the top of the withers corresponds to the contact between a foal and its

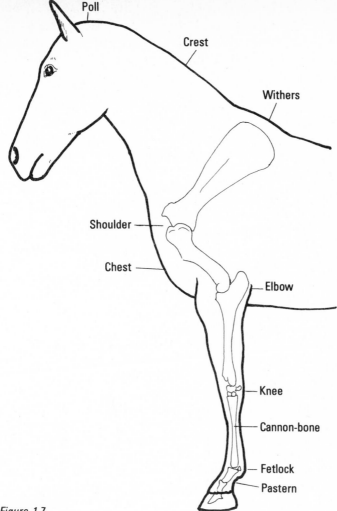

Figure 1.7
Anatomy of the forequarters.

mother both during suckling and when the mother stands with her head looking over the foal's back. The caressing of the chest corresponds to what an adult horse feels when a foal stands close up to it in a plea for protection and comfort.

An indication that your horse is beginning to accept you will be when he rubs his head against you using the side of his face above the angle of the mouth. This is equivalent to the "fencing" that companionable horses do to one another. They nibble one another gently with their lips, push the sides of their 21 heads against the neck or head of their companion and rub their faces up and down. You should respond as a horse would, by not pulling away, allowing your horse to rub his head against you. He may now let you rub your hand on the side of his face. Don't be put off by his attempts to nibble with his lips but be on your guard not to get accidentally bitten. He may nip you in play, but your sudden movement when you wince will alarm him and he will throw up his head and may make off. If he fences with your hand this is a good sign. Respond by extending the range of your rubbing movements, up the neck to the angle of the jaw and round the face from the sides onto the bridge of his nose. If he dips his head appreciatively, run your hand up the front of his head between the eyes. He will enjoy a quite firm pressure here as you rub your fingertips up and down his forehead. He may now rub the whole of the front of his head against you, pressing quite hard and moving his head up and down. This is a sign that he has accepted you as a companion.

When the horse has accepted the contact of your hands on both sides of his neck you may be able to pass a rope from one hand to the other encircling his neck. You need to be very circumspect at this stage. He may take fright if he sees the rope swinging about. A rope's end looks rather like a snake and horses do not seem to like snakes. Once you have the rope round his neck move it up to lie close behind the ears and hold on firmly enough to resist his movement, but do not press the rope into him by pulling when he is relaxed. Remember that when a horse is required to pull a heavy load, such as a plough, he is fitted with a collar round the base of his neck. He throws his shoulders against this collar and he can then pull with all his weight. If you put a rope round the base of a horse's neck he can throw his weight against it just as he would when pulling a plough, and it will be impossible to restrain him. In contrast, quite a light pressure of the rope round the top of the neck can act as a gentle signal; so get your rope into its proper position quickly.

You have to be careful if the horse throws his head up. You need a rope long enough to allow him all the movement he asks for without jerking the rope taut or pulling it out of your hand. If he feels too much pressure he may decide he has been trapped. His response is to throw himself upward and backward to break free. If he succeeds, he will develop the habit of trying it again, which will be a great nuisance. If he does not succeed, because the rope is too strong and it is fastened to something strong enough to hold him, he may fight hard enough to break his neck. Because of this it is very important to avoid letting him frighten himself. If he jerks, give way at once and take up the slack again a moment later when the initial force of his jerk has spent itself.

On no account should you attempt to throw a rope over his neck. He will interpret the movement of the rope as a threat. The impact of the rope against the skin feels like a punishment and the horse will make off. He will associate the threat and punishment with your approach, especially if he sees the halter swinging from your hand, and he will keep away from you. Whenever you approach, he moves away, keeping his distance, and it is hard to break him of this habit. You need to go back to the earlier stage of tempting him to approach a bucket.

While the horse has his nose in the bucket, he will probably allow you to rub him on the neck at the front of the shoulder but he may make it difficult for you to get a rope round his neck from below. He may bear down on you, making it hard to get your hand high enough up on the far side to pass a rope toward you over his neck. As soon as you reach up with your hand on the near side, he throws his head up and again the rope is out of reach.

The solution is to pass the rope over from above without him noticing what you are doing. You bunch up the rope in your right hand and rub the near side of his neck with the whole handful while he continues to feed with his nose in the bucket. Gradually you work your hand upwards toward the top of his neck and then over the top in front of the withers. Finally you loosen your hand to allow the free end of the rope to slide down on the far side of his neck. You keep your hand on the top of his withers, still holding the rope. Then with your left hand you reach under his neck and grasp the free end of the rope. If he now throws his head up, you will be able to restrain him with the rope round his neck, now held with one end in each hand. At the earliest opportunity work the rope up his neck till it lies close behind the ears. Once the rope is round the top of his neck you will find that everything suddenly becomes very much easier.

If he manages to break away after you have caught him, it will be of no use to try to catch him by chasing after him. He will outrun you easily. Remember that the survival of the horse 23 in the wild depends on his ability to outrun a predator. Horses spend a good deal of time practising chasing games so as to be better able to escape when chased in earnest. One horse canters ahead, turning sharply first to one side and then to the other. Another chases after, cutting the corners and trying to get close enough to nip the shoulder of the leader. If the pursuer seems to be gaining, the leader fends him off by kicking out. Horses appear to enjoy this game very much. You are unlikely to be able to beat them at it. Start stalking him again with a painstakingly gentle, cautious approach.

Some principles of learning and teaching

Remember that all stages of your approach to the horse count for him as a learning situation. His main aim in life is survival. For a large herbivore which in the wild would make a succulent meal for any predator, the price of survival is a constant vigilance. The situation in which the horse finds himself is thus continually being reassessed, second by second, to determine whether a state of alarm is appropriate.

In general terms he has three "states" to choose from. In addition to "alarm" there is "placidity", in which he may graze, sleep, or just stand about, and there is "play". At any moment he has to be able to switch instantly to the alarm state. He is particularly good at remembering situations in which the alarm state has been appropriate at some moment in his previous history. If he comes to associate your nearness with an alarm state you will have to be very patient in re-educating him.

In contrast, he is not very good at remembering what he himself happened to do at a particular time. He may not realise that the alarm was set off by his own action. He just tends in future to avoid getting himself into the sort of situation in which he felt the alarm. He does, however, recognise situations where he has not been alarmed and he will tend to move into situations where he has previously been rewarded, such as with food.

In grazing, for example, he knows that he will be better fed if he keeps moving than he would be if he stayed still, because unless food is very plentiful he can soon exhaust the small patch of ground that he can reach without moving his feet. It is this principle that leads him to come to the bucket, and later to come to your hand for a reward of pony cubes.

The process of modifying behaviour by systematic reward is

an important part of any teaching situation. Remember that the horse is learning all the time. A reassuring caress is just as much a reward as a morsel of food. It happens to be true that any behaviour that is followed by some kind of reward is more likely to be repeated than actions that are not systematically rewarded. The effect is often small, but it is usually cumulative. In man the positive effects of reward are often large and dramatic. A single trial may suffice, if it succeeds, while failures, even painful failures, are often not taken too seriously. The opposite is true for the horse. Alarm situations are learned, almost indelibly, at a single trial, whereas changes in behaviour induced by positive rewards build up only very slowly.

A curious feature of the domesticated horse, and one which distinguishes him from many other animals, is an apparent propensity to tolerate and co-operate with man, particularly when the horse is in the "play" state. He is prepared to accept, as a valid and apparently satisfying reward, the caresses of his human companion's hand and the encouraging tone of his voice. He seems eager to try to understand what his human companion would like him to do. With other humans we can communicate by language, though this is not our only means of influencing one another. The horse does not understand our spoken language so it is up to us to develop a special language which he will understand.

Do not underestimate the role of telepathy here. There is no doubt that the horse can sense your mood and sometimes you can sense his. Be on the alert for this because if you respond appropriately this can help to build up a bond between you. Apart from this you must exercise patience, repetition of rewards, and scrupulous avoidance of anything likely to alarm the horse. This is not to say that you may never use a rebuke, just that the rebukes you administer must be like those accepted between horses in establishing the hierarchy of dominance within a herd. Your rebuke must not look like an attack by a predator.

In particular, remember that any sudden movement in the horse's field of view will prompt him to throw his head up. He does this as a test for alarm conditions. With his head up he can command a larger field of view and he is thus better able to spot the approach of danger. If he bangs his head, or comes up against the head-harness with a sharp jerk, this will confirm the alarm and he may quickly become "head shy" so that you 25 will find it hard to get his bridle on. It is for this reason that the progression from a rope round his neck to the putting on of the headcollar must be made carefully and with infinite tact.

After you have got one hand on each side of his neck and have passed a rope from hand to hand over the top, continue your gentle rubbing and keep on talking to your horse in a quiet, friendly and encouraging tone. You can move round with your shoulder under his neck so that your head is side by side with his and he is looking forward over your shoulder like a mare protecting her foal. He may accept quite a strong pressure of your shoulders against his chest. If he leans his neck down on your shoulder this is a good sign. It means he likes you.

Putting on the headcollar

You are now in a good position to move a hand round from rubbing the side of your horse's face to resting on the bridge of his nose. If your headcollar is of the kind that has a buckle in the noseband as well as in the headpiece (*Figure 1.8*) you can now get the headcollar on quite easily. First, pass the headpiece over his neck and fasten the buckle, then put the

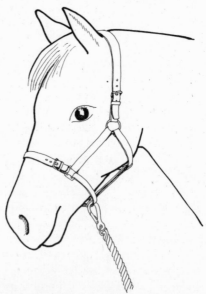

Figure 1.8
Headcollar. Note that the buckled noseband is placed well up on the bony part of the horse's face and that it is adjusted to leave plenty of room for the horse to open his jaws for grazing.

nosepiece on and fasten that too. Now feed him a few cubes as a reward. If your headcollar doesn't have a buckle in the noseband you will have to allow him to play about with it a little until he lets you slip it over his nose. Keep it in place by holding the cheekpieces against his face until he relaxes again, then cautiously pass the headpiece over his neck, being very careful not to make any sudden movement near his face. After a few trials and provided you have managed to avoid giving him a fright, he will accept the headcollar without too much fuss and you can start to lead him about.

When you do succeed in getting a headcollar on a horse, you must be very careful to make sure that he never gets the chance to tread on the lead-rope. With the rope trapped under his hoof he will get a nasty bang on the head if he throws his head up. He may break the rope or the headcollar and, of course, if this happens later with the reins, he will probably break some part of the bridle, as well as giving himself a fright.

It should be stressed that you should always be careful to use a fairly thick lead-rope, one that is comfortable in the hand. On no account should you attempt to make do with a piece of string. This could cut deeply into your hand if the horse were to throw up his head suddenly. Also remember not to wind the lead-rope round your fingers because this makes it difficult to let go if the horse takes fright and throws his weight against the rope.

It may sometimes be convenient to leave the headcollar on overnight. Naturally you take off the lead-rope so that the horse will not step on it or get it caught somewhere. You should also be careful to see that the nosepiece is slack enough to allow him plenty of room to open his mouth to chew. The headpiece should be adjusted to hold the nosepiece high enough to bear on the bony part of the nose. If it rests on the softer cartilaginous part lower down he may be able to slip his nose out of the nosepiece by rubbing his face against his foreleg. It is then only a matter of time before he shakes the headcollar off altogether. In tightening up the headpiece make sure that the throatpiece does not get drawn too tight as this would be very uncomfortable. The horse needs free play for his gullet during swallowing and, of course, you must not restrict his breathing.

If you want your horse to wear his headcollar continuously for several days, do check it at frequent intervals to make sure it is not chafing anywhere. If he develops a sore on his face you 27 won't be able to put a bridle on him until the sore has had a chance to heal. If he already has his headcollar on when you go to catch him in the field, remember not to snatch at it.

Putting on the halter

If you prefer it, a simple halter will be quite adequate for leading your horse from one place to another. However, because the headpiece of the halter has no buckle that can be undone, you will need a slightly different technique to get the halter onto the horse's head. The horse has to allow you to get your hands near his ears and this may prove something of a problem until he is used to you. The top of the halter has to go round his poll just behind the ears. Many horses are quite sensitive in this region and throw their heads up. The ears may then be quite out of reach.

Prepare the halter by checking that the nosepiece is well slackened off. Then hold the top of the headpiece in one hand while you approach and start rubbing his neck. Stand close up to his shoulder. This can be on either side, but for convenience

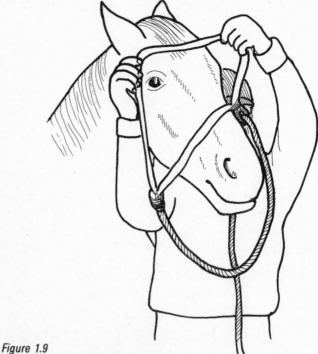

Figure 1.9
Putting on the halter. The arm passed up the far side of the horse's neck discourages him from moving off.

I will describe the moves you make when standing by his left shoulder. Have the top of the halter in your right hand together with the rest of the halter loosely coiled up or looped over your elbow to keep it from swinging about too much. Rub him on the front of the neck with the knuckles of the right hand and rest your left hand on the bridge of his nose. Gradually move your right hand up the far side of his neck close up behind the ear. Keep stroking and talking to him to keep him placid. Then, choosing your moment, reach across the front of his face with your left hand, grasp part of the top of the halter and lift it toward you over his ears (*Figure 1.9*), all the time keeping up the reassuring pressure of your right hand and wrist against the far side of his neck. Then, without letting go of the two sides of the halter, bring both hands down to the sides of his face. Again choosing your moment, manoeuvre the lower part of the nosepiece to go under his jaw. Draw the lead-rope tight but not too tight, and fasten it with a simple hitch (*Figure 1.10*). This knot serves two purposes. It prevents the halter from being shaken loose, and it saves the horse from

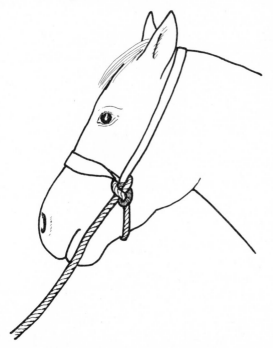

Figure 1.10
Halter in place, secured with a simple hitch.

having the noose of the nosepiece pulled tight round his face when the strain comes on the lead-rope.

Catching your horse in a loose-box

If a horse proves very reluctant to be caught in the field you have to proceed in stages. First herd him into a confined space, such as a stable yard. This will be much easier if there are other horses with him. Let them all run together without attempting to separate them. From the yard you drive them, or some of them, into a fairly large loose-box. If several go in together this is fine, so long as the horse you want is among them. Then you let these others out of the box one by one, leaving your quarry on his own with the door shut. He will probably charge around for a bit. Leave him to settle while you put the other horses back where they came from. Then gently open the top half of the door and start talking to him.

When you approach a horse in a loose-box at any time, the same principles apply as when approaching in the field except that, because the possibility of escape is limited, the horse is more likely to make a defensive threat. You must therefore be particularly alert to watch for any sign that he is about to swing his hindquarters toward you. Start talking to him as you first approach the box. If he appears restless, spend a few minutes talking to him over the half-door before venturing in. When he is reasonably settled you can go in, and again just stand against the wall for a few moments, talking gently all the time, until he gets used to your presence. Thereafter proceed as in the field, approaching from the side and nuzzling him first behind the elbow and on the root of the neck before approaching his face. Carry through all the routine already described until you eventually persuade him to accept the headcollar.

Leading the horse forward

When you are holding the lead-rope to a headcollar or halter you will be standing a step or two away from the horse instead of being in close contact with him as before. It is very important therefore to avoid confrontation. Now that you have stepped out from under his neck with him looking over your shoulder, you have suddenly become a much more prominent feature in his visual field. Take great care not to look like a threat. In particular do not face him and stare into his eyes; for if you do, he will take you as an aggressive adversary and in turn he will adopt his own aggressive pose to face you, head up, eyes

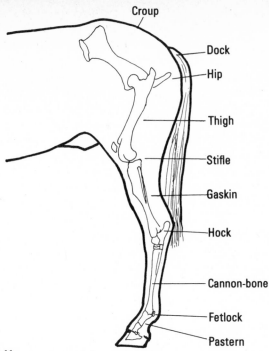

Figure 1.11
Anatomy of the hindquarters.

staring, nostrils flared and perhaps snorting. He will not want to walk forward in response to your pull on the rope. If you pull, he just pulls back.

Your best strategy is to stand beside him, facing in the direction you want him to go. Talk to him. If he doesn't move, swing your outside hand at full stretch backwards behind you and tap him under the belly with the rope's end, quite gently. While doing this, do not change the attitude of your head or of your leading hand. If you are lucky he won't see that it is you that is giving him the nudge. The effect of a tap on the belly in front of the stifle (*Figure 1.11*) is to prompt him to move that hindleg forward. Meanwhile you are urging him forward with the pressure of your lead hand just under his chin, with your voice, and with the exercise of your will power. One step leads to another so he should begin to walk forward. Reward him at once with your voice. If he is very reluctant to move, you can reinforce your prompt by using a crop. Again, use it in the outside hand behind your back while standing alongside the horse and facing in the forward direction. Do not hit him too 31 hard. This is a prompt, not a punishment, and a tap on the belly in front of the stifle is all that is needed.

Another trick you can use to persuade a particularly obstinate horse forward begins by taking a look at the position of his feet. He will probably have one forefoot in front of the other. If you move his head strongly round toward the side of this forward foot, while still urging him forward, this will make him put more weight on that leg. It will then be easier for him to lift the other foreleg and to take a step forward with it. Here you are taking advantage of his natural tendency to move his body round in such a way as to straighten his neck. As soon as he starts to move, you bring his head back to the "straight ahead" position and walk forward. Again, one step leads to another.

Practise walking and running, forward or in circles, with the horse sometimes on your right and sometimes on your left. Keep your lead hand well out to one side so that he does not tread on your heels. He will soon accept the headcollar and you will be able to lead him about quite happily.

As you are walking along, pay attention to the nodding movements of the horse's head. The nodding should be regular and even. If the head movements are alternately larger and smaller, the horse is probably lame. The first thing to do is to check the feet. You should, in any case, do this each day, just as one should take a quick look at the tyres before taking a car out on the road.

Checking your horse's feet

To examine your horse's feet you must first persuade him to co-operate. At first it may help to have someone to stand at his head to remind him not to walk on, but when he is used to the routine this should not be necessary. There are advantages in keeping to the same sequence so that the horse knows which foot you want to lift next. Start with the near fore. Stand facing his tail, your left shoulder alongside his. Turn your left hand over, thumb-down, and run your hand firmly down the back of his left foreleg from shoulder to fetlock. Take hold round the pastern and base of the fetlock and lift, saying "Come on, up! up!". Push your elbow into the back of his knee to encourage him to bend the knee, and nudge his shoulder with your own shoulder to tell him to put his weight on the other leg. If he leans against you, relax your pressure suddenly and then take it up again. He will adjust his legs to avoid falling over when he feels the collapse of your supporting shoulder. Be ready for him to lift his foot rather quickly, and when he does so put your right hand under the upturned toe of the hoof with the sole of the foot uppermost. If he waves his foot about or makes as if to kick out, drop the foot, yell at him "Stop that!" or "Keep still!" and give him a good thump in the ribs. After only a couple of seconds' pause, start again. A sharp rebuke like this is effective only if it is used sparingly and thus preserves a marked contrast with the gentle treatment consistently used at other times.

If he starts to put his weight on you, suddenly drop the foot by a few centimetres without letting go. It is important not to let him get into the habit of leaning on you as this gives him a chance to lift another leg to kick with. Whenever you are at close quarters like this with the horse you will be able to feel even very slight movements, as he shifts his weight, and as he prepares to move a limb. Be alert for these preparatory movements and give answering pressures, where appropriate, to check or to encourage the horse's movement. So long as you keep the foot doubled up with the fetlock and pastern joints well bent in the toe-down direction, he will keep the other joints in the leg bent also. Move the foot about a bit to encourage him to relax, talking all the time. The assistant standing at the horse's head can help also. By moving the horse's head to

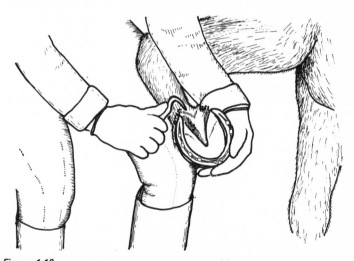

Figure 1.12
Cleaning out the hoof. Always work with the hoofpick pointing away from the soft part of the frog.

33

one side or the other and either pulling it forward or pressing back as appropriate, one can encourage the horse to shift his weight over the legs. The object is to get him comfortably supported on three legs with no weight on the leg that is to be lifted.

When the horse has settled with his foot in your hand you can rest it on your knee. Then, keeping the toe up with one hand, you have your other hand free to operate the hoofpick. Hold the hoofpick with its point directed always toward the toe of the hoof. First clear the compacted mud from alongside the shoe. This will make it easier to distinguish the outline of the frog (*Figure 1.12*). Clear the grooves at either side of the frog and the indentation at the heel. Check that there is nothing sticking into the frog or wedged in the grooves. Test the heel for soreness by pressing here and there with your thumb. Check that the shoe is still firmly nailed, and that the clenches have not risen to form dangerous sharp points. Assess the wear on the shoe and the amount of growth that has appeared between the inner edge of the shoe and the sole. The walls of the hoof grow steadily, like our own nails, and even if the shoes are not worn out it will be necessary to ask the farrier to remove the shoes and trim the hoof every six weeks or so.

When you have finished with the near foreleg, let it down gently and move on to the near hindleg. Again, start by running your left hand firmly down the back of the leg, from the hip to the fetlock, and take hold round the pastern and base of the fetlock just as for a foreleg. Be particularly alert for sudden movements and be ready to jump away to the side, pushing against the horse's thigh to get clear. The safest place to stand is level with his hip. He is most likely to kick backwards, but he can also kick forwards with the hindlegs. To kick out sideways, he has to tip his pelvis over to the other side and you may be able to see this coming, or will feel it if you are in contact with his thigh. Don't be put off by the prospect of such emergencies. They may never happen. But it is as well to have some awareness just in case.

After checking fore and hind on the left side, do the fore and hind feet on the right side, this time using the right hand to run down the back of the leg. If the same routine is used regularly the horse soon gets accustomed to it and you should have no trouble.

It is a good idea to give the shoes a few taps with a hammer from time to time so that the horse gets used to the feel of it.

34

This will make the farrier's job easier for him when the time comes.

Some horses lift their feet more readily if you adopt a slightly different technique. For the left foreleg, stand facing the tail as before, but put your left hand on the withers and use your right hand to lift the foot after sliding that hand down the back of the leg from elbow to fetlock. For the right hindleg, put your left hand on the horse's hip and slide the right hand down the back of the leg from hip to fetlock before grasping the base of the fetlock to lift the foot. Change hands for the other side.

Grooming

Having checked the feet, look the horse over for cuts and abrasions. This check is conveniently combined with a rough grooming. Use a close-bristled body-brush for the face and head, keeping to the direction in which the coat lies naturally. For the rest of the horse's body, starting with the neck, use first the stiff-bristled plastic curry comb, to dislodge any caked mud that may have been picked up in lying or rolling. Then go over him again with the body-brush. Elaborate grooming is not appropriate for a horse living out, as the scurf and grease that accumulates next to the skin provides some protection against extremes of weather. Excess accumulation is washed off by the rain or worked out of the coat by rolling. For a horse that is kept in a stable, on the other hand, regular and thorough grooming is necessary to keep the skin and coat in good condition.

Horses appreciate careful grooming. The time spent will yield dividends in terms of goodwill as well as in appearance. It is particularly important to rub down after exercise if the horse has sweated at all. The hairs become stuck together as the sweat dries and this will be uncomfortable as well as unsightly. The sweaty marks under the saddle need special attention. Brushing helps the skin and underlying tissues to recover from being squeezed by the pressure of the saddle under the weight of the rider.

2 Fitting Tack

The rider's tack

The conventional riding cap, with its hard crown and stiff peak, reduces the severity of head injury in the event of an accident. This is important because head injuries are by far the most serious of those that commonly occur. For the cap to be effective it is, of course, necessary that it should stay in place on the rider's head, and for this reason one should wear a chinstrap. In practice, one can fall off a horse any number of times without actually hurting oneself at all, provided that the ground is fairly soft and one does not land on an obstruction, such as a boulder or a fence post. The secret is to relax and curl up in the air so that one lands in a ball and rolls away.

The cap also provides useful protection in less dramatic circumstances. When you are attending to your horse he may indicate his friendliness by rubbing his head against you and, if he has his bridle on, you may be accidentally struck on the head by the bit. This can feel like being hit with a hammer and although you are not likely to be seriously injured, it can be very painful if you are not wearing your hard hat. In addition, the peak of the riding cap may help to avoid getting your glasses bent or dislodged.

The function of calf-length riding boots is to keep the rider's leg from being nipped between the stirrup leather and the saddle. One may be tempted to achieve the same result with ordinary wellingtons, but these usually have quite a deep tread on the sole compared with the smooth sole of the riding boot. A deep tread has two disadvantages. The stirrups tend to bounce against the projecting ridges of the tread so that it is difficult to get your feet back into the stirrups once they have slipped out. A more serious hazard is that the boot may jam in the stirrup and not pull free easily if you have a fall.

In competitive riding the organising body specifies what clothes are to be worn for each type of event. One needs to consult the relevant rule book because details of the rider's turnout are sometimes taken into account in the judging. Apart from these considerations one may wear what one chooses. Avoid anything that will flap loudly in the wind as this may upset the horse. Remember also that the horse may be given a fright by the sudden change in your apparent size and shape when you are putting on or taking off a jacket or other garment. Do not attempt this while in the saddle; always dismount first, and preferably have someone else hold your horse. If he were to make off with you in the saddle, and with your arms still tangled in the sleeves, you would have great difficulty in controlling him and you might easily find yourself involved in a serious accident. If you find trouble with chafing against the saddle this may be avoided by the liberal use of baby powder. Gentlemen will appreciate the importance of closely-fitting underpants.

Choice of bit and bridle

In choosing tack for the horse, our first requirement is a bridle. It is through the bridle that the rider communicates with that most sensitive part of the horse, his mouth. Where we use our fingertips to "feel" things and to manipulate them, the horse uses his lips. The bridle is a device to support the bit in a suitable place in the horse's mouth while allowing it to move under the influence of the reins. Because it is the bit itself that lies in the horse's mouth there have been countless attempts to solve the problems of controlling the horse by altering the design of the bit. In the days when fierce stallions were ridden into battle without saddle or stirrups quite horrifying pieces of ironmongery were used. In contrast, most modern bits appear very benign. There is still, however, a bewildering variety of bits to choose from and each has its own advocates as a cure for this or that vice of the horse.

An alternative attitude, and one that will be adopted here, is to regard the vices as curable by training rather than by force, and to recommend a simple snaffle, for example the Fulmer bit (*Figure 2.1*), for most occasions. The most common design has a joint in the middle. This rests against the horse's tongue and gives him something to fiddle with to keep him interested. Some horses have the habit of picking up the joint of the bit with their tongue to bring it between the back teeth where they will grind away at it. This can be avoided by using a plain bar without a joint.

Each end of the bit is fitted with a ring for attachment of the reins and of the cheekstraps of the bridle. After the bit has been in use for some time the edges of the holes in the bar some-times develop a sharp burr. It is then possible for the horse's lip to get nipped between this burred edge and the ring, and the

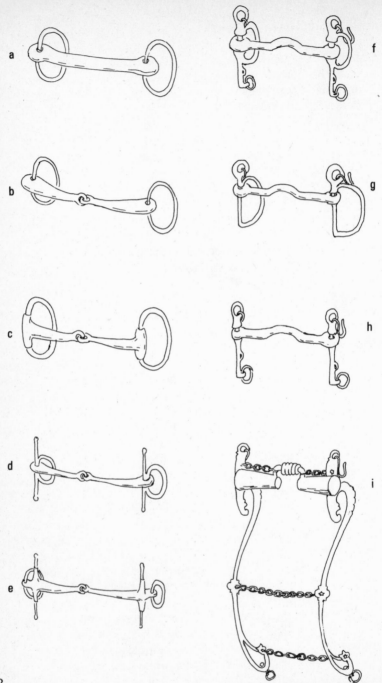

a

b

c

d

e

f

g

h

i

38

Figure 2.1 (OPPOSITE PAGE)
Types of bit. On the left: snaffles. On the right: curb bits, all worn with a curb chain (not shown).

a) Simple snaffle. Some are arched upwards as well as being curved in the horizontal plane. The concavity goes toward the lower jaw in each case. b) Simple snaffle with a single joint. c) Eggbutt snaffle. d) Snaffle with cheekpieces on the rings. e) Fulmer snaffle with cheekpieces attached to the bar. f) Pelham, used with two reins, the upper acting as a snaffle rein, the lower with a curb action. g) Kimblewick. A version of the Pelham to be used with a single rein. Intended to bring on more curb action when the tension in the rein is increased. h) Weymouth bit. The curb bit usually used in conjunction with a simple snaffle in a double bridle. i) Seventeenth century bit illustrated by William Cavendish, Duke of Newcastle, in his famous *General System of Horsemanship*. Notice the very long cheekpieces giving enormous leverage to the curb action. Some present-day "Western-style" riders also use a very long cheekpiece on a curb bit, usually with a plain bar through the horse's mouth.

lip becomes sore. This burring should be watched for, so that it can be scraped away and rounded off. The "egg-butt" snaffle is designed to avoid this problem.

As a precaution against lip injuries one may fit rubber discs to the bit to lie at each side of the mouth to keep the lip away from the ring. There is a trick to make it easy to get these rubber discs over the rings of the bit (*Figure 2.2*). Take a length of stout string (binder twine does very well) and tie the ends together. Pass a loop of the string through the two rubber rings, through one ring of the bit, and then back through the rubbers again. Hook the two free loops of string over your foot. You will then have both hands free to pull the rubber onto the bit. It will slide over the metal more easily if it is first wetted.

In addition to their function as anchorages for the cheek-straps and the reins, the rings on the bit, if large enough, will help to prevent the bit from sliding right through the horse's mouth from side to side. Some bits have elongated cheek-pieces fixed to the rings for this purpose. In the Fulmer bit the cheekpieces are joined to the bar instead of to the rings.

The severity of the bit depends on the thickness of the bar. A narrow bar concentrates the pressure exerted on the horse's mouth, to give a more severe action. If the horse dislikes the pressure, he will pull against the bit. This just makes matters worse and leads to a continual battle between horse and rider. The implication is that if you are having difficulty persuading your horse to accept the bit, you are probably using too severe a bit and should try a thicker one.

The length of the bit between the rings is judged with the 39

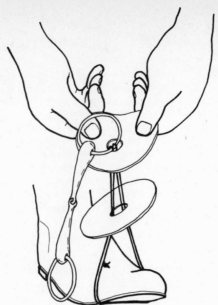

Figure 2.2
Trick to get rubber discs over the bit rings. A loop of string is passed through the bit ring, doubled over and threaded through the two rubber discs, and then anchored with the foot. This leaves both hands free to pull on the rubber discs.

joint pulled out straight. There should be about a centimetre of clearance on each side between the lip and the ring.

Putting on the bridle

The components of the bridle, apart from the bit and the reins, are: the two cheekstraps, the browband, and the headpiece (sometimes called the pollpiece), with which the throatlash is incorporated (*Figure 2.3*). The browband should be long enough to allow the headpiece to ride clear of the ears, and the throatlash has to be long enough to leave plenty of room for the gullet and windpipe.

There are three different systems for attaching the reins and the cheekstraps to the bit. Usually they are attached either with a buckle or with a stud-fastening. Alternatively, they may be stitched on, an arrangement which has advantages for some purposes, such as for racing where lightness is important, but which makes it inconvenient to experiment with bits of different patterns.

To assemble the bridle, or to reassemble it after cleaning, start with the headpiece and slip on the loops of the browband. Note that the browband goes to the front and the throatlash

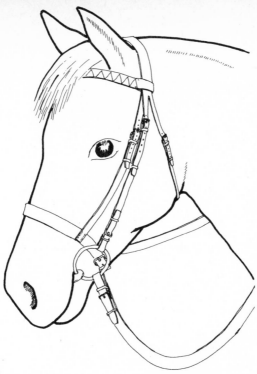

Figure 2.3
Bridle in place to show the position of the various fastenings. Here the cheekstrap and the rein are attached to the bit ring with a buckled fastening. (See also *Figure 2.4* where the cheekstrap is sewn to the bit ring and the rein is attached with a stud-fastening.)

goes to the rear. The long strap of the throatlash goes on the right so that the buckle finishes up on the left, with the pin away from the horse's face. Now put on the cheekstraps. If in doubt, have these long rather than short at this stage. There should be no doubt as to which is the top end of the cheekstrap – it has a plain buckle, while the lower end has either a stud-fastening or both a buckle and a tail.

Before attaching the bit, look closely to decide which way you want it to rest in the horse's mouth. Most bits are unsymmetrical. The gentle curvature of the bar between the rings, or the way the rings are set onto the bar, should be arranged in the mouth to be concave toward the lower jaw. An arch, or "port", in the bar goes uppermost, to leave room for the tongue underneath. Stud-fastenings are designed to go against the horse's face, so the tail of the strap is passed   41 through the bit ring from outside inward. The buckle-type fastening goes on the other way round – pass the tail through the bit ring from inside outward. The pin of the buckle will then be on the outside, away from the horse's face. Stud-fastenings are to be preferred for the attachments to the bit because they have fewer projections that can get caught. Horses often rub the sides of their heads against anything handy. If the bridle gets caught, the horse will throw up his head and something is apt to get broken or torn.

The only buckles that need to be unfastened for putting the bridle on and off are the buckles of the throatlash and of the noseband. There are, however, two points of difficulty: firstly, getting the bit into the mouth, and secondly, getting the head-piece over the ears. If your horse is well trained he will take hold of the bit for himself when you offer it in your left hand, and he will lower his head so that the headpiece can be easily passed over his ears with your right hand. Things do not always go as smoothly as this and your horse may throw his head up to put his ears well out of your reach.

If he already has a headcollar or a halter on you will need to take it off to get the bridle on. To keep control of him while you are changing over, put the reins over his head before taking off the headcollar. Keep the reins close up behind the ears and get into position with your right shoulder under his neck, as already described for putting on the halter. Take hold of the two cheekstraps, one in each hand, and check that there are no tangles. Put the two straps together in the left hand and steady the horse's head by placing your right hand on the far side of his face and on the bridge of his nose. Cautiously bring your left hand also onto the bridge of his nose. This will bring the bit up against his upper lip. Transfer the cheekstraps to the right hand, keeping this hand in place on the bridge of the horse's nose (*Figure 24*). You can now use your left hand to manoeuvre the bit between the lips while your right hand continues to restrain the horse's head. Be ready to move your right hand upwards to lift the bit as soon as the horse opens his mouth. It may help if you hold a few pony cubes up to his mouth. Then, when he moves his lips to take hold of these, he will grasp the bit at the same time.

If he does not at once open his teeth to let the bit in, push your thumb between his lips at the side of the mouth. If this still doesn't work, squeeze the lip against one of the tushes (the isolated small teeth between the front teeth and the grinders).

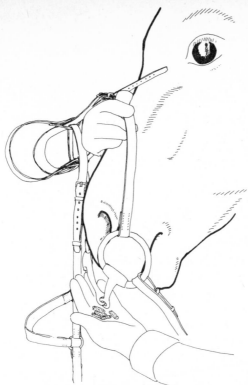

Figure 2.4
Getting the bit into his mouth. The pony cubes held against the bit help to indicate to the horse that you want him to open his mouth. The arm round the far side of his head, together with the hand on his face, serve to encourage him to keep his head still while you get the bridle on.

This will nearly always be effective. As soon as he opens his teeth, slip the bit in and hold it in place by sliding the cheek-straps up his face. Then, with one hand holding both cheek-straps against his face to steady the horse's head, the other hand is free to lift the headpiece up toward his ears. Keep your hands in contact with his head and take care not to let the cheekstraps slip down as this might allow the bit to drop out. Talk to him all the time to reassure him so that he doesn't get too excited. It may help to pause for a moment from time to time. When you have the headpiece up against the horse's forelock fold one of his ears in under it, using the flat of your hand. Check that the browband is in a reasonable place and then tuck the other ear in also. Then rearrange the mane and forelock and get the browband straight. Reward him with a few pony cubes.

43

Now check the position of the bit. The cheekstraps should be adjusted to hold the bit just against the corner of the mouth without wrinkling the lip. With a jointed bit, or if the horse is lifting the bit with his tongue, hold the bit out straight while making this check. Finally, fasten the throatlash, leaving it loose enough for you to put three fingers between the strap and the angle of the jaw.

Nosebands

Some horses have the habit of opening their mouths and lifting their heads when they feel the pressure of the bit in the mouth. The effect of this is to move the bit into the corner of the mouth and a pull on the reins will then just pull the bit up higher into the corner without exerting any effective control. The noseband restricts the movement of the jaw so that when the horse tries to open his mouth to evade the pressure of the bit, some of the pull of the reins is transmitted to the horse's nose. This helps to keep the head down and the reins can then exert their controlling action by pulling across the line of the lips.

The regular, or "cavesson", noseband (*Figure 2.3*) is fitted above the bit. It is held in place by a strap over the poll that passes through the loops of the browband to keep it neatly tucked away under the headpiece of the bridle. The noseband should be placed high enough to be well clear of the bit, yet not so high as to bear against the protruding lumps of bone at the bottom end of the ridges on either side of the face below the eyes. To be effective, the noseband should not permit the horse to open his mouth too far. A clearance of about one finger's breadth is about right. Many people have the cavesson noseband much looser than this, in which case it functions purely as decoration.

The dropped noseband has a much stronger action, being fitted below the bit, but it needs more careful adjustment. The nosepiece bears on the soft part of the nose and it must not be allowed to slip down onto the nostrils themselves. Usually there is a special ring linking the nosepiece to the supporting strap, with spikes designed to engage with the stitching of the straps to keep them at the proper angle. Ideally, the angle between the nosepiece and the headpiece should be maintained by a stitched-in leather connecting link. It is important that the nosepiece should be short enough to keep the rings of the noseband well clear of the bit. The chinstrap goes in a groove behind the lower lip and it can be fastened quite tightly when you have a particular need for it, as when tackling a series of jumps. For more general use it should be slackened off a little, but if it is too loose it will fall away from the lip altogether and just flap about. If your bit has rubbers on it, the dropped noseband goes inside the rubbers, so as not to interfere with the action of the bit.

Various types of crossed noseband have been devised to combine the functions of the regular and the dropped nosebands, or to ensure that the point of pressure on the front of the nose is kept well up away from the nostrils. The two parts of these combined nosebands are adjusted separately, using the principles already given for the regular and for the dropped nosebands.

Saddles

The saddle distributes the pressure exerted on the horse by the weight of the rider, making the ride more comfortable for both. In addition the various pads fitted to the saddle provide a purchase for the rider's legs and thus make it easier for him to stay in place when the horse is making sudden movements.

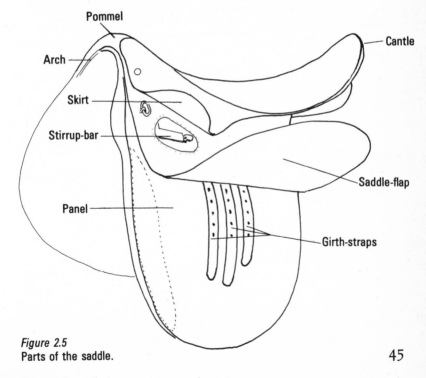

Figure 2.5
Parts of the saddle.

Along the mid-line of the horse's back a row of bony lumps can be felt. These are the spiny parts of the individual vertebrae of the backbone. These bony lumps are rather sensitive and the horse will try to escape from any direct pressure on them. Just beside the vertebrae you can feel the soft masses of the muscles of the back. Here the horse will tolerate quite a lot of pressure so long as it is applied evenly. The framework, or tree, of the saddle consists of two padded beams that rest on the muscles of the horse's back, together with two arches that hold the beams in place. The arches curve over the central row of bony lumps without touching them. The seat for the rider is fitted on top of the tree and the whole is held in place on the horse's back by the girth.

The padding under the tree is extended in a sheet that hangs down the sides of the horse to provide some thin padding under the buckles of the girth. The whole of this padded sheet is called the "panel" (*Figure 2.5*). Additional rolls of padding are often fitted on the outside of the panel. A sheet of relatively stiff leather is hung over the girth buckles to protect the rider's legs. This sheet is called the "flap". It is usually of the same profile as the panel. The hooks, or "bars", on the saddle-tree that carry the stirrup leathers are accessible through a slit in the saddle-flap. A second small flap, called the "skirt", covers the bar and also the buckle of the stirrup leather.

The front arch of the tree forms a hard lump on top of the front of the saddle. This is the "pommel". The rear arch is shaped to the rider's seat to form the "cantle", the highest part of the back of the seat. In between, the part the rider sits on is formed of stretched webbing, padded and covered with fine leather. In some saddles the construction of the tree allows some slight bending of the cantle toward the pommel. This "spring tree" makes the seat even more comfortable.

Saddles are of several different kinds according to the type of riding for which they are intended (*Figure 2.6*). They differ in the shape of the flaps and in the size and positioning of the pads providing a purchase for the rider's legs. For example, the show saddle has small straight flaps to display as much as possible of the horse's shoulder. Then, because the dressage rider sits with fairly straight legs and uses long stirrup leathers, the dressage saddle also has straight flaps, rather like those of a show saddle but somewhat larger and with small pads at the front and back of the panel to assist the rider in applying controlling signals with his thighs.

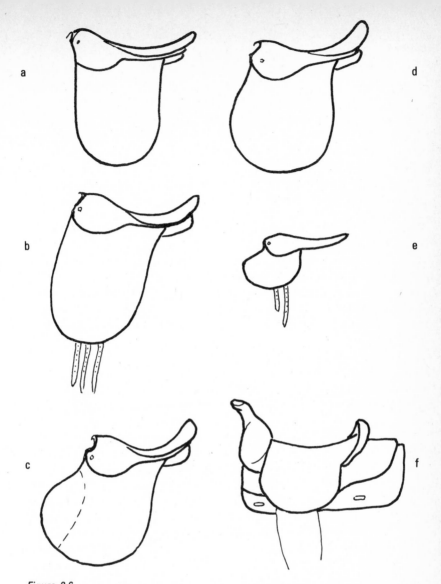

Figure 2.6
Types of saddle. a) Show saddle, with small straight flaps. b) Dressage saddle, with long straight flap and long girth straps so that the girth buckles do not interfere with the contact between the rider's legs and the side of the horse. c) Jumping saddle, with large knee pads. d) General-purpose saddle, as used for hunting. e) Racing saddle, reduced to bare essentials to save weight. f) Western saddle. As well as the pillar used for roping, the pommel carries a large padded crossbar that comes above the rider's thighs. A built-up cantle provides additional security for the rider's seat. Eyelets for two girths (cinches) are shown. The stirrups are supported by broad sheets of leather, instead of by the narrow straps used with the other saddles illustrated.

For show-jumping, the saddle-flaps extend well forward of the pommel and large and elaborate pads are fitted under the flaps to prevent the rider's knees from sliding forward when the horse lands after a jump. A general purpose or hunting saddle comes in design somewhere between the "straight-cut" dressage saddle on the one hand and the "forward-cut" jumping saddle on the other.

Examples of more extreme designs are the racing saddle in which each component is reduced to a minimum in size in order to save weight, and the "western" or "Spanish" saddles which have the pommels and cantles built up to form a very deep seat to give security to the rider during the sharp turns and other manoeuvres involved in roping cattle.

The cavalry trooper's saddle, which is still used by mounted police and others, has the beams of the saddle-tree extended backwards behind the cantle. This spreads the weight of the rider over a greater area of the horse's back and also provides a platform from which to suspend the weight of the saddlebags.

Positioning the saddle

The fit of the saddle is governed by the shapes of the beams of the tree and of the two arches. Each of the beams is twisted so that at the front of the saddle the two beams lie at an angle, like a steeply pitched roof, while at the back they are much flatter. The steeply pitched part goes on the narrow part of the horse's shoulders just behind the withers. Further back, the horse's body widens out like a barrel. In profile, the withers are higher than the rest of the back, so that if the saddle is put on too far forward it will slide backwards down the slope. If the saddle is too far back the narrow part of the saddle will ride up on the wide part of the horse's body and the front arch of the saddle will be strained. If you start by putting the saddle on well forward of what you think is the best place, you will find that it will shake down into a stable position when you come to tighten the girths. If you have occasion to move the saddle forward, remember to lift it clear of the horse's skin so as not to rub the hairs of the coat the wrong way.

Horses differ from one another considerably in the shapes of their backs and it is important to select a reasonably well-fitting saddle. In particular, the arches must be high enough to avoid contact with the bony spine even when the weight of the rider comes down heavily. In some saddles the front arch is set back somewhat to allow room for high narrow withers. In the course of time the padding under the tree becomes flattened and it may be necessary to have the saddle restuffed. One should resist the temptation to put padding under an arch that is not really high enough. Even with the padding in place there will be some pressure on the spine and this will be uncomfortable for the horse and will restrict his movements.

Before putting the saddle on, run your hand over the horse's back to check that there are no sore places where the saddle will bear on them. If the horse is uncomfortable under the saddle he may express his resentment by bucking you off.

The girth fits close behind the horse's elbows in a natural hollow. When tightening the girth, do not be too sudden. Feel round where the girth is going to lie to make sure there are no lumps of mud or sore places which will make the girth uncomfortable. Have the horse take a couple of steps before pulling up the last hole to avoid trapping a fold of loose skin behind the elbow. It may help if you lift each foreleg in turn and pull it forward from the knee to stretch the skin under the girth.

Some horses take a deep breath just as you are trying to tighten the girth. Slip a couple of fingers under the girth and feel for the moment when he relaxes for the next breath, and then pull up. The girth should not be so tight that it is difficult to slip your fingers under it. Nor should it be so loose that you can easily lift it more than one or two centimetres away from the horse's side.

The stirrup leathers are looped over the bars which are firmly attached to the tree of the saddle on either side. It is usually easier to get the leathers into place before the girth is tightened up. The hinged thumbpiece at the end of the bar may be turned up to keep the leather from slipping off when the saddle is being carried about, but it should always be turned down again to the "open" position when riding. If you are unfortunate enough to come off the horse with your foot caught in the stirrup the possibility that the leather will slide off the bar provides some insurance against being dragged along by the foot, but one should not rely on this. Be sure that the stirrups you use are amply wide enough for your feet to slide out easily, and avoid riding in any sort of footwear that can get caught in the stirrup.

Do not expect the two leathers of a pair always to remain equal in length. In use, the rider inevitably puts more weight on one stirrup than on the other, particularly when mounting, so that the leathers are unevenly stretched. Some compensa- 49 tion can be achieved by periodically swapping them over. Hang the two leathers up side by side by their buckles and compare the positions of the holes, making a mental note of the markings to help you when you come to adjust the lengths of your stirrups. The buckle is to finish up close to the bar with its pin pointing upward, so you pass the tail of the leather through the slot at the top of the stirrup, up under the bar and outward through the buckle. When not in use, the stirrups can be prevented from swinging about by sliding the stirrup iron up the inner part of the leather until it lies up against the bar. Then tuck the hanging loop of strap back through the stirrup to keep it in place and out of the way where it will not get caught on one of the stable fittings or on a gatepost.

Special equipment for early training

Lunge and lungeing cavesson   In the preliminary training both of horse and of rider it is convenient to keep the horse within range of an unmounted instructor. The lunge rein is a single length of webbing about 10 m long, with a swivel and snap hook at one end. It is attached to the horse by way of a lungeing cavesson, which is a stiffened and padded noseband fitted with three rings, at the front and on either side. The lungeing cavesson can be used with or without a bridle.

Side reins   One advantage of the use of the lunge rein is that the horse is kept on course with no need of steering by the rider's hand. Sometimes, however, a horse on the lunge will tend to drift inward in ever decreasing circles instead of keeping well out to the full extent of the lunge rein. This can be corrected with side reins running from the bit to the rings on the saddle just in front of the pommel. The length of the rein can be adjusted. A short piece of rubber is incorporated so that the horse can move his head without jerking the bit. The direction of the pull on the bit is very nearly the same as when a rider is holding the reins, and with suitable adjustment the effect is similar to that of a rider having very steady hands.

Side reins are especially useful in the training of beginners. The regular reins can be attached to the side rings of the headcollar so that the novice rider can accustom himself to handling the reins with no danger of jabbing the horse's mouth. The novice horse can be worked on the lunge with side

reins to get him used to the feel of a pull on the bit.

Long reins   The unmounted instructor can apply the normal control to the bit through long reins which allow him to walk behind the horse. The reins need to be long enough for the instructor to keep out of range of a kick from the hindlegs. For a novice horse without a saddle, the reins are passed through rings on either side of a broad strap called a "roller" which is fitted round the horse in the position normally occupied by the girth. Long reins can be used in teaching children to ride small ponies. To avoid getting the reins tangled in the rider's legs, tie a couple of loops of string to the rings on either side of the front of the saddle and pass the reins through these so that they do not fall below the rider's knee.

Special equipment for intermediate stages

Martingales   Inexperienced riders tend to lift their hands when they get apprehensive. The horse can feel that the reins are changing the direction of their pull on the mouth and he responds by lifting his head even more than before. One thing leads to another till the rider is trying to pull the bit straight up through the corner of the horse's mouth, while the horse gets more and more excited and starts throwing his head about and dancing up and down. To prevent this happening it is essential to keep the pull of the reins working across the line of the horse's mouth so as to avoid pulling the bit up into the corner where it is so much less effective. The running martingale achieves this by providing a sort of pulley which changes the direction of the reins.

The broad strap of the martingale has a loop at one end which is threaded on the girth at its lowest point, between the forelegs. The other end of this strap forks into two tails with a ring at the end of each. These rings are threaded over the reins to provide the pulley action already referred to. A neck strap holds the martingale up when the reins are slackened, so that the horse does not step over the hanging loop and get tangled up.

To fit the martingale, first put on the neck strap. This goes round the base of the neck and should be adjusted to lie in the groove of the chest. The broad strap of the martingale goes through the loop stitched to the neck strap. Check that the buckle adjusting the loop of the martingale has the pin on the side away from the horse. Pass the loop through between the horse's forelegs and thread it onto the girth. It is most con- 51 venient to do this when you are first putting on the saddle. While tightening the girth, check that the martingale remains in the midline. A thick rubber ring fitting tightly round the main strap of the martingale in front of the neck strap prevents the martingale from sliding down. It should hold the martingale close against the horse's chest like a breastplate.

If the reins separate into two parts with a buckle, undo this buckle to fit the reins to the martingale. Hold the martingale with the strap horizontal and free from twists. The rein coming from the bit passes up through the martingale ring from below and thence to the top of the neck to join the rein of the opposite side. Before refastening the buckle between the two halves of the reins check that the reins of both sides are free from twists. If the reins are in one piece, you will need to undo one of the fastenings to the bit. Bring the whole of the rein round to the side that is still attached to the bit and thread the free end of the rein up through the martingale ring of the same side, over the neck, and down through the martingale ring on the other side. Check that the rein is not twisted, and refasten it to the bit. It is a good idea to fit rubber stops on the reins between the martingale rings and the bit. These rubber stops prevent the martingale rings from sliding down to get entangled with the bit fastenings when the horse lowers his head.

To adjust the running martingale shift the buckle that controls the length of the loop round the girth. When the horse's head is in a reasonably normal rest position, the rein, pulled toward the top of the pommel of the saddle, should be just slightly deflected downward by the martingale ring. With this adjustment the rein will leave the bit in a line directed toward the horse's shoulder, even when he throws his head up.

The running martingale described above is the most generally useful design. However, catalogues and books on saddlery describe various other kinds of martingale, some more elaborate than others.

Draw reins The force exerted on the bit when using the running martingale is the same as the force applied by the rider's hands. If the rider releases his pull the horse can throw his head up quite freely to its full extent. The running martingale has no effect when the horse's head is lowered beyond the rest position.

In the training of the horse one may wish to encourage him to hold his head with his face more nearly vertical. With a suitable degree of impulsion, this can produce an arching of the neck which, together with a rounding of the back, will give the horse a splendid appearance of controlled power and energy. The effect is achieved with the draw reins in combination with leg-aids.

The draw reins are formed of a single strap about twice as long as the normal reins. Each end finishes in a single loop. To fit the draw reins, lay the centre part over the horse's neck and feed the ends through the rings of the bit, from outside inward on each side. Check that there are no twists, pass the two ends between the horse's forelegs and thread them onto the girth, as for the martingale.

When the rider pulls on the draw rein, the bit ring acts as a pulley so that the force on the bit is almost double that exerted by the rider. The direction of the pull on the bit is halfway between the directions taken by the two parts of the rein as they leave the bit ring. That is to say, with the rider's hands above the withers, the bit is pulled downward toward the horse's shoulder. Because of the mechanical advantage of the pulley action, it is comparatively easy to prevent the horse from throwing his head up. For the same reason a particularly supple hand is needed to avoid restricting the forward movement of his head if the draw reins are used during jumping.

Do not rely on the draw reins to keep the horse's head in position by main force. If he were given the chance to pull repeatedly against the draw rein the effect would be just to exercise those muscles by which the horse lifts his head, whereas what you want him to do is to get into the habit of using the muscles that keep the nose in. The best technique is to use the draw reins tactfully in conjunction with the ordinary rein, to suggest to the horse the head attitude that you want him to adopt. Use the draw rein occasionally to resist his attempts to push his nose out, but relax it so long as he holds his head in of his own accord.

An effect very similar to that aimed at with the use of the draw reins can be achieved simply by leaning well forward in the saddle and holding the regular reins well down beside the horse's shoulder. This gives the same direction of pull on the bit as you get with the draw rein. You do not, of course, get the extra purchase, but this is no bad thing as it is the pulling by the rider that encourages the horse to pull back. The important part of the relevant signal with the rein here is the checking action rather than the pulling.

53

The Market Harborough   This is a combination of draw rein and regular rein. The girth attachment resembles that of the running martingale but in place of the two tails ending in rings there are two long straps ending in snap hooks. These straps are fed through the bit rings, as described for the draw reins but this time from below, and the snap hooks are clipped each onto a D-ring sewn to the regular rein of the same side. Several such D-rings are provided on each side to give the possibility of some adjustment. When the horse's head is down, the attachment to the girth goes slack and the effect is that of an uncomplicated regular rein. When the horse raises his head the regular rein goes slack between the snap hook and the bit and the effect is that of a draw rein.

Special equipment for advanced work

Spurs   After the rider has acquired a supple and secure seat and can confidently control his lower leg independently of his knee, he can attempt to polish up on the performance of the various manoeuvres called for in dressage tests involving lateral work. Here the occasional judicious use of the spur can help. It is a mistake to think that the spur is the answer to the problem of a beginner who has difficulty in getting his horse to go. Beginners often allow their toes to point out sideways. If they were wearing spurs, this involuntary movement of the foot would bring the spur onto the horse's side. The horse is not to know that the imperative command conveyed by the spur does not represent the wish of the rider. He responds briskly and this may upset the rider because he does not realise what he has asked the horse to do and is consequently quite unprepared. The situation is very much worse if the rider has the habit of kicking his horse on with his heels. A kick with the spur will be very painful for the horse. Do not be surprised if he rapidly comes to resent being ridden and bucks the rider off.

Before a rider can permit himself to wear spurs he must be quite sure he can keep his heels away from the horse all the time except when he wants to apply the spur deliberately. When the time comes to use the spur, a little nudge is all that is required. Sometimes this may be emphasised by a slow stirring action with the heel. Jabbing is definitely to be avoided.

The spurs used nowadays are very much less severe than in earlier times, being reduced to a simple blunt peg, supported on an arch that fits on the boot just below the ankle bones. The longer arm of the arch goes on the outside, with the peg pointing slightly downward.

Double bridle While the spurs make it possible to develop accuracy in the responses to the leg-aids, the double bridle serves a similar purpose in relation to the controls exerted through the reins. Such fine control is needed on ceremonial occasions and for advanced dressage. Although the double bridle incorporates a curb this does not mean that it is a suitable device for controlling a headstrong horse. Indeed, the more severe the bit in the mouth of an unschooled horse, the more likely is it that a battle will develop between horse and rider. A strong pull on a severe bit will be painful to the horse and he will react by pulling strenuously in an attempt to free himself from the painful situation.

Two bits are used in the double bridle, each with its separate set of reins (*Figure 2.7*). One is a simple snaffle bit which when

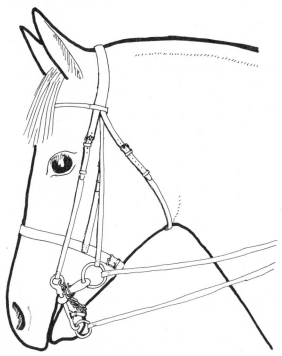

Figure 2.7
A double bridle. Note that the buckle on the headstrap supporting the snaffle bit is arranged to lie on the far side of the horse's head so as not to interfere with the buckle of the noseband.

used in the double bridle is called the "bridoon bit". It is supported in the mouth by a separate strap, the headstrap, which buckles on the offside of the horse's head so as to avoid interference from the buckle of the noseband. The curb bit is of more complicated shape (*Figure 2.1*). The bar, or "cannon", that goes in the horse's mouth is usually not jointed but it may be curved or have an arch, or "port", in the middle. The way the bit goes in the mouth is the same as for the snaffle. The port goes uppermost and the curvature is arranged to be concave toward the lower jaw. The cheekpieces are shorter above the cannon and longer below. The ring on the upper cheek is fastened to the cheekstrap of the bridle. The reins go on the ring at the bottom end of the lower cheeks. Alongside the upper ring there is a hook for the curb chain and about halfway down there is another small ring for the chain-retaining strap.

When fitting the bridle, the curb chain is loosened and the two bits are fed into the horse's mouth together. The headstrap is adjusted to hold the bridoon just against the corner of the horse's mouth. The cheekstraps are then adjusted to hold the cannon of the curb bit about halfway between the tushes and the bridoon. The curb chain usually consists of twisted links which by appropriate twisting of the chain as a whole can be made to lie flat in the groove just above the lower lip. A loose link in the middle of the chain goes toward the back at the lower edge of the chain and a small strap passed through this loose link is attached to the small rings on the cheeks of the bit on either side to prevent the chain from getting lost if it should become shaken loose from the hooks.

The effective length of the curb chain is adjusted by selecting different links to go on the hooks. Because these hooks are attached to the cheeks above the cannon and the reins are attached below, the effect of pulling on the curb rein is to pivot the cheeks about the cannon and to pull the curb chain tight under the jaw. With correct adjustment the pinching of the jaw between cannon and curb chain should take effect when the cheeks are tilted through about 45 degrees. This gives a very positive effect on the horse for a delicate touch on the curb rein.

The Pelham bit   The Pelham bit (*Figure 2.1*) is a curb bit that can be used without a bridoon. Two sets of rings are provided on the cheeks for the attachment of two sets of reins, one pulling at the level of the cannon, as in a snaffle bridle, and the other pulling at the lower end of the cheek to bring the curb chain into play. The adjustments are the same as for the full double bridle. The Pelham allows the rider to accustom himself to the action of the two sets of reins while the horse still has only a single bit in his mouth. It may be useful in the transition stage between working entirely on the snaffle and starting work with the double bridle. The Pelham is sometimes used with a single rein which, instead of being attached directly to the bit, runs on each side to a short yoke strap, or "rounding", that joins the snaffle ring to the curb ring.

The Kimblewick   A similar arrangement to that sometimes used in the Pelham is found in the Kimblewick (*Figure 2.1*). Here the rounding is made of metal and it is incorporated into the cheekpiece. With a single rein, the rider has no control over the relative proportions of snaffle and curb action. When the pull on the rein is increased, the rein slides down the rounding and this brings on more curb action. These designs are thus more in keeping with the notion that the curb is to be applied as a punishment than with its use to achieve precision by delicate control.

3 First Steps

Mounting

It must be a dramatic experience for a horse, having for the first time accepted the pressure of the saddle on his back and the feel of the girth round his chest, suddenly to have the whole thing pulled violently to one side as the rider puts his foot in the stirrup to mount. Accordingly, it is better, if either horse or rider is a beginner, for the rider to be given a leg up. This is not nearly so easy as it looks. Both rider and assistant have to exert themselves, and their efforts need to be precisely synchronised. Some effort is needed to lift even a small child. Do not expect to lift a grown man with a flick of the wrist.

Before mounting, check that the bridle is correctly adjusted, that the girth buckles are about even on the two sides of the saddle, and that the girth is tight enough. Stand facing the saddle on the left side of the horse. Put your left hand on his withers and with the right hand draw the reins through the left hand to hold the bit square and firm in the horse's mouth. Do not pull too hard or he will go backwards. If he swings his head about, talk to him and pet him a little to get him settled. Do not rush things. Choose a quiet moment at which to mount.

For a leg up, the assistant stands facing the rider's left shoulder. He is going to lift the rider by the left ankle. The rider raises his left heel to bend the knee and to bring his lower leg to the horizontal, and puts his right hand on the centre of the saddle, the left being on the withers holding the reins. If a stick is carried, it goes in the left hand on the far side of the horse. Now we come to the difficult part. Rider and assistant have to synchronise their moves.

The simplest way is to count "one, two, three" out loud. The assistant puts his right hand under the rider's left ankle and the other hand under the middle of his shin (*Figure 3.1*). On "one" and "two" the rider sinks on the right leg with slightly bent knee and bounces up again. On "three" he sinks, bounces, and springs upward to take his weight on his hands while he swings his right leg up and over the horse's back. Meanwhile he must stiffen his left knee to resist the upward push of the assistant against his ankle. He should try not to straighten his left knee too much because this would make his

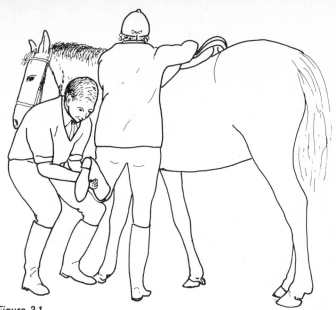

Figure 3.1
Preparing to give a leg up. The assistant is ready to bring his elbows under the weight of the rider so that he can lift with his leg muscles rather than with his arms. Agreed signals are essential to ensure synchronisation of effort between rider and assistant.

leg slip through the assistant's hands. The assistant times his lift from the count and prepares by bending his knees and elbows to get, so far as possible, underneath the rider's left leg. He has to lift the rider's weight a long way, right up to the point where the rider's left knee is about level with the top of the stirrup leather. He should keep the rider's knee close to the saddle, and when the rider swings his right leg over the back of the horse, the assistant should turn to bring the rider's ankle against the saddle also (*Figure 3.2*).

The rider must be careful not to land as a deadweight on the saddle. As he rises he leans forward, pivoting over the left forearm. The palm of the left hand is on the withers ready to take the weight. If the left elbow is held tightly against the body just in front of the rider's left hip, the weight can be taken entirely on this left forearm. The right arm is used simply for steadying. Then, as the right leg comes down into position beside the saddle, the rider's weight can be gently eased back into the saddle. Of course the right foot must be lifted high enough to avoid kicking the horse on the flank. If the horse is at all nervous, it may help to have a second assistant standing at 59

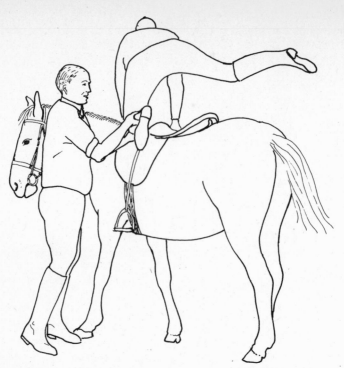

Figure 3.2
Later stage in the leg up (started in *Figure 3.1*). You may be surprised how effective a lift can be achieved by proper synchronisation. The assistant is in the act of moving the rider's foot nearer to the saddle.

his head, holding the reins close up behind the bit and fondling the horse's nose, talking to him, or giving him a couple of pony cubes to distract his attention.

In mounting with the stirrup you can choose either side, and you can choose to start facing forward or facing to the rear of the horse. Take first the most usual case of mounting from the left, facing to the rear. Prepare, as before, with your left hand on the withers and the reins drawn in to hold the bit square and steady. Have the crop in the left hand, on the far side of the horse (*Figure 3.3*). Make sure your horse knows what you are going to do, by taking hold of the stirrup leather with your right hand and putting your weight on it. This will pull the saddle round to give the horse much the same sensations as he will get when you put your foot in the stirrup and start to get up. The point of giving this warning move with your weight on your right hand is that you will be in a secure posture if the

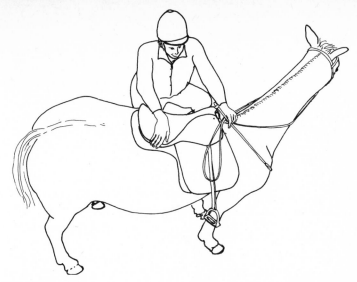

Figure 3.3
Position of the hands just before mounting. Notice that the crop and spare rein are on the far side of the horse from the rider, hinting to the horse that he is not supposed to step to the side. Here the horse's head is turned toward the rider, discouraging him from moving toward the rider and overbalancing her as she prepares to mount. If the horse develops the habit of moving away, it may help to hold his head turned away from you.

horse reacts. If he were to start playing up when you are standing with one foot on the ground and the other in the stirrup you would be at a distinct disadvantage. You would need to keep a tight hold on the withers and to disengage your foot quickly from the stirrup, otherwise you could easily be thrown on your back under the horse's feet. This would be a terrifying experience both for you and for the horse; but you can avoid it if you watch what you are about.

If the horse swings his quarters away from you, shorten the right rein to pull his head round to the right. If he then leans against you to push you off balance while you are trying to get your foot up, give him a good punch in the ribs and speak sharply to him. Don't pull so hard on the reins. Assert yourself, but don't get angry. This will not help. The horse is trying to understand what you want him to do and he is doing his best by responding to all the various pulls and pushes that he can feel you making. Some of these are accidental. You may not even realise what you are doing to him, but he is not to 61 know which of the pushes and pulls are accidental and which are deliberate commands. He responds to everything, and if you get excited, so does he. He may even come to enjoy the romp of dancing around with you, as though this is what you want him to do.

You will need to take particular care if your horse is for some reason especially eager to go forward. This may happen in the course of a ride. Suppose you have been cantering through a wood and have come to a gate for which you have had to dismount. Then, after negotiating the gate, you will be faced with the problem of getting back into the saddle. Meanwhile the horse will be eager to continue the exhilaration of the previous canter. If you are not careful, he may make off as soon as he feels your weight on the saddle even before you have managed to get your leg over him. At this point the reins will be in your left hand which is probably at the same time grimly hanging on to the mane. Your right hand will be clinging to the saddle to keep you from sliding off and you won't have a hand free with which to shorten rein. It will be hard to recover from this situation because the horse will be feeling unaccustomed bumpings from the saddle and this may well encourage him to gallop on.

To avoid all this, before attempting to mount, turn your horse to face some suitable solid obstacle. For example, put him with his nose hanging over the closed gate, facing the direction from which you have just come. The obstacle will hold back his urge to break away into a gallop and you can safely proceed with the business of mounting.

If your horse will not stand still when you put your weight on the stirrup leather with your right hand, you will need an assistant to hold his head and distract him with talk, with caresses, and with pony cubes. Keep trying until he gets used to the idea and stands quietly. Throughout all these pre-liminaries, your left hand remains on the withers and from time to time you may readjust the reins by pulling more of one rein or the other through your left hand with your right.

When you are ready to get up, and the horse is steady, turn sideways, facing toward the rear of the horse and take hold of the stirrup leather with your right hand just at the top of the stirrup (*Figure 3.4*). Turn the stirrup toward you, lift your left foot and fit the stirrup over it with the tread against the ball of the foot. If you have any difficulty in reaching the stirrup, let it down a few holes. You need to be able to pull the stirrup

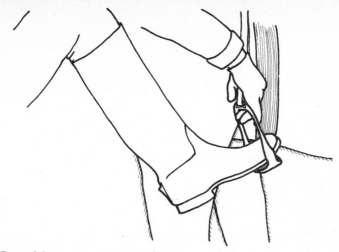

Figure 3.4
Pulling the stirrup near you before mounting. This brings your weight nearer to the horse and makes mounting easier.

toward you with your foot in it, otherwise you will never manage to get your weight over the stirrup.

Several things now happen in rapid succession. Pull the stirrup toward you with your foot in it, lean your shoulders in toward the horse, bounce once or twice on your right foot and then spring upward off your right foot to get your weight over the stirrup. As you begin to rise, quickly shift your right hand to reach over and grasp the far side of the seat of the saddle at the back edge of the flap, and use this handhold as a purchase, together with the left hand on the withers, to pull yourself up and forward over the saddle (*Figure 3.3*). Tuck your left elbow into your body, swing your right leg well up, and pivot over the left forearm until you are ready to lower your weight gently into the saddle. Throughout this manoeuvre try, if you can, to keep your left toe from digging into the horse's side. Your right hand comes free naturally as you let your weight down onto your seat.

An alternative routine, which definitely avoids digging your toe into the horse, is to start by turning forward instead of back. When you take hold of the top of the stirrup with your right hand, ready to put your left foot in it, turn forward, with your right shoulder against the horse. Keep your left hand on the withers even though you need to stretch a bit. Turn the stirrup toward you and put your left foot in it as before, but this time the toe will be pointing toward the horse's elbow. Pull the stirrup toward you with your foot in it, spring up as before, this time reaching with your right hand for the far side of the pommel. Swing up and over, and let yourself down gently into the saddle. Speak to the horse and take up the reins to prevent him from moving off.

Once you are in the saddle feel under the pommel with two fingers to make sure that the arch of the saddle is clear of the horse's backbone. Do not ride on a saddle that touches the horse's spine along the mid-line.

Adjusting stirrups

When the stirrup is hanging free the leather lies flat against the horse's side with the stirrup at right angles to its working position when the rider's foot is in it. You put your foot in from the outside, so that when your toe is pointing forward, the twist of the leather will cause it to lie flat to follow the surface of your boot. If your foot goes into the stirrup the wrong way round, the twist of the leather will bring an edge to bear uncomfortably against your shin.

The tread of the stirrup should go under the ball of the foot and your heel should be a little lower than the sole of the foot. To get the feel of this position, take hold of the mane at the withers, or hold on to the pommel of the saddle, and stand up in the stirrups, with knees straight. Then, without bending either knees or hips, raise and lower yourself by moving your ankles (*Figure 3.5*). Rise on the ball of the foot and then relax the ankle to sink your heel as far as it will go. Do this several times to force your heel lower and lower each time. Now sit back again in the saddle.

When your heel is lower than the sole of the foot, the calf muscles are tensed and will form a bulge on the inside of the lower leg. Your leg has a hollow between this bulge and the knee. The side of the horse is rounded like a barrel and the hollow in the side of your leg between the calf muscles and the knee should fit snugly against the bulging side of the horse. This does not by itself govern the position of the leg because you can slide your leg up and down over the horse's side while still keeping the hollow of your leg against the bulge of the horse. When you do this, however, you alter the position of your knee in relation to the saddle. If your saddle has knee rolls on it, as with a jumping saddle, you will find a hollow surrounded by these rolls. Your knee should nestle

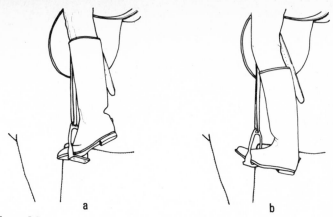

Figure 3.5
Exercise to get the feel of the stirrup against the ball of the foot. Steady yourself against the withers; stand in the stirrups; then without bending at the knee, raise and lower yourself by bending only at the ankle.

comfortably into this hollow. There are, thus, three things to think about when gauging the length of the stirrup leathers:

1) The heel is to be lower than the sole of the foot, with the tread of the stirrup under the ball of the foot;
2) The hollow of your leg below the knee is to fit over the bulge of the horse's side;
3) Your knee is to fit snugly into its nest in the knee rolls of the saddle.

To judge whether the two leathers have been adjusted to equal lengths, stand in the stirrups with your knees straight. Check that the saddle is not displaced to one side by looking to see that the pommel is centrally placed over the withers. You may be able to move the saddle to one side or the other by putting more weight on one stirrup or the other while you bounce up and down on your ankles.

When you wish to adjust the stirrup leathers, do not take your foot out of the stirrup. Lift your knee sideways away from the saddle and grasp the free end of the stirrup leather, placing your thumb on top next to the tongue of the buckle (*Figure 3.6*). Relax the pressure of your foot on the stirrup and pull the leather upward and outward. This will pull the buckle away from the bar. Relax the pull of your hand slightly to allow the leather to dip down between your hand and the stirrup bar. **65**

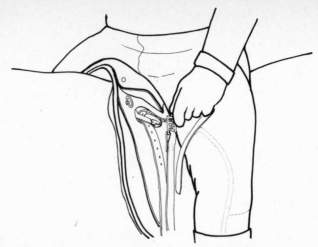

Figure 3.6
Adjusting the length of the stirrup leathers. Keep your toe in the stirrup and work the buckle along the stirrup leather by moving hand and toe up or down together.

This will loosen the buckle and you can manipulate the tongue of the buckle with your forefinger. To lengthen the leather, push down gently with the foot, meanwhile relaxing slightly with your arm. The buckle will slide away from the bar. To shorten, raise your hand while relaxing your ankle. The buckle will slide toward the bar. Feel for the desired hole in the leather with your thumb and work the tongue into the hole using your forefinger and a slight increase in the pressure of your foot while lowering your hand. When the buckle is positioned to your liking, shift your grip to that part of the leather running down from the buckle to the stirrup. Pull up on this while relaxing your foot. Then, keeping your fingers well away from the buckle, put pressure on the foot while still holding up the outer part of the leather with your hand. The inner part of the leather will slide over the bar to bring the buckle hard up against the bar with a click. Smooth away the free end of the leather, tucking it into the keeper on the saddle-flap, if you have one, and adjust the other side similarly. Once you have mastered this routine, you will be able to adjust your stirrups at any time without having to stop or to ask for assistance.

It is usual to ride with a longer leather for dressage than for jumping. Some riding schools advocate riding as "long" as possible for hacking and for general school work, instructing their pupils to shorten up by two holes for jumping. The idea of this is to stretch the pupil's hip joints. I prefer to use the safe jumping length for all occasions, with special periods of riding without stirrups to exercise the hip joint. This plan makes it easy to take advantage of any casual opportunities for jumping that may arise during a hack. It also provides more security for the rider if the horse should unexpectedly be startled by anything.

Checking the girth from the saddle

The tightness of the girth often changes when your weight comes into the saddle. This may be because the saddle changes shape slightly, or just because it comes to fit more snugly onto a different place on the horse's back. Another factor, mentioned earlier, is that many horses take a deep breath just when you are trying to tighten the girth. Then they relax once you are up, and the girth goes slack. To check the girth from the saddle, lean forward and feel the girth just below the bottom edge of the saddle-flap (*Figure 3.7*). You should be able to slide thumb and two fingers in easily, but you should not be able to pull the girth more than one or two centimetres away from the horse's side. To adjust the girth, move one leg forward, without taking the foot out of the stirrup, and lift the saddle-flap so that you

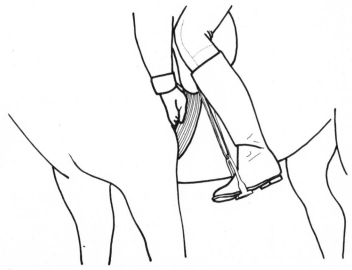

Figure 3.7
Checking the tightness of the girth.

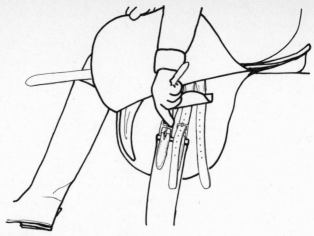

Figure 3.8
Adjusting the girth from the saddle.

can get your hand on the girth straps. Place your thumb on the protruding tongue of the buckle and feel for this tongue underneath with the forefinger (*Figure 3.8*). Use the other fingers to take a firm grip on the girth strap. Pull upward on the strap and use the thumb and forefinger to manoeuvre the tongue of the buckle into the next hole. Your thumb finds the hole and your forefinger feels where the tongue of the buckle has got to so that you know whether to pull harder or to let down the tension to allow the tongue into the hole.

If your girth has a second buckle, or if you are using two webbing girths each with a single buckle, both buckles will need to be adjusted, using the same technique for each. Check that the buckles are at about the same level on the two sides of the horse.

The safe position for the beginner

The procedures for mounting and checking stirrups and girth soon come to be virtually automatic. I have described them in detail so that you can help a friend who is getting into the saddle for the first time.

The beginner suddenly finds himself unusually far from the ground and may feel some apprehension. I usually go through the following routine to establish confidence. You, as instructor, hold your hand above the horse's withers and have the mounted pupil hold on to your hand to balance himself. The

Figure 3.9
The safe position for the beginner. The rider is much less stable if he allows his feet to move back behind the vertical.

pupil then stands in the stirrups with knees straight and adjusts his body until he is in balance and not exerting much force on your hand. The pupil then moves his weight up and down using the ankles only and without bending either at the knees or at the hips (*Figure 3.5*). This allows him to feel the close fit of the legs against the side of the horse. The pupil now lowers his seat gently into the saddle, bending at knees and hips. You next move your hand slowly forward, telling the pupil to follow by bending forward at the hips and stretching his hands forward, but all the while keeping his lower leg hanging straight down. Keep going until the pupil's chest is against the horse's withers (*Figure 3.9*) and his hands are almost round the horse's neck, elbows well in front of his knees. Have the horse walk on a few paces with the pupil still in this position. Emphasise that he is to keep his lower leg straight down. Then rock him gently from side to side at the shoulder to demonstrate that he is quite secure so long as his feet hang straight down. He will be much less stable if he allows his heels to come back. Demonstrate this also. Then let the pupil relax back into the normal position in the saddle. You are now ready to lead him on with a leading rein or to work either on the lunge or with long reins.

Handling the rein
It is through the rein that the rider influences the feel of the bit 69

in the horse's mouth. You train the horse to pay attention to the bit. He in his turn moves the bit about in his mouth and reacts against the pull of the reins. You can, to some extent, feel what he is doing, so the reins provide a channel of communication in both directions between horse and rider. Unfortunately the portion of rein hanging between your hand and the bit has appreciable weight and, if you are not careful, it can swing about and produce unwanted effects on the bit. To the horse, any change in the feel of the bit in the mouth will be equally important, and he will react to a "signal" which you may have allowed to pass along the rein accidentally. You may not be aware of having done anything to the reins. Meanwhile the horse may behave as if you have been shouting at him. It is for this reason that you need to give a good deal of thought to the way you handle the reins.

Start with the rein lying over the horse's neck just in front of the withers. Bring the hands forward with the knuckles upward, thumbs toward one another, as though reaching for the keyboard of a piano (*Figure 3.10*) and lay hold of the rein with three fingers of each hand. Separate the hands to take up the slack in the rein. Grip the rein lightly between thumb and forefinger in each hand, turn the hands to bring the thumbs uppermost and bring the hands to about 10 cm to 12 cm apart. The hands should come to rest just above the withers and in front of the pommel of the saddle (*Figure 3.11*). The rein running to the horse's mouth passes between the fourth and fifth fingers. The loose, spare loop of rein lies forward over the forefingers. The fingers are curled in a half-clenched fist (*Figure 3.12*). The position of the hands is such that, from the side, the line of the rein passes straight from the bit to the rider's elbow.

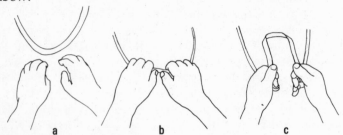

Figure 3.10
Taking hold of the rein. a) Reach forward as to a keyboard. b) Take hold with three fingers of each hand. c) Separate the hands and turn the thumbs uppermost.

Figure 3.11
A reasonable rest position on a general-purpose or on a jumping saddle. The seat-bones are in the lowest part of the dip in the saddle; the back is upright and the rider looks ahead in the direction of the horse's ears. The upper arm hangs freely with the elbow by the rider's side. The hand is over the withers at such a height that the rein appears from the side to run in a straight line from the rider's elbow. The stirrup leathers are vertical, with the heel below the toe and the stirrup against the ball of the foot. On a dressage saddle, with the stirrup bars nearer to the dip in the saddle and the rider's legs rather straighter, the heel would come nearer to a vertical line down through the rider's shoulder and hip (see *Figure 6.4*).

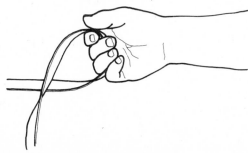

Figure 3.12
The normal grip of the fingers on the rein.

The rider's upper arm hangs vertically from the shoulder, with the elbow just clear of his waist. The aim is to keep the same light pressure on the bit all the time. This is called "contact". However, the horse does not usually keep his head still, so the rider has to be ready at any time for his hands to make the necessary compensating movements, otherwise the rein will occasionally go slack and then pull tight with a snap.

The jerk on the bit when the rein snaps tight after flopping free counts to the horse as a shouted command to stop, such as you might use in an emergency. Of course, if the jerk is repeated at every step, the urgency of the command rapidly fades. The horse learns to disregard it, except as a continual nuisance. The consequence is that he pays less attention to the command to stop when you really need it, and also he may show little inclination to go forward freely when you want him to do so.

There are several movements that can be used to keep the reins from going slack. The most obvious is the forward and backward movement of the elbow as the upper arm swings from the shoulder. This movement should be accompanied by adjustments of the angle at the elbow to keep the forearm moving along the same line like a piston. Then there are the horizontal movements of the forearm and of the hand swinging in toward your body, separately or together. The forearm swings, like a gate on its hinges, about the vertical line of the upper arm. The hand swings, again like a gate on its hinges, about the wrist, which is held with its axis vertical, thumb uppermost.

By using these movements in various combinations, and also by moving the shoulders to lean forward or to lean back, a considerable range of movement of the horse's mouth can be compensated for without needing to shift the position of the hands on the rein. If the horse makes an even larger forward movement with his head, then you must let the rein slide through your fingers. Take up the slack again as soon as you get a chance.

Shortening rein

The simplest movement for shortening rein to take up slack is just to separate the hands while sliding them along the reins. This is effective only when your hands are near the buckle joining the two reins at the centre. To take up more slack you need to draw the rein through each hand in turn, and to do this

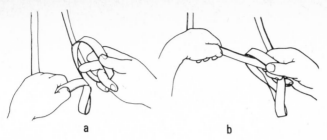

a   b

Figure 3.13
Shortening rein without disturbing the contact with the horse's mouth. Hook a finger of the right hand into the loose rein lying over the forefinger of the left hand. Slide the left hand down the rein toward the horse's mouth. Resume the grip and repeat with the other hand.

quickly you have to use both hands. One pulls while the other slides. The pulling hand has to do two things at once. It has to pull the rein through the sliding hand, but it must not let go of its own rein. The trick is to close the hand firmly on the rein to grip it in several places (*Figure 3.13*): between thumb and forefinger, between the ring finger and the little finger, and between the ring finger and the palm. The ends of the first and second fingers can then be lifted a little to form a claw, without loosening the grip of the other fingers on the rein. By turning the hands toward one another with the back of the hand upward, the loose rein lying over the forefinger of the hand that is to slide can be hooked into the claw of the other hand. The claw closes on this rein while the sliding hand relaxes its grip and is then moved quickly toward the horse's mouth without at any stage losing its contact with the rein. The sliding hand then resumes its grip and the hands exchange roles to move what was previously the pulling hand down the rein in its turn. It may be necessary to repeat the manoeuvre a few times to find the best position for the hands on the reins.

There are some situations in which it is not convenient to use both hands. For example, if one is sitting forward at the gallop with hands low down on the horse's shoulders, the horse's neck is between your hands, and the two-handed manoeuvre is not possible. Shortening rein in these conditions must be achieved by each hand on its own. This is done by inching the rein through the fingers. Grip with thumb and forefinger, relaxing the other fingers (*Figure 3.14*). Separate the fingers to slide the third and fourth fingers along the rein away from the forefinger. Grip with the third and fourth fingers, relax the thumb and slide the forefinger along the rein to close the

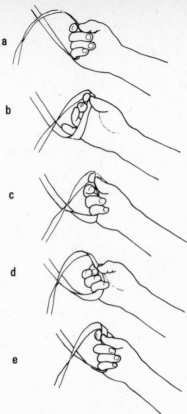

Figure 3.14
Shortening rein with one hand only.

spaces between the fingers. Then take up the pressure again with the thumb and move the thumb and forefinger to pull the rein through the other fingers. Repeat the whole sequence several times. Usually you will be able to move the rein only a little way through the hand at each step, but with a little practice you will find it easier. It is certainly a most useful manoeuvre.

Taking a contact
The positions of the fingers when holding the rein are very like the positions taken up on the handle of a suitcase. You should not, however, pull too hard on the rein. Nor, on the other hand, should you ever allow the rein to go completely slack for then you will have no chance of feeling what the horse is doing to the bit, and he in his turn will not be able to feel what you are

doing with your hands. For any communication to be possible, there must be some tension in the rein, and to maintain this tension you have to be continually adjusting the rein in your hand, allowing a little to slide through and then taking up again, as well as moving your hands to compensate for the movements of the horse's head. What you need is a delicate control of the fingers such as you might use to hold a small bird, using just enough firmness not to let the bird escape and at the same time being very careful not to crush it. Remember that the horse feels the bit in his mouth pressing on his lips and tongue with exactly the same force as the rein exerts against your fingers.

It is important for both horse and rider to distinguish between "leaning on the rein" and "feeling" it. Keep some tension all the time, as otherwise the rein can snap taut unexpectedly, but you should not need to carry the whole weight of the horse's head. If the horse is in some doubt about what is happening to the rein, he may throw his weight against the bit to try to pull the rein free and thus escape from being pestered by the confusion of signals in his mouth. It is a mistake for the rider to fight back by just pulling harder in his turn. What he has to do is to convince the horse that the movements of the bit mean something. The steady pull doesn't mean anything in itself. It is the *changes in pull* that matter.

To appreciate this point, try the following experiment. Bring the tips of the fingers of one hand against the palm of the other. Hold still for a moment, and observe that you soon feel hardly anything, even if you are pressing quite hard. Now move some of your fingertips ever so slightly. The movement is instantly noticeable. There is nothing particularly mysterious about this. It is a well-known fact of sensory physiology that tactile sense organs soon adapt to steady conditions and that they are much more effectively excited by changing stimuli.

It is easier to learn how to adjust the tension in the reins if you have some way of knowing in advance what it is going to feel like when you are handling the reins correctly. One way to approach this is to try out the feel of a few known tensions. You can do this at home. You will need a strap about the same width as the reins, and a few manageable objects of known weight in the range from 1 kg to 5 kg. A bucket and a brick will do very well. The bucket will weigh about 1 kg empty, and about 4 kg with the brick in it.

Hang the bucket from the strap and take the strap in one

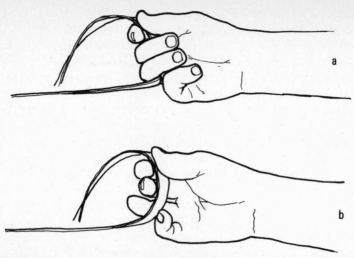

Figure 3.15
Using the fingers to give the "alerting" signal with the rein. The fingers curl and uncurl in rapid succession, alternating between the two positions illustrated. The grip of the thumb and forefinger prevents the rein from sliding and maintains a steady tension as a background to the fluctuations in tension produced by the movement of the fingers. The effect is to make the bit feel interesting in the horse's mouth so that he pays attention to it.

hand with the same grip as you would use on the rein (*Figure 3.12*). Let your hand hang down so that the pull of the strap comes against the second and third fingers. With the bucket empty, the pressure of thumb and forefinger is enough to prevent the strap from slipping, and it is easy to jiggle the bucket up and down using the other fingers (*Figure 3.15*). This is the sort of tension to aim at for routine use. If you have less tension than this the rein is apt to go slack accidentally and then to snap taut again to give an unwanted jerk to the horse's mouth.

Now put the brick into the bucket and take the strap in your hand as before to see what this sort of tension feels like. You will find it is now much more difficult to jiggle the bucket up and down with the fingers because the whole hand is engaged in the task of holding on to the strap. You may need as much tension as this, or even a little more sometimes, for certain special situations, such as to restrain an over-eager horse from rushing at a fence. But if you find you need such a tension for more than a few seconds at a time you should do something about it.

76

If you were to relax your arm completely while sitting in the saddle, the hand would hang vertically down from the shoulder. Now imagine the hand drawn forward by the rein (*Figure 3.11*), still with the arm completely relaxed. The rein will need to pull against the weight of the hand and forearm to bring the hand forward from the vertical position. If you grip the rein with the normal grip (*Figure 3.12*) you will be able to feel how much tension is needed to support the weight of your hand. Do not hold your hand out deliberately. Let your shoulder, elbow and wrist go quite slack and just hold on to the rein with thumb and forefinger alone. If the horse now moves his head, your hand will go with it.

When you are actually riding it is not appropriate to let your muscles go completely slack. It is better to aim for a somewhat springy condition with supple joints. Any stiffness is to be avoided, but your joints should not be so loose as to be floppy. The normal rein tension is just a little more than that needed to support the weight of the hand and forearm. You provide this slight extra tension by bearing down gently with the elbow while still allowing the hand to be carried by the rein. Make yourself aware of the feel of the rein against your fingers. Be attentive to what the horse is doing to the bit. If you make the bit interesting to him he will move his mouth forward to restore the contact whenever you let your hand go forward. You maintain his interest by sending messages along the rein with your fingers.

The messages that you want to send along the rein to the bit consist of small changes in the pull. It is much easier to send such messages if they are superimposed on a light tension than if there is a strong pull going on all the time. Your first message after mounting is to tell the horse that you are ready to move off. For this you use the "alerting" signal.

Alerting the horse
While you are settling yourself in the saddle after mounting and while you are adjusting girth and stirrups, the horse should stand quite quietly. If he does not, you speak to him, calling "Stand!", and give a brief pull on the reins. Be careful not to bang his sides too much with the stirrups or with your legs, as he will take this as an encouragement to move on. If he is very restless, lift your heels well away from his sides and turn your toes in. This will feel "pigeon-toed" and will bring your knees firmly onto the saddle. Give repeated brief pulls on

the reins, keeping your hands as low as possible, rubbing his neck to calm him. Keep on talking to him, calling sternly "Stand!", and "Hold!", or "Wait now!". A steady pull is of no use. He may throw his head up, or start to walk backwards, or he may rear. Lean forward, rub his neck, and give repeated brief pulls on the rein. If he does not settle quite quickly it may help to walk on a few strides, halt and try again.

In the more usual situation, the horse will stand calmly and wait for you to give the signal that you are ready. You take up the reins and adjust your grip so that, with your elbow hanging beside your hip, the rein is just taut from your hands to the bit. Now, keeping your grip with thumb and forefinger, and without changing the position of your hand, you make a series of rapidly repeated movements with the other fingers, curling and uncurling them against the rein (*Figure 3.15*) to send along it a series of small pulls that have the effect of tickling the horse's mouth with the bit. If you watch the horse's head while you are jiggling the rein, you will see him prick up his ears and lift his head slightly. At the same time he will start to move the bit about in his mouth with tongue and lips. You may hear the bit clicking against the rings. All these are signs of alertness, indicating that the horse is attending to the bit. You are now both ready to move on.

The command to move forward is given with the legs, but it is not understood unless the horse has been warned, by the alerting signal, that the command is coming. Before this he has been asked to ignore quite large movements of your legs while you are making your adjustments to girth and stirrups, and you have discouraged him from responding to your legs by pulling the rein whenever he attempts to move forward. You are now suddenly going to change the significance of the feelings that the horse gets from the movements of the saddle and of your legs against his side. You have taught him that a pull on the reins means "Stop!", and that he should ignore the movements of your legs. Now you wish him to alter his responses. To do this you need a new set of signals.

Driving the saddle forward

While you are sitting in the saddle you are never quite still. All the little movements of your head or shoulders, the movements of breathing and everything else, all these are reflected in small subtle changes in the feel of the saddle against the horse's back. If you make a deliberate effort to relax your back, the horse will feel it. Similarly, when you brace your back, after first relaxing, the horse will feel it even if you do not at the same time do anything deliberate with your legs.

There are many different ways of bracing the back. It may, for example, be hollowed, or it may be rounded, and you can alter the pressure against your individual seat-bones, putting more weight on one side or on the other. For the "move on" command, what you want is a bracing action that pushes the saddle forward. You do this by moving your pelvis as though to sit on your "tail", or to tuck your tail in under you. If you practise this at home, sitting on a stool with your feet off the floor, you will find it is quite easy to make the stool slide forward. This is the movement you need in the saddle, though it does not need to be too exaggerated.

As you brace your back, the pressure of your legs against the saddle will alter. You emphasise this effect slightly by first lifting the lower legs on both sides a couple of centimetres sideways from their rest position, keeping your knee on the saddle, and then closing the legs again against the horse during the bracing of the back.

Walking on

The command to move on is made up of a number of components carried out in sequence. You sit quietly in the saddle, keeping your legs still so that the horse will realise that the adjustment stage is over. You take up the reins and make the alerting signal by tickling the bit. You open your lower legs slightly and then, all at the same time, you brace your back to slide the saddle forward, close your legs, and relax the tension in the rein. Each component plays its part in encouraging the horse to move off. The preliminary preparation is essential. The horse must be "listening" for your command, so you must indicate that you have finished fussing about with the stirrups or with your clothing, and you must get him to wake up and be attentive.

It is not necessary to bring the heels back, indeed it is preferable not to do so. The leg pressure should be applied over the girth with the foot in its normal position. A slight clenching of the calf muscles is really all that should be necessary. One often sees youngsters trying to start their ponies by kicking their heels backwards with all their might and at the same time waving the reins about. It is not surprising that their poor ponies do not know what to do. The "heel back" is part of 79 a command to turn, but the horse does not know which way to turn, as the commands are given on both sides at the same time. The rider is trying to get the pony to move on, but the jerks on the reins mean "Stop!". To make matters worse, a youngster will often resort, in frustration, to beating his pony with the crop, often still holding the rein in the crop hand so that each blow of the crop is accompanied by a jerk on the bit.

Effects of jerks

A jerk on the rein produces a bang on the mouth, whether the jerk is deliberate or accidental. The horse hardly needs to be taught that a brief pull on the rein means "Slow up" or "Stop". But a jerk is something much more severe, a real "shout", with an element of punishment in it. Repeated jerks are both confusing and distressing. The horse tries desperately to escape from the attack on his mouth. He throws his head about, opens his mouth, pulls wildly at the reins and may plunge all over the place. Great tact will be needed to calm him. It is accordingly most important for the rider to develop techniques of handling the reins that avoid jerks so far as possible. The occasional deliberate jerk will then have a useful effect. In contrast, repeated jerks without special significance come to obscure all the signals one wishes to convey along the rein and the horse tends to stop "listening" to the rein and just goes on persistently fighting against it.

The situation to aim for is one in which both horse and rider contribute to maintaining a steady light tension in the rein. The rider allows the muscles of his hand and arm to act like very soft springs. Any movement of the horse's mouth is followed up smoothly by the rider's hand without allowing the tension in the rein to rise and without ever letting the rein go slack. The horse, for his part, learns not to lean too heavily against the bit and he also seeks to regain contact when the rein begins to go slack.

To teach the horse not to lean on the bit, you give when he pulls. This has the effect that, when the horse moves his mouth forward in an attempt to pull the rein free, he does not, in fact, achieve any change in the feel of the bit in his mouth. If his head movement fails to produce the desired effect, he gradually gives up making it. As soon as he brings his nose back in, you follow in with your hand, keeping up the contact. Occasionally you indicate to him that you don't want him to poke his nose out, by giving a brief pull on the reins just as he starts his head movement. You can also give one or two brief jerks if he persists in holding his head out and down for more than a moment or two. If he starts to graze, don't attempt to lift his head up by a long strong pull on the reins. Just nudge the reins and use your legs to ask him to walk on. He can't both walk on and graze at the same time.

If he gets into the annoying habit of repeatedly lunging downward and forward with his head, you must avoid letting him have the satisfaction of pulling you off balance because this rewards his misbehaviour. He is trying to pull the rein free, and if you topple forward he will have succeeded in his objective of relieving the pull of the bit in his mouth. If you are quick enough to catch the moment when he is just starting this lunging movement, you can discourage him by a brief pull on the reins. Another strategy is to grip the reins very firmly and to bring each hand across his neck to block the forward movement of the rein. When he throws his head down, he pulls your fists hard into the top of his neck. As well as helping you to avoid overbalancing forward, this will make the reins feel to him quite solid and unyielding. If you can manage it so that he never succeeds in snatching the rein from you, but always finds the rein solidly blocked when he tries this trick, he will eventually decide there is no profit in it and will give it up.

When you have got into the way of making the bit interesting to the horse by tickling with the reins, he will come to seek this interesting sensation. He will "feel" for the bit by a gentle forward movement of his head. If, at the same time, you have allowed your hand to move forward a little, he will step forward to try to bring himself closer to the bit. Of course, his step does not have this effect, because as he steps forward he carries you forward at the same time. But he is not to know this, since you reward his forward movement by yourself resuming the gentle pressure on the bit. In this way you teach the horse to go forward when you move your hand forward, even though the logical effect of your hand movement would appear to be to reduce your contact with the horse's mouth.

Emergency stop

After mounting and setting the horse in motion the next important manoeuvre that you need to master is how to stop. In this context it is well to remember that only the most vicious and unfriendly horses will deliberately try to throw you off. This means that if you take up the right position in the saddle, 81 namely the "safe position" illustrated in *Figure 3.9*, you can survive any but the most violent movements that the horse is likely to make. Keep this in mind and don't panic.

Most important: keep your heels away from the horse. Many beginners, when they get apprehensive, try to hold on by wrapping their legs round the belly of the horse. This reaction, which is apparently instinctive, has two serious disadvantages. It brings the knee away from the saddle, making the rider much less secure in his seat, and it brings the rider's heels against the horse's side. The pressure of the heels against the belly feels to the horse like an urgent command to gallop, and this is just what he is likely to do. Meanwhile the apprehensive rider goes all stiff in the body and rattles about in the saddle. Because the knees are not against the saddle the rider's centre of gravity doesn't stay in place over the mid-line of the horse. Then every time the rider's weight comes down in the saddle, that is to say, at each stride of the horse's progress, the impact tends to throw the rider further and further off balance until he eventually falls off.

To avoid all this, concentrate on pushing your heels well away from the horse. Push them forward a bit, rather than back. This will bring your knees firmly against the saddle, which is just where you want them. If both knees are firmly against the saddle, your weight will be in the right place, over the mid-line of the horse. Think of keeping the centre-line of your chest over the centre-line of the horse's neck. If the horse is not galloping on wildly, a few brief pulls on the rein will tell him to slow down and stop. Don't attempt to stop him by main force. The reins do not work like the brakes of a car, where the harder you press on the brake pedal the more effective the brakes will be. With the horse, a strong pull on the reins just encourages him to pull harder against you and the effect is to deprive you of any chance to "speak" to him through the bit. Instead of pulling like mad it is better to give with the reins, letting your hands go well forward, round his neck if need be, and then gradually you can take up a light contact. When you have managed this you can start to signal to the horse with brief pulls. If he does not seem to be responding to this and it feels to you that you are being run away with, the rule is: "Steer for the open spaces, and turn your horse into a circle". You gradually make the circles smaller and smaller. Also try turning the horse first to one side, then to the other, all the time concentrating on keeping your heels well away from him.

Eventually he will run out of steam and you can get him back under control – and enjoy the exhilaration in retrospect.

It is really a sign of serious bad management for a beginner to be run away with. The beginner should never be offered a ride on a horse if there is any doubt about the horse's response to the "stop" command. Furthermore, the first thing to teach a beginner, once he is in the saddle, is how to stop, and he should practise this repeatedly. Another principle is: when you first get up on a horse that is strange to you, set about practising the stops right away, even after only a few strides. In this way you build up your own confidence, and you also tell the horse that you know what you are doing, and that you do not mean to allow yourself to be trifled with.

The essential parts of the command to stop are: heels away from the horse, knees in, sink in the saddle if you can, think about stopping, and apply a few brief pulls on the rein. The horse will feel you relaxing into the saddle ready for the stop, and it is surprising how effective a little telepathy can be. After some practice, he will stop for you in response to the feel of the saddle alone as you put your knees in and relax your spine. The voice command of "Whoa!" can also be effective, but only if the horse has first been taught this in association with the signals of saddle and reins.

Lunge and side rein

The risk of a beginner suffering a runaway is, of course, very much reduced if the instructor retains control of the horse with a lunge rein. The beginner can then accustom himself to the horse's motion without any fear.

At first, the reins should be attached to a headcollar or to the side rings of a lungeing cavesson instead of to the bit. In this way the horse is saved the problem of interpreting the violent movements of the bit that can be caused accidentally by inexpert handling of the reins. Side reins can be fitted to discourage the horse from wandering if he is not used to keeping out to the full length of the lunge rein.

The beginner should practise the leg movements needed for the "walk on" command and should get used to keeping his heels away from the horse once it is in motion. He should also pay attention to relaxing his spine slightly, so that the shoulders and pelvis can move independently. The pelvis has to be allowed to rock from side to side with the movements of the saddle that are inevitable while the horse is walking. 83

Meanwhile the shoulders and upper part of the rider's body have to remain in balance over the horse's mid-line. The arm exercises which I shall describe later on are intended to help the rider to learn how to balance himself in the saddle. They also help to make the rider's balance independent of the rein.

The first stage, however, is to get the beginner to relax at the knee. So long as he keeps his heels away from the horse, the knee will be pressed into the saddle. Then, without moving his knee from its position on the saddle he should swing his lower legs about, forward and back, together and independently, and in and out sideways. From time to time he should halt, stand in the stirrups using a hand to maintain balance, and rise and fall on the ankles alone, keeping knee and hip straight, as described earlier. The aim of this exercise is to train the rider to keep his heel below the line of the stirrup so that he will get the full benefit of the effect of the bent ankle on the firmness of his grip with his knees.

Movements of the horse at walk

As soon as the horse begins to walk on, the beginner will experience unfamiliar sensations from the movement of the saddle. Indeed, even before that he will have felt some movement in the saddle because no horse ever stands absolutely still. The movements of the saddle are caused by changes in the activity of the horse's muscles. These changes are of two kinds. When a muscle is active it feels harder to the touch. It is not so easily deformed when you squeeze it, as you can see for yourself by feeling your biceps while you alternately tense and relax the muscles of the arm. The saddle rests on the muscles of the horse's back, so that when these muscles become tense or relax, the saddle sinks in to a lesser or greater extent. The muscles of the two sides of the back may change independently, leading to a rocking of the saddle from side to side.

The other way the horse's muscles affect the position of the saddle is a consequence of the way the muscles act to keep the animal's weight from collapsing onto the ground. One may think of the body as being supported on the bony skeleton, which is made up of stiff, virtually incompressible, rods. However, the bones are not rigidly coupled to one another and the flexibility of the joints makes it quite impossible for the bony skeleton to stand up by itself. Each joint needs to be stiffened by the pull of the tendons that pass from one bone to another across each joint, like the rigging of a ship. In most cases there is a muscle involved as well as a tendon. Muscles and tendons are all springy and they stretch when they are pulled upon; but whereas the springiness of a tendon is a constant characteristic of that tendon, the muscles can have their springiness altered by messages from the animal's nervous system.

When we look at the hindlimb of a horse from the side (*Figure 1.11*) we see that the joints between the bones are arranged in a sort of zig-zag, so that the weight of the body would collapse the leg against the ground if the muscles were not working at each joint to keep it from folding. I have spoken of the muscles as springy, but the body does not bounce up and down all the time like a weight supported on simple springs. The reason for this is that muscles have a sort of "shock-absorber mechanism" built into them. A muscle will develop more tension if it is being stretched than it can when it is shortening. The effect is just like that of the combined action of the shock absorbers and springs of a motor-car, though the actual mechanism is quite different.

When a horse is standing still the combined thrusts of its legs pushing against the ground must exactly balance the effect of gravity. If the limbs do not push hard enough, the body will fall; and if the limbs push harder than just enough, the body will be thrown upwards. If the body is moving, there are other factors we must take into account. Extra force is needed to set the mass of the body into motion, and once it is moving we need other forces to bring it to rest or to change the direction in which it is moving.

As well as pushing with the legs against the ground there are other effects that must be achieved by muscular action. Imagine trying to set up a table without fastening the legs to the top. Although the table-legs are quite stiff, they will not carry the weight of the table-top unless they are prevented from tilting over. It is essential to stiffen the angles between the legs and the top. In the same way, the horse's legs have to be prevented from slewing round as well as being made stiff enough to carry the weight.

The varying thrusts of the legs tend to produce twistings of the trunk and these in turn have to be resisted by the muscles of the back. You can feel corresponding changes in the muscles of your own back when you put your weight first on one leg alone and then on the other. By adjusting the actions of these trunk muscles one can move the body about without taking the feet off the ground. You will see the horse doing this while 85 grazing, as he moves his head to reach for fresh areas of grass to crop.

The slow movement of the body of the grazing horse involves changes in the amount of support provided by each of the legs. From time to time one of the legs is completely unloaded so that the thrusting muscles can be relaxed. Other muscles are then brought into play to fold up the leg, lift the foot, swing the leg forward into a new position, and then to let the foot down again onto the ground. The thrusting muscles are then brought back into play to provide limb support to the trunk in a new direction. If you continue to watch, you will

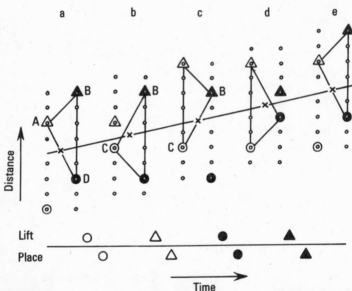

Figure 3.16
Five successive stages in a steady progression at the grazing walk. In each stage the relative positions of the feet are indicated by the following symbols (which are also used in later diagrams): Triangle = forefoot; Circle = hindfoot; Open symbol = left side; Filled symbol = right side. x = position of the centre of gravity. The small circles indicate four possible positions for each foot: 1) Full ahead, i.e. just arrived on the ground; 2) Half ahead, i.e. this foot has been on the ground for one, and only one, segment of the forward progression; 3) Half trailing, i.e. even after one more segment of forward progression there will be no urgency about lifting this leg; 4) Trailing, i.e. about to be lifted. The head is toward the top of the page in each case. *Below*: the moments of lifting and placing. When the left hindfoot is lifted, the body is supported on the triangular support ABD. During the movements of the left forefoot and right hindfoot the centre of gravity passes across the line CB. The body is stable at all times, there being always at least three feet on the ground.

86

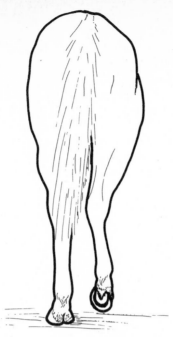

Figure 3.17
Resting a leg. The quarters are higher on the weight-bearing side.

notice that the horse always lifts his feet in the same sequence: left hind, left fore, right hind, right fore, and so on. When each leg is in the air, the trunk is safely supported on the other three legs and there is no danger of overbalancing (*Figure 3.16*).

You will sometimes see a horse dozing with the weight very unevenly distributed between the hindlegs. One leg may be bent with just the tip of the hoof resting on the ground (*Figure 3.17*). The haunches then appear markedly unsymmetrical, the resting side being carried very much lower than the weight-bearing side. There are similar, though less pronounced, differences to be seen between the forelegs, and you can feel these when the horse is walking along. If you rest your hand on the side of the withers just beside the backbone you can feel the shoulderblade pushing upwards at each step when the weight comes onto that leg. Then as the horse moves forward over the weight-bearing leg, you will see the point of the shoulder, down at the level of the chest, moving backward toward you. When the foreleg is swinging forward, the shoulderblade can be felt to sink away from the backbone. The chest is displaced sideways at each step. It bulges toward the swinging leg because the muscles are more relaxed on that side.

As you sit in the saddle at the walk you will feel the effects of these changes in the horse's body. The saddle rocks from side to side and at the same time surges forward and backward over the horse's back. The surges arise from the fact that the legs do not push straight upward. When the axis of a leg is tilted forward, from the foot, as it is toward the end of the support phase of the stride, it tends to topple forward and thus pushes the trunk forward. When each foot is set down after a swing phase, it props against the trunk and checks the forward motion. The sideways rocking of the saddle comes from the rolling motion of the horse's body as the support thrusts alternate between the limbs of the two sides.

The sequence of leg movements

To understand what is going on, feel the way your own pelvis moves when you are walking with long strides. As you move over the supporting leg and while the other leg is swinging forward, you will feel your body first rising and then falling forward. During the forward-falling phase, the supporting leg gives an extra push, when you straighten the ankle and push the hip down on that side. The swinging leg gives a little after touchdown, to absorb the momentum of the falling trunk onto a flexible and springy support. The centre of gravity of the trunk is lifted up over the forward leg by two mechanisms. It first rises passively like a pole-vaulter, and then it is actively lifted by straightening the leg. During the strong thrust of the supporting leg, the hip on that side is first pushed passively upward by the initial impact, and then it is later brought level again by the activity of the back muscles. The hip on the side of the swinging leg is actively lifted while the free leg is passing the supporting leg and during the development of extra thrust by the supporting leg at take-off. The hip is then moved forward and downward to extend the swing leg ready for landing.

The ordinary, or "medium" walk of the horse is slightly different from the grazing walk. When grazing, the horse slowly moves his trunk forward over stationary feet, with occasional steps by one leg at a time. Between the steps there is a pause with all four feet on the ground (*Figure 3.16*). When he walks on without grazing, he first lifts his head, then he takes a sequence of steps without any pauses between the movements

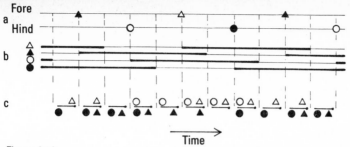

Figure 3.18
Timing diagram for the walk. a) footfalls of the forelimbs and hindlimbs; b) durations of the support phases (heavy lines) and of the swing phases (faint); c) patterns of support, with the head to the right in each case. (Symbols as in *Figure 3.16*.) The cycle is arbitrarily divided into eight epochs at the moments of lifting and placing of the feet. Each support pattern shown applies to the whole of the corresponding epoch. The pair of forelegs and the pair of hindlegs each move like the legs of a man walking, each foot of a pair being lifted only after the opposite foot has come to the ground. The two pairs are out of step, the hindlegs moving earlier than the forelegs, so that sometimes there are only two feet on the ground. At the trot the feet spend relatively less time on the ground. Forelegs and hindlegs move like the legs of a man running, this time they are almost exactly out of step. Consequently, at the trot there are two phases in each stride where all four feet are off the ground (see *Figure 4.2*).

of the individual legs. Indeed, he starts to move the next leg before the previously stepping leg has touched down (*Figures 3.18, 3.19 and 3.20*) so that there are moments in the cycle during which the body is supported only by a single pair of legs. One consequence of this is that each leg now has to develop a greater thrust, at least half the body weight, instead of only a quarter when standing still, or a third when one leg is being swung forward.

You can perhaps visualise the movements of the walking horse by thinking of two men striding along one behind the other, out of step by a quarter of a cycle (*Figure 3.18*). Look at the forelegs first (triangles). Each foreleg swings forward in turn, but only after the leg of the opposite side has already come to the ground to take over the support of the body. Thus, in *Figure 3.18*, the left foreleg (open triangle) continues to support the body until the right foreleg (filled triangle) has been placed on the ground. The hindlegs (circles) also execute a walking sequence like that of a walking man, each hindfoot coming to the ground before the opposite hindfoot is lifted. Because the swings of the forelegs are out of step with the hindlegs, there are times when two legs are both swinging 89

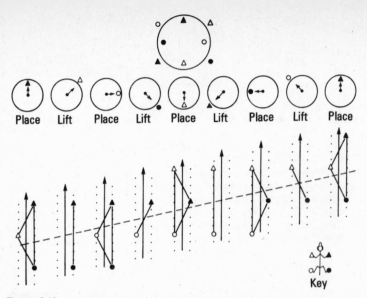

Place **Lift** **Place** **Lift** **Place** **Lift** **Place** **Lift** **Place**

Key

Figure 3.19
Succession of support patterns at the walk. *Above*: moments of lifting and placing arranged like the hour-markings on a clockface to show the repetitive nature of the cycle. Symbol inside the circle = moment of placing; symbol outside = moment of lifting. *Below*: support patterns at successive stages.

forward at the same time, leaving the body supported only on the other two, as indicated at the bottom of the figure.

Figure 3.19 shows the sequence of support patterns in the ordinary walk, for comparison with the grazing walk illustrated in *Figure 3.16*. The moments of lifting and placing of the individual legs are arranged round a clockface to emphasise the repetitive nature of the walking cycle. *Figure 3.20* combines this clockface layout with the side views of a walking horse at different moments in the progression.

The forces developed against the trunk by each of the legs follow a sequence like that described above for the human walk. Because the thrusts at the shoulders are not synchronised with those at the hips, the trunk is set into complicated twisting motions. As a result, the saddle executes oscillations of all possible kinds: swaying from side to side, surging forward and back, and vertical movements of rising and falling. Three sorts of rotary motion also occur: rolling from side to side about the longitudinal axis, pitching in the fore-and-aft plane, and yawing from side to side about a vertical axis.

90　　　The body of the rider is not rigidly fastened to the saddle. As

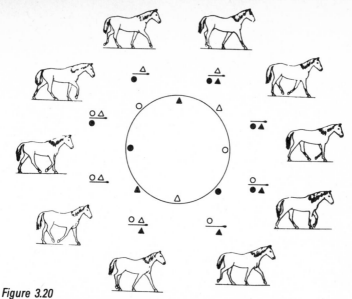

Figure 3.20
The cycle of movements at the WALK. The support patterns shown in *Figures 3.18* and *3.19* together with corresponding side views, are here set out in appropriate positions around the clockface of *Figure 3.19*. The outline drawings are taken from Muybridge, E. (1893) *Descriptive Zoopraxography, or the Science of Animal Locomotion Made Popular.*

the horse's body moves, so the rider's weight is continually being moved about by the movements of the saddle. Every so often, when the movement of the saddle changes direction, the rider's seat comes up against some part of the saddle with a jolt. The skilled rider absorbs these jolts by the flexibility of his spine. The horse also feels the jolts transmitted to his back from the saddle. In this way the horse can distinguish at once between carrying a rider on his back and carrying an inert load. He can also readily distinguish the involuntary swayings and jerkings of a beginner from the smooth movements of the skilled rider.

Movements of the horse's head

In addition to the complicated movements of the saddle, the rider has to contend with the movements of the horse's head. These head movements affect the reins, and if the rider is not careful the horse will feel the bit moving in his mouth in ways that do not reflect the intention of the rider. The horse does not know that the rider has not initiated these movements of the bit, and consequently may well become confused.

The head of the horse is relatively very heavy because, although it contains air spaces in the nasal cavities and elsewhere, it also contains the large masses of ivory forming the grinding teeth. This heavy weight on the end of the long neck forms a massive pendulum which needs large forces to set it into motion and to change its speed or direction of movement. The muscles that pull on the neck to move the head also pull on the trunk. In this way, the horse can use the momentum of its very heavy head to assist in moving other parts of the body.

For example, when the horse lifts his head the muscular effort involved has the indirect effect of tending to lift the hindquarters, because the support at the shoulders acts as the fulcrum of a lever. When the horse is walking briskly you will see that he lifts his head each time he needs to bring one of his hindlegs forward. As well as lifting the head and neck up and down, he may nod his head alone, pivoting at the base of the skull, just behind the ears. In consequence the rider feels the reins moving forward and back quite a long way. It is very important that he should learn to let his hands follow this movement smoothly. The necessary movement of his hands will be quite different from the movements of his shoulders that result from his being moved about by the saddle. The rider's arms have, therefore, to be very flexible. They have to give easily when the rein is drawn forward and they must be brought smoothly back again a moment later to take up the slack when the horse's mouth moves in again toward his chest.

Arm exercises at walk

The smooth control of the rein is perhaps the most difficult thing that the beginner has to master. It is for this reason that I advocate that, when the beginner is having his first lessons with reins and stirrups and with the horse on the lunge, the reins should be attached to the rings at the side of a cavesson or of a headcollar rather than to the bit itself. The rider can then get used to the movement of the horse's head without accidentally jerking the bit in the mouth.

When you are a beginner you may at first instinctively try to use the reins as an aid to balance. This should not be allowed to become a habit. It is as well to start without holding the reins at all, concentrating on learning the proper position for the feet and practising the suppleness of the back that will allow you to move with the saddle rather than being moved about by it.

When you have begun to keep your back supple and have

learned to swing the lower leg without moving the knee off the saddle, you can try some more adventurous moves. Hold both arms out sideways as far as they will go, palms uppermost. Then, keeping the elbows up and out, swing the arms forward at the elbow to bring the hands in front of the shoulders. Swing the arms out again to their full extent, again turning them palm upward. Repeat several times. This exercise helps to lift and expand the chest, and it lifts the shoulderblades away from the pelvis.

Leg-aids

Now combine the arm movements with movements of the legs. Pay attention to the sideways rolling of the saddle at each step. Notice that the saddle follows the movements of the horse's shoulders. When the left foreleg is on the ground you will see the point of the left shoulder moving back toward you. At the same time the saddle tips up slightly on the right side and down on the left. Emphasise this tilting by lifting your right leg sideways at this time, moving the foot about five centimetres away from the girth, but keeping the knee firmly pressed against the saddle. Then, as the weight comes onto the horse's right foreleg, bring your own right leg in against the horse's side and put a little more weight on your right knee. Take care that your foot does not move backward as you bring it in. It should remain on the girth. Make corresponding movements with your left leg also until your knees and pelvis are rocking from side to side in time with the movements of the horse's shoulders.

The alternating contact of your legs with the sides of the horse will have the effect of encouraging him to walk on. For this reason these movements are called the "leg-aids" for the walk. If your leg movements are too exaggerated, the horse may break into a trot; so if you are not ready for this, be careful not to give him too much of a thump with your leg. The combination of arm exercises with leg movements and rocking sideways in the saddle will help you to relax your spine until your shoulders can move independently of the movements of your pelvis. It also helps you to dispense with the rein as an emergency hand-hold.

Rein exercises at walk

You are now in a position to take up the rein and to get yourself used to the movements of the horse's head. At first have the 93 reins attached to the cavesson or to the headcollar with the horse on the lunge. Later you can try the same exercises with the rein in its normal position attached to the bit. You will probably find that it is very hard to concentrate on what is happening to the rein without your arm getting unacceptably tense. It helps to have something else to think about and for this I recommend changing hands.

Changing hands The aim of this exercise is to achieve such flexibility in the arm that the rein feels as though it is kept taut by the weight of your hand alone. The arm pivots freely without any pull being exerted at the shoulder. With your hands in the rest position, just above and slightly in front of the pommel of the saddle and with about ten to twelve centimetres between your thumbs, you will see that your forearm is not quite in line with the rein. If you swing your hands inward toward your body, keeping the thumbs on top, this will pull on the rein. If you swing your hands outward until the forearms point to the sides of the horse's mouth, the rein will go slack. You can use this sideways swinging of forearm and wrist, together with some forward and backward movement of the elbow, to allow the rein to come and go with the movements of the horse's head.

To practise this without thinking about it, keep changing the reins from one hand to the other and back again. The technique for getting both reins into one hand is as follows. Suppose you want to get both reins into the right hand. Roll your hands over to bring the thumbs toward one another and get ready to cross your hands to bring the left hand behind the right. Open the fingers of the right hand slightly, keeping a grip on the edge of the right rein with the second and third fingers and lifting the thumb (*Figure 3.21*). Then pass your left hand across behind and to the right of the right hand, laying the left rein into the fingers of the right hand on top of the rein that is already there. Close the fingers and thumb of the right hand and let go with the left. You now have the two reins in the right hand, the two parts that go forward to the bit being separated by the width of your hand, so that you can steer as necessary, simply by rotating the hand horizontally at the wrist. To separate the reins again, take hold of the left rein with the left hand just where it passes from the right hand toward the bit, and allow the loose central part of the left rein to slide out of your right hand without letting go of the right rein.

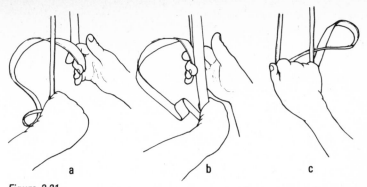

Figure 3.21
Taking both reins into one hand. Keeping control of the rein by curling the fingers, open the right hand and lay the left rein into it behind the rein that is already there.

Lightening the hand   In the rein exercise to lighten the hand on the rein, you repeatedly perform the following sequence of moves. Start with the reins in both hands as normal. Put both reins in the right hand. Hold the left hand out to the side fully extended from the shoulder, palm uppermost. Take the reins into the two hands and separate them. Put both reins in the left hand. Put the right hand out sideways from the shoulder. Separate the reins into the two hands. Put both reins into the right hand, left arm out. Separate the reins again, and so on. Throughout all these moves, the rein is to be kept just taut, the hands coming and going with the movements of the horse's head at every stride, and your legs swinging on and off the horse in time with the rolling movements of the saddle.

After you have been given a chance to get the feel of this exercise with the rein attached to the headcollar, the reins may be shifted to their proper place on the bit. You can now tell whether you are being successful in your handling of the rein because any jerk on the bit is likely to make the horse slow down and you will have to work harder with your legs to keep going.

Long reining
At this stage you can change over from the lunge to the long reins with these fastened to the rings of the bit along with the regular reins.

You, the rider, are now supposed to be in control of the horse. Your instructor is there just to make sure that the horse does not make off in response to some unintended stimulus from your legs, and to give you confidence. You can now practise "Walk on" and "Stop". You can also make the horse go faster or slower by adjusting the urgency of your leg movements and by adding occasional brief pulls to the steady tension you maintain on the rein.

Action of the "aids"

If someone tickles you in the ribs when you are lying down, this makes you lift your knee and bring your elbow down to cover the place where you are being tickled. The effect of your leg on the horse's side is rather similar. You will see from *Figure 3.18* that when one foreleg is past the halfway stage in its support phase, the horse is ready to lift his hindleg on the same side. You apply your leg to the horse's side during the support phase of the foreleg. This makes him bring that leg back more briskly, thus pushing the body forward, and it encourages him to lift the hindleg a little earlier. The combined effect is to speed up the walk.

Another way to speed up the walk is to encourage the nodding action of the horse's head. You do this by rhythmical adjustments of the tension in the rein. You pull a little when the horse is bringing his nose in, and you relax the rein a little extra when his nose is moving forward. As well as these rocking actions of the rein on the horse's head, which have the effect of increasing the vigour of the steps, you can also use the reins to adjust the speed over the ground. So long as the horse is contributing to the role of the rein as a signalling system, by gently seeking to maintain the "contact", then a slight reduction in the pressure of the bit will tell him to move forward and take longer strides, especially if at the same time you are active with your leg-aids. Similarly, a slight increase in rein tension will tell him to take shorter strides.

The effects of the rein on the speed over the ground can be independent of the effects on the vigour of the stepping action produced by encouraging the horse to nod his head. But to get these two valuable kinds of rein-aids to work, you must first persuade your horse to abandon the habit of playing at tug-of-war with you, and you must develop a sufficiently springy control of your hands to avoid the accidental jerks on the reins that inevitably follow those moments when you have allowed the rein to go slack.

With the horse on the long reins, you can practise adjusting the speed of the horse over the ground and you can also attend to the "character" of the horse's stepping action, distinguishing between a lazy, slouching action and a more lively, alert action in which the legs are picked up more briskly and raised higher at each step.

Steering

When you want the horse to move straight ahead, you make sure that the pressure exerted by the rein is equal on the two sides of the bit. You also apply your leg-aids symmetrically, at the level of the girth, and keep your weight centrally placed in the saddle. To change direction you alter the symmetry of all three kinds of signal.

To turn right, you first move your right hand back toward you by about a centimetre or so. The horse feels the bit move in his mouth and he will shift his head to bring the bit back to a position where it feels the same to the lips on the two sides. Do not attempt to pull the horse's head round as though you are turning the steering wheel of a car. Just give a sufficient signal to tell him to move his head. As soon as you can just see his eye on the right side you have gone far enough and you can resume a symmetrical pressure on the two reins. You do not need any more head movement than that which just brings his eye into view. The purpose is simply to indicate that a turn is coming and that it is going to be to the right.

The main command to turn is given with the leg. The effect of the squeeze of your lower leg against the horse's side is to increase the vigour of the activity of the legs of that side and, in particular, to tell the horse to lift the hindleg on that side. To make a turn to the right, you need more activity in the legs of the horse's left side. You indicate this to the horse by applying the left leg-aid a little behind the girth, while the leg-aid on the right remains as before directly over the girth. One effect of the asymmetry of your legs will be to alter the distribution of pressures between your seat and the saddle. As your left leg goes back to give the leg-aid for the right turn, the whole of the saddle twists very slightly to the right. You can emphasise this rotation of the saddle by shifting your weight to put more weight on the right knee. It is the combination of the changing feel of the saddle together with the new unsymmetrical position of the leg pressures that is effective in telling the horse to make the turn. He will actually turn quite readily, without the need for any rein signal, in response to the leg-aids accompanied by small shiftings of the rider's weight.

97

During early training, with the horse on the long reins, the rider may exaggerate each of the components of the aids for turning, first to one side and then to the other, so as to get the feel of what is required and of the way the horse responds. When the rider can manage the steering, and can demonstrate the effectiveness of his commands to stop, the long reins can be dispensed with and the rider can practise on his own. Gradually the intensity of his signalling movements should be reduced until he is able to give effective commands to the horse without his aids being conspicuous to the onlooker.

By the time the rider is ready for competitive dressage work, the aids should be virtually invisible. The rein-aids are almost imperceptible nudges executed by the fingers alone and applied during the steady contact with the horse's mouth. For the leg-aids, all that is needed is a small movement of the foot inside the boot, to alter the pressure against the stirrup. This has two effects: it alters the tenseness of the calf muscle, which the horse can feel because the rider's calf is resting against the horse's side; and it alters the tension in the stirrup leather. The leather does not hang absolutely straight down from the bar on the saddle because the horizontal distance between the bars is less than the width of the horse's body. Accordingly, when the tension in the stirrup leather is increased, it presses harder against the flap of the saddle. The horse can feel this change of pressure, just as he can feel the change in the feel of the saddle when the rider puts more weight on one knee than on the other. Eventually, both horse and rider develop the habit of "listening" intently to one another by feel so that they can each respond to even the smallest hint of an indication by the other.

Just as the rider practises the movements that he must make to help his horse to understand his wishes, so he should be on the lookout to feel for the changes in the horse's muscles that accompany the horse's movements. For the horse to move any leg, he has first to shift his weight onto the other legs. The horse may also make use of the changes in the momentum of his head as he swings his head about, sideways as well as up and down. The horse is continually on the alert for signs of approaching danger and you can tell when something catches his attention by the way his ears are suddenly aimed in a new direction. By paying attention to the movements of the horse's ears and head, and to the changes in the feel of the horse's muscles as conveyed to him through the saddle, the rider can learn a great deal about the horse's intentions. In this way he can avoid being taken by surprise. If the rider notices the signs that the horse is about to make some move, he will have time to make a signal of his own, either to encourage or to discourage the horse. Encouraging the horse to do something that he was going to do anyway has the effect of reinforcing the significance of your command, and this is a most important part of the process of building up fluency in the communication between horse and rider.

Hacking

When the rider has acquired the ability to walk on and to steer, and so long as there is no uncertainty about the effectiveness of the command to stop, it will be quite beneficial to go for a quiet hack in company with two or three more experienced riders, even though there has as yet been no practice in trotting. It is noticeable that horses like to keep together in a group; so where the experienced riders go, the beginner can accompany them without too many problems. He should keep practising his steering and his control of the speed over the ground. He should be particularly careful to avoid being taken too near the hindquarters of another horse. He should always maintain a clearance of at least one horse's length. If he gets too close, the horse in front will feel threatened and may kick out. Don't rely too much on assurances that "my horse doesn't kick". Just keep your distance and be safe.

Do not venture onto roads where there is likely to be a lot of traffic unless everyone in the party is experienced enough to be in control of their horse. If there is a beginner in the party, who is not yet secure at the trot, the others should not trot either, because when one horse trots, all the others are likely to imitate him. It is also important not to let the beginner become separated from the others. If, for some reason, he gets stuck and falls behind, go back and join him, because his horse may become agitated as soon as the others move away, and could become more and more difficult for the beginner to control. This principle is especially important if there are gates to be negotiated. Do not ride off after a friend has dismounted to open and shut the gate, until your friend is safely back in the saddle. If you are alone and your horse is getting worked up because you have been left at the gate, turn your horse away from the others and point his nose over the closed gate while you mount up. Talk to him and pat his neck to quiet him. Run your hands up and down his neck just beside the crest. 99

If during the ride you happen to stop for a chat to a pedestrian, you may have difficulty in keeping your horse quiet. He will not understand why you want him to continue standing still while you remain sitting on his back. He will keep trying to walk on and he may become excited if you repeatedly restrain him. It will be better to allow him to walk around in small circles while you continue your conversation. This gives him something to think about so that he doesn't get quite so impatient. Alternatively you can dismount, but even then he may wonder what all the delay is about and may start pawing at the ground. This is a polite way of telling you to get a move on. Remember not to ask your horse to stand about too long in a cold wind when his coat is wet with sweat from earlier exertions.

Shying
In the wild, the horse depends on his vigilance for survival, so you will find that, as you ride along, your horse's attention is continually being distracted, to one side or the other, often by things you yourself do not bother about, such as a piece of paper blown by the wind. He may stop suddenly, or he may swing suddenly to one side. In an extreme case he may stop very suddenly with a quick stamp of all four feet and throw his head first down and then violently upward, following through with an upward and sideways rearing lurch of the forequarters as he jumps to the side. It may thereafter be very hard to persuade him to go back to that spot.

If your horse shies like this, be very careful not to dig your heels in and pull on the reins. This will only excite him further. Put your heels firmly away from the horse, forward if possible, to bring your knees hard into the saddle. Reach forward with your hands and shoulders to get your hands onto the side of his neck where the contact will have a soothing effect. Try to relax, and speak reassuringly to the horse, patting him on the neck and rubbing your hands up and down beside the mane. Wait quietly for a moment or two before trying to move on again.

It is a great help to have another quiet horse to walk alongside, and slightly in front, to help you get your own horse past a point where he has shied. Here you are using the principle of "giving a lead". Because horses like to keep together, they will often tackle obstacles, when they are in a group led by a confident leader, that they would repeatedly shy away from and refuse if presented with the same situation when on their own.

Giving a lead

The strategy of giving a lead may be employed to deal with many other awkward situations. For example, the beginner will often find that he has difficulty in persuading his horse to leave a group of other horses. The root of the problem here may be either that the rider is not sufficiently unambiguous in his commands, or that the horse has not learned that leaving the others is one of the things he is expected to do. The beginner is likely to feel rather frustrated when his horse will not move off when asked. There is a strong temptation to kick the horse on and, as the rider's exasperation grows and his movements become more and more vigorous, he tends not to notice that at the same time as kicking backwards at the horse, he is also throwing his shoulders and arms about and accidentally jerking the reins.

In response, the horse starts throwing up his head and generally "playing up", sometimes even walking backwards. It is important that the rider should restrain himself. If he allows himself to get excited when his horse is misbehaving, the result will be a "shouting match", and a shouting match based on a misunderstanding doesn't usually solve anything. The rider should make an effort to keep calm and to proceed quietly, and step by step, through the routine described earlier for walking forward.

First of all, calm the horse by rubbing your hand up and down his neck alongside the crest and talking soothingly to him. Then ask for his attention by tickling the bit with the rein. Finally, drive on with seat and legs while at the same time easing the rein. If this does not work you may need to ask one of the other riders to give you a lead.

The idea of giving a lead in this context is that the horse's natural desire to keep with others can be directed to the lead horse as well as to the stationary group. If the lead horse is moving, it exerts a particularly strong attraction. Accordingly, if your horse refuses to leave a group of stationary horses, have another rider come alongside you, preferably between you and the others, and give your "walk on" commands just as he passes you. The two of you then ride round one behind the other on a fairly large circle, coming back close to the group of stationary horses each time round. As you pass the group, emphasise your walk-aids with legs, rein and seat, and pay particular attention to the steering. After a few trials you can try going round the circle on your own without the lead horse. In this way you allow your horse to become accustomed to walking past other horses without stopping.

Heading for home

The liking for the company of other horses produces another effect that can be troublesome for the beginner when he starts to go out hacking. Horses seem to know their way about the countryside quite well and they know which gateways or turnings will take them back to the stable. If they have made up their mind that the rider is somewhat ineffective in asserting his will, they will try to go home when they feel like it, without waiting for the rider's indication. They will sometimes show great reluctance to be ridden away from the stable, or past a turning toward home that they have taken on a previous excursion. Firm leg-aids are needed in situations such as this.

Do not expect to be able to exert your will by exaggerating your commands through the rein. You must, of course, be quite firm in your intention, so that any effect of telepathy will work in your favour, but do not try to pull the horse round by his head. I described earlier how to stop a runaway by steering strongly into ever decreasing circles. This is the only situation in which there is any point in pulling the horse's head round toward your knee. The effect of this is to slow him down and eventually to stop him. When you remember this you will see that to pull the horse's head round when he is standing still, in an effort to get him to move away from the direction he has chosen, is not going to have much chance of success. You are asking him to move on in response to a command to stop. It is better to turn the horse's head only slightly, just enough to bring his eye into view on the side to which he is to turn. Then get him to walk on, straight ahead at first if need be, even if this is not the way you want to go eventually. Then get him to make the turn at the walk, using strong leg-aids, behind the girth on the outside of the turn and on the girth with the inside leg. Turns on the spot may be useful here (described in the next chapter), but until you have mastered these, it is better to get the horse moving first, and then to make the turn at the walk.

If the horse persists in making for home, bring him firmly to a halt, speak to him, set his head ready for a turn, and walk on, as described above, making the desired turn firmly with your legs once he is in motion and using as light a hand on the rein as possible. Any jerking or pulling on the rein at this point just undermines the effectiveness of your leg command to walk on. If you still have difficulty, ask one of your companions to ride his horse across in front of you and try to get your horse to follow on. As a last resort, dismount, lead your horse a few yards in the direction you wish to go, and then get up again. Watch out for any suspicion of an intent to turn for home and give firm leg-aids to make clear to the horse what you want him to do.

Walking backwards

If you find yourself in a conflict of wills with your horse, watch out in case he starts to walk backwards. This reaction is a particularly dangerous habit. When the horse is fighting against the bit he does not look where he is going and he may walk backwards into trouble. For example, he may back into oncoming traffic or over an edge into a ditch. On no account should a beginner be put up on a horse that has this vice, because the beginner's reaction to the undesired and unexpected movement is often to tighten up on the rein as though this will put on the brakes. What happens is precisely the opposite. The pull on the rein is an encouragement to back and the horse just goes backwards faster than ever.

To cure a horse of this habit you need an experienced rider who knows how to manage the spurs and who can deal with any sudden reaction of the horse. As soon as the horse starts to back, the rider should apply firm pressure with the spurs well behind the girth on both sides. Be careful not to have a tight rein but be on the alert for any sudden move the horse may make. If necessary the action of the spur can be reinforced by a sharp blow with the crop, applied just behind the boot, but not always on the same side. Remember here that, to be effective, any punishment like this must be extremely prompt. If you delay even a couple of seconds, the horse will not associate the punishment with what he has been doing. It will just reinforce his notion that he is in a situation from which he must exert himself violently to escape.

Pulling

A horse will go forward much more eagerly once you have reached the homeward leg of your hack. Here is your chance to practise the stops. It is better to stop many times, and to ride 103 with a light rein in between, rather than to allow your horse to pull against you all the way home. The tug-of-war is an irritating bad habit. Some horses will open their mouths and throw their heads about to evade the bit while pulling very strongly, almost hard enough sometimes to pull you right out of the saddle. Do not put up with this. Even more important, do not encourage the horse by pulling against him. Give when he pulls and quickly take up the slack again as soon as you can. Try to keep a constant gentle pressure in spite of all his head shaking. If he starts to go faster, make a definite stop with a few brief pulls on the reins, returning at once to the gentle contact as soon as you get any response.

It is important not to get too tensed up. Keep your heels well away from the horse, because if you cling on, this will only make him want to go faster. Run your hand up and down his neck beside the mane. Speak to him calmly. Although you are practising stops, do not let your companions get too far away ahead.

Up hill and down hill
It is very good practice, both for horse and for rider, to take any opportunity that presents itself, when out hacking, to walk up and down hills, banks and other rough places. But be careful to avoid slippery places. Even a quite moderately inclined metalled road can be quite treacherous. A surface that is admirable for the wheels of a motor-car can be quite dangerous for horses. Their iron horseshoes make no indentations in a hard road so that there is nothing to grip with, and the horses slide all over the place. On a hill they can easily fall and hurt both themselves and their riders.

When going up a steep hill, sit well forward in the saddle, gripping with your knees and reaching along the horse's neck with your hands (*Figure 3.22*). Let the reins be fairly slack to allow the horse to make the plunging movements with his head that he needs. If you have to hold on with your hands, use the neck strap if there is one, or hang on to the mane. Do not try to save yourself from slipping back by pulling on the rein. Aim to get your weight well forward, over your knees if you can. If you start to slide in the saddle, get your feet out of the stirrups quickly and hang on to the pommel of the saddle so that, if you do slide right off, you will land on your feet. Horses seem to enjoy going up hill. On a moderate slope they will canter if given half a chance. Very steep slopes are taken in

Figure 3.22
Going up hill. Lean well forward with your weight out of the saddle, arms round the horse's neck if need be. Have a slack rein and grip with your knees. If you start to slip, hold on to the mane, to the neckstrap, or to the saddle. Do not try to save yourself by holding on to the rein.

a series of bounds and it is essential to lean well forward with your seat out of the saddle and with your weight on your knees to avoid being thrown about violently by the saddle each time the horse surges upward.

You also need to keep your weight on your knees when going down hill.

When you realise you are about to go down a steep place, pause and check the girth. You don't want the saddle to go sliding along the horse's neck. Then put your feet well forward, knees almost straight, heels out and toes in, and check that the stirrups are under the ball of the foot (*Figure 3.23*). The cushioning action of the ankle joint provides an important contribution to your security. Lean your shoulders a little forward, if anything, rather than back, to make sure you are not pressing on the saddle with your seat-bones. It is permissible for your seat to brush the saddle momentarily from time to time, but if you are sitting back with your weight on the saddle, the sudden movements as the horse lifts up each of his hindlegs in turn will throw you forward quite sharply. If you overbalance forward you will have nothing to hold on to. So 105

Figure 3.23
Going down hill. Weight on your knees, feet slightly forward rather than back, heels away from the horse. Let the horse have his head free.

keep your weight out of the saddle, grip firmly with your knees and balance yourself with knee and ankle. Let the rein go reasonably slack, so as not to restrict the movements of the horse's head. Just give a touch on the rein occasionally on one side or the other to keep the horse aimed in the desired direction.

You will feel that the movements of the saddle are very much more pronounced than they are on level ground. This is because the horse prevents himself from pitching forward by strong thrusts of the forelegs. The horse doesn't have a collarbone to connect his shoulderblade to the skeleton of the trunk and in consequence the increased forces that the forelegs have to bear when the horse is going down hill produce large movements of the shoulderblades under the saddle. You will feel yourself being thrown from side to side as well as plunging downward in a series of lunges.

The horse will hold his head a long way down and, because the hill is sloping away in front, you will feel a very long way from the ground. Don't let this worry you. Horses are quite used to going down steep hills and they don't mind going down quite fast. The essential thing is to aim straight down if the slope is at all steep or slippery. Then if the horse starts to slide, he will just sit down on his hindquarters and slither along until he gets a grip or reaches the bottom. So long as he is going straight down he can keep his forelegs out in front of him and he can easily remain upright. On no account attempt to go down a steep slope at an angle because, if the horse should happen to lose his footing, you will both go rolling down together, with serious risk of injury both to horse and rider.

The extensive movements of the saddle, as the horse negotiates the uphill and downhill slopes, compel the rider to bend his back. To retain his balance he has to keep his shoulders vertically above his seat while his pelvis is being rocked from side to side and while his weight is being pushed alternately forward and backward. This is a very good exercise and it helps considerably in developing the rider's suppleness. It is also very good for the horse, strengthening his muscles.

Another advantage of practising riding up and down steep places is that it brings home to the rider the importance of the shock-absorbing action of the ankle. He will get the benefit of this only if he rides with the stirrup under the ball of the foot. This should become a matter of habit.

The position of the foot
When you are out hacking take the opportunity to check the position of your foot in the stirrup. You should not be able to see your toe, but you can lean over from time to time to take a peep. The toe should be pointing forward, not out to the side. If you let your toe turn outward this will bring your knee away from the saddle. Your legs will hang round the horse in an attitude like the legs of a frog. At each jolt, the heels come up against the side of the horse, giving him a signal that you do not intend. If he were to pay attention to this signal, it would mean "Gallop on", but usually he will have realised that he need not bother to respond. He can ignore this continually repeated signal and treat it as meaningless "noise" – irritating but not significant. The consequence is that when you really do want to signal to him with your legs he will not be "listening".

If your knees are not firmly against the saddle, you will be at a disadvantage if the horse is suddenly startled. His reaction is to drop his weight four or five centimetres while he splays his feet out ready to make off in any direction. You will feel the jolt as the saddle first drops and then is suddenly supported again. You will hear the stamp as all four feet come down together in their new positions. The horse's ears are pricked up and his 107 head will make a sudden movement. The horse may either make a dead stop or he may jump to one side. In any case, if your knees are not firmly against the saddle, it will be possible for the saddle to move some way under you before you detect it. This delays your reaction and you may be unbalanced to such an extent that you fall off. With the knee against the saddle you not only get an early warning, but the saddle pushes against your knee and this can itself start you moving in the direction of safety.

To check that your feet are in the correct rest position just over the girth, try the effect of relaxing the pressure against the stirrup. If your foot is too far back, the stirrup will slide forward under your toe as soon as the sole of your foot lifts clear of the stirrup. Similarly, if your foot is too far forward, the stirrup will drop back under the arch of your foot. With your foot in the correct position, the stirrup leather will be vertical and the stirrup will remain in place under the ball of the foot when you lift the front of your foot up and down. Try to do this without lifting the heel, so as not to disturb the position of your knee against the saddle. Repeat on the other side. As well as consolidating your habit of keeping the foot in position over the girth, experiment with other positions, forward for a stop and behind the girth ready for a turn, and get used to the feel of these positions so as to be able to put your foot where you want it when the occasion demands. Return to the rest position: stirrup leather vertical, heel away from the horse, toe pointing forward, heel well down below the base line of the stirrup, knee nestling in the hollow between the knee rolls of the saddle.

When your weight comes onto the stirrup, the leather will have to be vertical. This is why the rest position of the foot should also allow the leather to be vertical. The stirrup is placed under the ball of the foot so that, when the leg moves up and down relative to the saddle during the inevitable jolting of the horse's motion, this leg movement can be taken up by the ankle joint, to keep a steady contact with the stirrup.

The aim is so far as possible to avoid movement of the leg relative to the saddle except when making a deliberate signal to the horse. Nevertheless, because of the movements of the horse, and because of changes in the rider's posture when he shifts his weight, the forces between the leg and the saddle are continually changing. The soft tissues of the rider's leg are squeezed by these changing forces and this inevitably leads to some relative movement of the leg over the saddle. If the stirrup is under the arch of the foot, instead of under the ball, the leg movement comes up against the rigid stop of the stirrup leather, producing a jolt that disturbs the contact between horse and rider. If this happens when going down hill or at the take-off for a jump, when the horse's body rises suddenly, the rider may be thrown out of the saddle. The rider's weight, during active riding, should come on the inside of his knees: not on the stirrups (because he should be able to ride without stirrups) and not on the seat-bones unless the rider deliberately applies his weight there as a signal to the horse.

Training the rider's leg

Once you have some idea of what is needed, you can help yourself to find a comfortable way of achieving the desired posture by an exercise carried out unmounted. Stand on the bottom step of a staircase, facing inward, with your heels overhanging clear of the edge of the step. Steady yourself with a hand and then move up and down using only your ankle joint. Rising onto the toes is a familiar movement. Now try sinking as far as you can, allowing the heel to go down below the level of the step. Throw your weight up and down several times allowing the ankle to relax as much as possible to get the feel of having the heel below the ball of the foot.

The next stage is to have the feet well apart, as they would be on the horse, and set parallel to one another, that is, toes pointing forward. Repeat the "bouncing" to help free the ankle joint. Then lean forward, bending the knees, and move the arms well forward until the elbows are in front of the knees. The bounces continue until the shoulders come down almost between the knees. Practise balancing in this position, with minimal support from the hands, while bouncing up and down by moving the ankles.

To extend the exercise when mounted, rise in the stirrups, making sure they are under the ball of the foot, and balance yourself with a hand on the horse's withers or by holding on to the mane. Have the knees as near straight as they will go, then move repeatedly up and down with the ankles as before, emphasising the sinking deep down to get the heel well below the ball of the foot, and keeping the heels out, toes forward. One effect of this exercise is to firm up the muscles of the calf so that they may be used to press on the horse in the various ways needed for signalling in the "leg-aids". Another effect is to encourage the inward bracing of the knees that provides the basis of a "good seat". After some practice it will be possible to hold the position of "rising in the stirrups", with the knees straight and the seat out of the saddle, even without the stirrups, the weight being taken entirely on the inside of the knees. It is important to remember that in this exercise the reins may not, in any circumstances, be used for balancing.

Riding without stirrups

One of the problems facing the beginner is that he is not used to having the width of the body of the horse between his legs. The unfamiliar attitude of the hip joints becomes uncomfortable after he has been jolted up and down for a few minutes by the movements of the horse. This is particularly so because the horse's movements are also unfamiliar and the beginner needs time to learn how to relax so that his pelvis will smoothly follow the movements of the saddle without jolting the rider's back. A good way to get your hip joints used to the new movements is to spend a few minutes each day riding without stirrups.

You will need your stirrups to get mounted up and if you just leave them dangling, they will swing about and bang against the horse's side. To get them out of the way, lift them up and cross the leathers over the horse's neck in front of the saddle. This may leave an uncomfortable lump where your thigh passes over the stirrup bar. To avoid this, first pull the buckle of the stirrup leather a few centimetres away from the bar and then turn the two parts of the leather upward separately so that they lie flat under the skirt of the saddle (Figure 3.24).

Ride on at the walk, practising your leg-aids, swinging your weight a little from side to side in time with the horse. Remember to keep your toes pointing forward with the heel below the sole of the foot. Try to get the knee as straight as possible. This will emphasise the grip of your knees against the saddle and will give you an increased sense of security. If your leg-aids are so vigorous that your horse starts to trot, don't panic and grip with your heels because this will only send him on faster. Relax your lower leg, squeeze with your knees, and give a few brief pulls on the rein to tell the horse to slow down.

The leg-aids involve movements of the lower leg, out sideways away from the girth and then back again into position over the girth with a slight pressure against the horse's side.

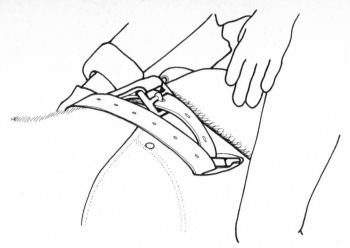

Figure 3.24
Crossing the stirrups. To avoid an uncomfortable lump under your thigh, pull the buckle of the stirrup leather away from the bar and make sure both parts of the strap are lying flat under the skirt of the saddle.

The knee stays in place against the saddle. Also try movements of the lower leg forward and back without touching the side of the horse. The aim here is to develop independence of the lower leg so that it can be used to control the horse without disturbing the grip of the knee against the saddle. Move the two legs in opposite directions, as in walking. Also move both legs forward or back at the same time, or move one leg at a time.

Practise also the arm and rein exercises described earlier, changing the rein from one hand to the other in order to free yourself from the feeling of wanting to hold on to the reins for balance. Then combine the arm exercises with the leg exercises until you begin to feel really confident in your balance in the saddle, and can move hands or legs quite independently when you need them for signalling to the horse.

Dismounting

When the time comes to dismount, bring your horse to a halt, take both feet out of the stirrups, and sit softly and quietly in the saddle. The horse will then know that you are about to get down. Put both reins in the left hand, with your hand on the withers as for mounting. Put the flat of your right hand firmly on the front of the saddle with the heel of the hand on the pommel (*Figure 3.25*). Bring your right elbow hard in to your

111

Figure 3.25
Prepare to dismount. Feet out of the stirrups, weight on your hands, right elbow hard against your side, and pivot forward over the right forearm.

side in front of your hip and lean forward, pivoting over your forearm. This will lift your seat out of the saddle. Bend the right knee and, carefully avoiding kicking the horse, swing your right leg backwards up and over the horse. Pause when the two legs come together on the left side of the horse, let yourself slide down gently for a few centimetres, and then drop to the ground. Keep hold of the reins and keep both hands in contact with the horse so as not to fall over backwards. Be prepared to bend your knees as you land on your toes; you are going to drop quite a long way.

Unsaddling
If the horse is not going to be mounted again immediately, by yourself or by someone else, put the stirrups up into their 'parking' position so that they do not swing about. Slide the stirrup up the inner part of the leather, right up to the bar, and then tuck the free loop of leather through the stirrup. This will hold the stirrup in position. If you have some distance to go to

the place where you will take the saddle off, first loosen the girth a couple of holes. As soon as your weight is out of the saddle, the girth will suddenly feel tighter to the horse and he will appreciate being relieved of this tension.

When taking off the tack, take the saddle off first. If you remove the bridle first, the horse may walk away from you with the saddle still in place. His first thought may be to have a good roll, and this won't do your saddle any good! After parking the stirrups, take the reins over his head and loop them over your arm while you are manipulating the saddle. Undo the girth buckles on one side and lift off the saddle, sliding it first backwards a little over the horse's back so as to avoid rubbing the hairs of the coat the wrong way. Lay the girth over the seat of the saddle, horse side down. The sweat will wipe off easily, whereas any dried mud on the outside of the girth might scratch the saddle. Place the saddle over a gate or over the half-door of the stable until you have finished with the horse. Be careful if you have to lay it on the ground. Keep it well out of the way of the horse's feet. If the front of your saddle is fairly square, you may be able to balance it on the front arch; otherwise you will have to lay it down upright, resting on the back of the panel and on the edges of the saddle-flaps. Keep it away from grit and gravel.

When taking the bridle off, start by putting the rein over the horse's neck, just behind the ears, so that you will be able to retain some control. Have the headcollar or halter ready, looped over one elbow. Undo the buckles of the noseband and throatlash. Then put both hands up to the poll. One hand is to slide the bridle forward over his ears, the other is to discourage him from immediately throwing his head up. Pause with your bridle hand in front of his forehead to allow him to drop the bit. If you don't do this he may throw his head up with the bit still in his mouth. It will rattle against his front teeth and he may plunge about trying to get rid of it. Once his head is up, the bit will not drop out. Even if he does open his mouth, the bit will still be hooked round the lower teeth. An instinctive pull on the bridle doesn't help either. When the horse finally succeeds in getting rid of the bit, it may fly toward you and hit you in the face. You can.avoid all this excitement, simply by taking the bridle off gently and pausing to give time for the horse to drop the bit. Once the bit is out of his mouth you can take your hands away from his head. If he starts to move off before you are ready, take hold of both sides of the reins close up to his 113 throat. If you have remembered to put the rein just behind the ears you should have no difficulty in restraining him. Loop the headpiece of the bridle over your elbow in exchange for the headcollar and slip the headcollar into place. You will then have the lead-rope with which to restrain the horse while you lay the bridle aside with the saddle.

Give the horse a rub down, paying particular attention to the damp patches under the saddle and girth. Also rub round the ears and over the face in those places that have been in contact with the bridle. He will appreciate this and may rub his head strongly against you. He intends this in the most friendly manner, but you must be careful not to get your clothes covered in slobber. If you give him a few titbits, remember to keep your hand flat so that he doesn't accidentally close his teeth on your fingers. Don't have sweets in your pocket at this stage. He will smell them and may try to get at them with his teeth. Nibbling at you with his lips is a friendly gesture rather than a vicious attempt at a bite. If he gets too demonstrative, just give him a firm nudge on the side of his face with your knuckles. Don't slap his face or make any sudden movement because this will alarm him and he will become more reluctant to stand close to you. He will also be more difficult to catch. When you are ready to let him free, slip the headcollar off quietly, talk to him, rub his neck and walk away. Do not drive him away from you, leave him standing there. He may stare after you for a bit, then he will probably walk away and have a roll.

Collect up your tack, rinse the bit and go over the leather items with saddle soap, paying particular attention to the panels of the saddle. If these are left to dry they soon become encrusted with hard masses of dried sweat and hair which can eventually cause saddle sores. The sweat wipes off easily if you attend to it promptly.

4 Basic Movements

Impulsion

When you get your leg-aids working properly at the walk (closing your legs alternately against each side of the horse in turn when the shoulder of that side is coming back toward you) and if you can avoid jerking the rein, you will usually find that the horse gradually increases the vigour of his walk. He may walk faster, or step out more, or lift his feet higher at each step. At the same time the nodding of his head becomes more and more pronounced. You can accentuate the nodding by rhythmically varying the pressure of your fingers on the rein.

Apart from the grip of thumb and forefinger, which should be just enough to prevent the rein from sliding through your hand, the fingers are only lightly curled against the rein. The pull on the rein is just enough to carry the weight of your hand hanging against it and the flexibility of your relaxed arm and shoulder allows the hand to be moved freely backward and forward by the movements of the horse's head. Unless you deliberately intend it, there should be no fluctuation in the tension in the rein. You should feel the rein by pressing lightly with your fingers and you should be on the lookout for moments when the rein goes slack and then snaps taut again. If this happens, you will feel the slight jerk. The horse easily notices the very slightest jerk and responds by slowing down, unless he has decided that the jerks are happening all the time and that they can therefore be ignored.

You encourage the nodding by pulling a little when he gives and by giving a little when he pulls, at each nod of the head. The change that is produced in the horse's readiness to go forward by the combination of your repeated leg-aids together with the action of your hands, is called "impulsion". This is a very important idea. It is not the same as "acceleration" or "speed", and it is not quite the same as "eagerness" or "spirit". It is a contained eagerness to go forward. The horse holds back, waiting for the rider's authorisation, so that he is ready to surge forward promptly on command.

To build up impulsion you first practise changing the speed over the ground by adjusting the steady tension in the rein. You need to start by increasing the pressure on the bit surrep- 115 titiously, taking up the rein a little at a time and keeping the speed going by the action of your legs. If the horse slows up, at once ease the rein and increase the vigour of your leg-aids. After a few strides with increased rein pressure, relax the rein a little and watch for the horse moving his head forward, to follow your hand, and lengthening his stride. Then take up rein again cautiously, to meet the increased pressure that the horse is now putting on the bit. Keep the leg-aids going while the horse shortens his stride. After a few strides with this increased rein tension, relax the rein again and allow the horse to go ahead with longer strides.

Extended walk

You now have two sorts of variation in the feel of the rein to keep going at the same time. There is the regular coming and going with the nodding of the horse's head and there is the slower and more sustained variation to produce shortening and lengthening of the horse's stride. Persist with your practice of the changes in speed until you can obtain three clearly differentiated speeds at the walk. In the "extended walk" the horse steps out briskly, each stride being noticeably longer than those taken at the relaxed "medium" walk which is his more natural pace.

Collection

The "collected walk" is more difficult to achieve. Usually, when you increase the pressure on the rein, the horse will slow up and he may stop altogether. What you have to aim for, by tactful adjustments in the intensity of your aids with leg and rein, is a shortening of the stride with at the same time an increase in the vigour of the action of the horse's legs. The horse lifts his feet well up at each stride and arches his neck without pulling too heavily on the rein. He is responding to the leg-aids by increasing the vigour of all his movements. At the same time he is holding back in readiness for whatever you tell him to do next. He should not be fighting against your restraint, but holding himself in without leaning on the rein. As soon as you move your hand forward, he responds by surging forward. If you move one hand forward he advances more on that side and goes into a turn. You should practise these turns asked for by giving with the outside hand, as well as those produced by pulling with the inside hand and those produced by leg-aids alone.

Also try to recognise the general feel of the horse's movements. When properly collected, the horse feels more "bouncy" under you. Distinguish this controlled bounciness from the excited "tittuping" that horses sometimes perform when they are very keen to get on with something but cannot quite make up their minds exactly what is required of them. A horse that is accustomed to go forward freely and to lead other horses when out hacking, will start tittuping if he is held back and sees the other horses in the ride going past him or away from him. He may be fighting the bit that is holding him back if the rider gives in to the temptation to pull back at him, or, if the rider has a light enough hand, he may just throw his head up and down without pulling. He makes lots of little steps with his hindlegs and plunges up and down on the forelegs as though about to take off at a gallop. Indeed, he will gallop on as soon as the rider indicates that this is permitted. He may prance about all over the place, even going backwards, and seems obsessed with the idea of violent activity and pays no attention to what he is doing. To calm him you may have to turn him away from the other horses, caress his neck and talk soothingly to him. If there is room to walk on, this will usually settle him. Because of the problems associated with tittuping, you have to be very tactful with a lively horse when asking for collection. Be content with just a little collection to start with.

Transition from walk to trot

After practising the changes of speed at the walk you will begin to be able to feel changes in the horse's impulsion. By working with your legs and at the same time restraining his forward acceleration, by increasing the weight of your hands on the reins, you will feel the horse being "wound up" like a spring compressed between the forward drive of your legs and the backward restraint of your hands. When the horse is wound up, he will surge forward as soon as you move your hands forward to relieve the tension in the rein. To get the change of gait from the walk to a trot, all that is now needed is the appropriate signal from your legs.

The leg-aids for the walk are the alternating pressures, one at a time, of the calf muscles of your leg on each side. To tell the horse to trot, you squeeze simultaneously with both legs, each leg applying the same sort of pressure as you have been using at the walk. These leg-aids are applied over the girth. There is no need to kick backwards.

Just as you used a combination of signals to give the command to walk on – leg, rein and saddle – so you need a similar combination for the command to trot. Before asking the horse to walk on, you have learned to warn him that you are ready by giving the "alerting" command, tickling the bit with the rein. He then goes forward when you relax the rein at the moment of giving the aids with leg and saddle. To make the transition from walk to trot you first prepare by building up impulsion at the walk, using active leg-aids accompanied by a restraining hand. You will then have some tension in the rein which can be relaxed as part of the command to trot.

It may be helpful for the beginner if other horses are ridden alongside and all start the trot together. The beginner's horse will then trot by imitation and this helps the novice rider to learn the timing of his moves. The instructor first calls "Prepare to trot". Each rider then collects his horse and starts building up impulsion so that the horse can feel the relaxation in the rein as the rider's hand moves forward. At the command "and ... ter-rot!", all riders apply their leg-aids simultaneously and give with their hands. All the horses then start to trot at the same time.

Halt and rein-back

The preparation for each change of gait involves an effort by the rider to get the horse alert and ready for the next command. The rider makes his wishes known to the horse by "winding him up" between the forward drive asked for by the leg-aids and the restraint indicated by the reins. The combination of leg and rein should be used for the halt as well as for an increase in forward speed. Do not expect a clean halt in response to rein action alone. Remember that the effective part of your signal with the rein is the change in tension. Use brief pulls and make a distinct release of tension as you give between the pulls. A steady pull just encourages the horse to lean his weight against your hand. He may lunge his head forward to escape the steady pressure on the bit and try to pull you forward out of the saddle.

You build up impulsion by squeezing with the legs while restraining with your hand. Then, if you give with the hand while squeezing with the legs, the horse will move ahead. If, instead of giving, you increase the pressure on the bit, the horse will slow down. If he is already at the halt, he will walk backwards. Thus the preparation for the rein-back is the same

118

Figure 4.1
Rearing. A trained horse is here rearing up on command. The rider grips with his knees and bends forward at the hips so that his body remains upright in spite of the backward tilt of the saddle. The drill for rearing is very similar to that for riding up hill (see *Figure 3.22*).

as the preparation for the walk-on. The only difference is in the rein pressure. A decreased pressure means "walk on", and an increased pressure means "walk backwards", provided you start from a suitable state of alert collection.

Do not attempt to produce the rein-back simply by a strong pull on the rein alone. If you happen to raise your hands while you are pulling strongly, the horse may respond by rearing. If you are not ready for this, it can be very frightening.

Your reaction to rearing must be to grip firmly with the knees and to throw your weight well forward (*Figure 4.1*), arms round the horse's neck if need be. Relax the rein. If you need something to hold on to, grasp the mane rather than the rein. If you happen to tip backward and try to save yourself by hanging on to the rein, the effect may be just to overbalance the horse. He may then fall backwards on top of you. Pulling his head to one side may help because he can twist in the air to land on his forefeet. In any case, if the horse goes well up, get your feet out of the stirrups, so that, if you do start to slide, you can land on your feet.

If you feel that your horse is about to rear, quickly urge him to go forward with active leg-aids and relaxed rein as he cannot both go forward and rear at the same time. Then return to what you were trying to do before, but this time be a little more tactful.

When you first try the rein-back, the horse may not understand what it is you want him to do. To explain this to him, ride him toward a high wall that he cannot see over. Come to a halt square on to the wall and very close to it. Pause for a moment, then give strong leg-aids and brief pulls on the rein, keeping your hands low. The leg-aids tell the horse to get moving, but the wall prevents him from going forward. He may then realise that the pulls on the rein, which are in any case increasing rather than decreasing at the time when he is feeling the leg-aids, must this time mean "Walk back". Watch out for attempts to turn out to one side and indicate briskly with the rein that this is not what you want. If he takes one step back, reward him warmly by your voice and by your hand on his neck. Be content at first with even a single step back and go on to do something else. Leave the follow-up till later. This gives the lesson a chance to sink in. Too much insistence all at once can have the undesirable effect of building up resistance.

Movements of the rider at trot

When you have achieved the rein-back you will have begun to get the feel of having your horse wound up between leg and hand. Thereafter, you should have no trouble in making the transition from walk to trot, so long as you can avoid giving the horse accidental jerks on the bit, by the rein alternately going slack and snapping taut.

As soon as the horse starts to trot, the rider is faced with a whole set of new sensations. In place of the rolling and horizontal surging of the saddle, forwards as well as sideways, the saddle suddenly starts to hop up and down. The reins, which were previously moving forward and backward through fifteen to twenty centimetres at each stride, suddenly go slack. However, although the horse has stopped nodding his head, the rider himself is now bouncing about. This presents a new set of problems in the task of avoiding jerks on the reins. The horse's head is comparatively steady, but now the rider's hands tend to be thrown about by the bouncing of his body.

The first reaction of the beginner is to stiffen his back and grip with the legs. Both of these movements only serve to make matters worse. With a stiff back, the upward movement of the saddle has to lift the whole of the rider's weight all at once. This means a hard impact and severe jarring. If the rider can relax his back, then the shoulders can keep on going downward for a bit after the seat has struck the saddle. The first impact then has to lift only the lower half of the body. The descent of the shoulders and upper part of the body is cushioned by the springiness of the back. The shoulders thus land, and are thrown up, later than the lower part of the body. The effect of the springiness of the back is to distribute the forces on the body so that they act over a longer period of time. This means that the peak force at impact is much reduced and there is consequently a great deal less jarring.

The effect of gripping with the legs is twofold. It will usually bring the knee away from the saddle and at the same time it presses the rider's lower legs against the horse's side. Because the rider is bouncing up and down, his legs tend to thump against the horse. This will feel to the horse like a command to go faster, which may not be what the rider intends.

Instead of trying to wrap his legs round the horse's belly, the rider should think about keeping his heels away from the horse while pointing his toes forward. This will have the effect of pushing his knees against the saddle, which is where they will be of most use. With the knees against the saddle on each side, the rider's weight remains centred over the saddle even though everything is bouncing up and down. When the knee grip is slack, the occasional small sideways movements of the horse will have the effect that the rider does not always hit the saddle square in the middle at each bounce. If the impact is even a little to one side it will tend to tip the rider over to the other side. The next bounce will then be even further from the mid-line and after a very few bounces the rider is rattling about all over the place and feeling increasingly uncomfortable. He becomes more and more insecure with each stride.

With your knees firmly against the saddle you can take some of your weight on the knees. You can push your knees down as your seat comes out of the saddle. In this way your knee and lower leg stay in position on the saddle and do not move relative to the horse in spite of the up-and-down movements of your trunk. You can also use your thigh muscles to check the descent of your trunk, taking more weight on the knee each time the body comes down toward the saddle. This provides further cushioning of the impact.

Posting (Rising trot)

If, on alternate strides, you push down harder onto your knees, you can then, for these strides, absorb the whole of the impact when your body is coming down toward the saddle. 121

Doing this reduces the main up-and-down movement of your body to half as often as before. That is, you are thrown up and down in the saddle once for every two bounces of the horse, instead of at every stride. This mode of progression, called the "rising trot", involves much less jolting than the "sitting trot" in which the rider's seat comes down into the saddle at each bounce of the horse. The procedure of taking the weight intermittently on the knees is called "posting". At successive bounces the main part of the rider's weight comes alternately on his knees and on his seat. He should be taking some weight on his knees all the time.

Some beginners get the idea that they are meant to stand upright in the stirrups while posting at the rising trot. They actively throw the pelvis forward into a standing posture for one stride, letting their seat down into the saddle with a thump for the next stride, then again throw themselves forward, and again thump back, and so on. Often the stirrups will swing backwards and forwards as the weight on them comes and goes, and the rider's calves get nipped uncomfortably between the stirrup leather and the saddle.

There is no need for all this excess activity. Just keep yourself supple and let the horse do the throwing. Cushion yourself against the saddle by relaxing your back and putting weight on your knees. Let your knees follow the up-and-down movement of the horse and use your thigh muscles to catch you on the descent, using a bit more push against the knees at alternate strides so that your seat just grazes the saddle at the rising stride and just gently sinks into the saddle at the sitting stride. In this way you not only get a more comfortable ride, you will leave your lower leg free to be moved independently when you need it for giving the leg-aid signals to your horse.

The beginner should be given the chance to get used to the motion of the trot with the horse on the lunge and with the reins attached to the cavesson or headcollar instead of to the bit. To get the trot started he emphasises his walk-aids, builds up pressure in the reins and then gives the combined aids for "trot". Then, as soon as the horse starts to trot, the rider should relax his body as much as he can. Let the reins go slack, relax the back and shoulders and let the lower leg dangle. Think only about keeping the heels out and toes forward with a relaxed lower leg. Get used to the feel of the knees pressing snugly into the saddle. You can let your hands rest on your knees to encourage relaxation in the arms, and just jog round and round for two or three minutes each way, with rests at the walk in between. If you feel very insecure, hook two fingers of one hand under the arch of the saddle in front of the pommel to help you to keep your weight over the mid-line.

The next stage is to let go of the reins and hold your hands out to the side in a straight line from the shoulders, palms upward, as in the exercise already practised at the walk. The idea here is to develop the balance of the trunk without the rider being tempted to hold on with his hands. It is essential to achieve independence of the hands before you start to take up the rein. You can now start to move the shoulders forward, trotting all the time with a supple back. This brings more weight onto the knees. Bring your hands forward also, aiming to get your elbows in front of your knees and relying as little as possible on contact with your hands for balance.

While you are leaning forward, pay attention to the position of your feet. Don't let the feet come back. The lower leg should be hanging freely below the knee with the stirrup leather vertical and the stirrup on the ball of the foot. After a little practice you will find that most of your weight comes on your knees and that your seat is just grazing the saddle at each bump. Now sit up a little and use your legs to take more weight on alternate strides, letting your seat down gently into the saddle in between. You are now doing the rising trot. Practise this while circling on the lunge in both directions.

Notice that at each bounce your lower leg swings inward against the horse's side. The leg-aid for encouraging the trot is simply to emphasise these natural intermittent leg contacts. Squeeze a little at each bounce, using the calf of your leg which will be tensed up automatically by the increase in the pressure of the stirrup against the ball of your foot as your weight comes down. If the horse accelerates more than you want, push your heel out to the side so that your calves no longer touch the horse and your knee-grip is intensified. If, at the same time, you drop back into the sitting trot, the horse should slow down, even without a pull on the rein.

When you have become accustomed to riding with a supple back at the trot you can begin to take up the rein. At first have the rein attached to the headcollar so as not to jerk the bit accidentally. Practise changing the rein from one hand to the other without either jerking the rein or losing contact with the horse's head. Then put the reins back in their proper place on the bit and watch for the horse's reactions to your accidental and deliberate changes in the tension in the rein. Convince yourself that the horse will stop when you want, and you are then ready to ride at the trot without the lunge rein.

Movements of the horse at trot

The reason for the marked difference in the rider's sensations when the horse starts to trot lies in the very nature of the trotting action itself. At the walk the horse always has some feet on the ground, and the movements of the four legs are equally spaced out in time. At the trot, the timing is altered so that the two feet of each diagonal pair of legs are moved simultaneously and strike the ground at almost the same instant. The horse's body is then for a moment supported on this diagonal pair of legs before being again thrown up into the air to produce a period of so-called "suspension". All four feet are then off the ground at the same time until the horse lands on the feet of the other diagonal pair.

When the body is in "suspension" after being tossed upward, it is actually falling freely under gravity, just as when you toss a ball in the air it first rises and then falls. It takes some effort to throw the heavy body of the horse into the air, and there is a good deal of momentum to be absorbed on landing. This means that the horse's legs have to push very hard against the ground. They have to exert all their effort within a very short space of time and it is this sudden sharp push that produces the jolting motion of the horse's body. We are not much aware of the jolting of our own bodies when we run to cover the ground quickly, but it becomes much more obvious if we run on the spot, particularly if we make the action brisk enough to clear a skipping-rope. The horse usually lifts his feet well clear of the ground at the trot, so the up-and-down motion is very like that of a person skipping.

Just as the legs of the trotting horse have to catch the falling weight of the horse's body and throw it upward again at each stride, so they must also catch and throw the weight of the rider. If the rider allows himself to be thrown clear at each stride, he will still be coming down after the horse's body has already started to rise at the next stride. This is why the impact of the rider's seat with the saddle can be so severe if he tenses his back. For the rider's comfort it is essential to use the thigh muscles and to press down with the knees to cushion the impact.

The sequence of the horse's leg movements at the trot is

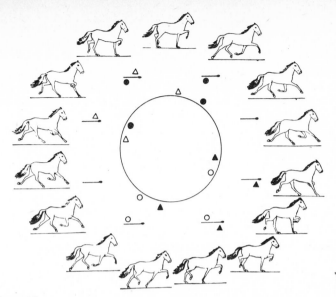

Figure 4.2
Cycle of leg movements and support patterns at the TROT. (Symbols as in *Figure 3.16*; clockface as in *Figure 3.19*; side views from Muybridge (1893).) The body is tossed from one diagonal pair of legs to the other.

indicated in *Figure 4.2*. When we compare this diagram with that for the walk (*Figure 3.20*) we see that the hindlegs are lifted relatively earlier and that the placings of the forelegs are much delayed. At the moment of transition from the walk to the trot, the horse has to take an extra-long stride with one hindleg in order to catch up with the diagonal foreleg. He can then use this diagonal pair of legs in a simultaneous push to throw the body up for the first stride at the trot. When in the air he delays the moment of placing the foreleg of the same side and brings the opposite hindleg forward to make an almost synchronised landing on the other diagonal pair.

This analysis explains the working of the leg-aids. It has already been mentioned that the effect of the rider's leg-aid on a given side is to increase the vigour of the movements of the horse's legs on that side. For the transition from walk to trot, both hindlegs need to make an extra reach forward. We ask for this by giving leg-aids simultaneously on the two sides.

Because of the substantial forces involved in the thrusts of the legs to catch and throw the body at each stride, the muscles of the horse's trunk also have to work hard to stiffen the body. **125**

The upthrusts of a diagonal pair of legs have a strong twisting action on the trunk, the direction of the twist being reversed for the alternating diagonals. The horse does not swing his head about much when he is trotting, but he has to catch and throw the weight of the head at each stride just like the weight of any other part of the body. The neck muscles thus must also be stiffened to provide intermittent strong lifting action on the head even though we don't see the head move much. Without some controlled intermittent muscular action in the neck, the head would tend to be jolted wildly up and down at each stride just as the rider is.

There is a very small nodding action of the head as the weight is taken at each stride by the neck muscles. This means that the reins move backwards and forwards a little, though not nearly so much as at the walk. It is the stiffening of the neck that brings the nose in a little at the start of the trot. That is why the rider has to be ready to take up the rein. He can help to speed up the trot by encouraging the swing of the head by alternately pulling slightly when the nose is coming back and giving when it is going forward. He must remember that his own shoulders are probably moving about much more than the horse's mouth. It is therefore essential to develop great suppleness in the arms to avoid accidental jerks on the bit.

Exercises at trot

Once the rider has become used to riding at the trot, there are several exercises that he can practise to develop his confidence and to increase both his enjoyment of riding and his security in the saddle. These exercises will also help him to develop feel for those changes in the horse under him which are indications of what the horse is going to do next. The horse usually has to shift his weight before making any new move. If the rider is alert to this he will feel the changes in the horse's muscles that bring about the shift of weight, and thus will be better able to anticipate the horse's movement. He can then either encourage or discourage this movement by the application of the appropriate aids. In this way he keeps up a continual conversation with the horse. The rider "listens" to the horse's movements and the horse "listens" for the rider's intentions as communicated through the rein, through the feel of the rider's legs against the horse's side and of the shifts of weight in the saddle, through the rider's tone of voice, and even through the rider's unspoken intention. This latter may perhaps be communicated by the rider's unconscious movements but we should not disregard the possibility of direct telepathy.

The objectives of these exercises can be summarised as: to develop suppleness in the rider's body and shoulders; to improve his balance; to confirm the grip of his knees against the saddle; to consolidate the correct habitual position for the rider's foot; to ensure that the rider can move his hands and lower legs independently of the movements of his body; and to develop the responsiveness of the horse to each of the various commands indicated to him by the rider's hands and legs and by the shift of the rider's weight.

In the early stages it will be appropriate, in the leg-aids, to make a fairly definite, even exaggerated, movement. Then, as horse and rider come to understand one another better, the aids can be reduced to nudges that are almost imperceptible to an onlooker. One should remember that the aids given both by the leg and by the reins are to act only as signals. They do not operate like the controls of a motor-car where the driver pushes harder against the appropriate pedal to produce more acceleration or more braking action. The signals to the horse are intensified by brisk repetition, not by submerging the signal in a strong pull or by kicking harder. At all times the rider's hands have to be supple enough to allow the horse to move his head freely whenever the need arises, either during the rhythmic movements of normal locomotion or in the sudden movements the horse needs to make in order to regain his balance after a stumble. The rider must learn not to hang on to the reins to preserve his own balance because this will inevitably mean inappropriate jerking of the bit in the horse's mouth.

Arm and rein exercises at trot

One may start by carrying out at the trot the exercises already performed at the walk. The rein is passed from one hand to the other, and the rider sometimes has the reins separated in the two hands and sometimes rides with both reins in the same hand. The arm not engaged with the rein is held out horizontally sideways straight out from the shoulder, palm up. All the time the rider is to maintain a steady light contact with the bit, making just sufficient difference between the pressures on the two reins to steer as may be necessary.

One variation on this exercise is to make more extensive movements with the disengaged arm. Instead of just holding it out sideways straight out from the shoulder, raise the arm straight upward and then sweep it right round backward and downward to make a complete circle, like a windmill, before taking the rein again into the two hands. Repeat with the other arm.

Handling the crop

You may from time to time have occasion to carry a crop and this is a good time to get used to managing it. The crop is normally carried with the butt end upward and with the tip pointing backward along the thigh toward the hip. The wrist strap fitted to many crops is not used during normal riding. It is provided merely to save dropping the crop when all the fingers are needed for some special task such as putting on gloves or the like. To change the crop from one hand to the other, first take both reins into the hand that is already holding the crop (*Figure 4.3*). Draw the crop through the slightly

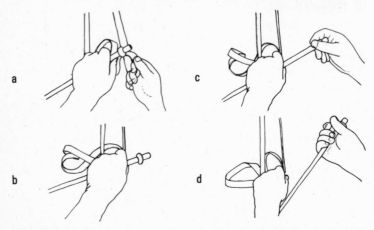

Figure 4.3
Changing the crop from one hand to the other. Take both reins into the hand that is carrying the crop. Draw the crop through into the other hand. Rearrange the fingers round the crop. Take back the rein into this hand.

relaxed fingers of the rein hand. Rearrange the crop in the free hand. Then take the rein back into the two hands.

This leads to the following practice routine:
1) Start with the reins in the two hands, crop in the left hand. Separate the hands;
2) Take both reins, together with the crop, into the left hand, hold the right hand straight out sideways from the shoulder;

128

3) Both reins still in the left hand, take the crop in the right hand and hold it out from the shoulder;
4) Take the reins into the two hands, crop in the right hand. Separate the hands;
5) Put both reins, and the crop, in the right hand, left arm out;
6) Reins in right hand, crop in left hand held out from the shoulder;
7) As (1), and repeat the whole sequence.

The exercise is carried out both at sitting trot and at rising trot. All the time the rider should be just feeling the reins to keep up a steady light pressure of the bit in the horse's mouth, and he should steer in a figure-of-eight to confirm that the rein-aids are working properly.

When you want to use the crop, remember to take both reins into the other hand. It is a mistake to attempt to use the crop while you still have your crop-hand on the rein. The object of using the crop is to reinforce a leg-aid that the horse has ignored. The leg-aid is a signal to increase forward impulsion, but if the hand wielding the crop is also holding the rein, there will inevitably be a jerk on the horse's mouth, meaning "Stop!", happening at the same time as the horse receives the blow from the crop. It is unfair to give the horse commands calling for both "stop" and "go" at the same time. He will just become confused and upset.

Before using the crop, reverse it in your hand so that the butt comes against the heel of your hand. You will need to practise this manoeuvre. It is easiest if you let your hand drop to your side while the point of the crop swings forward. You can then relax your fingers and work your thumb over the end of the butt (*Figure 4.4*). For the return to the carrying position you just reverse the sequence. Start with your hand down by your side holding the crop which you then rotate as you bring your hand up toward the rein.

The place to aim for with the crop is the side of the horse's belly just behind your heel. This makes quite clear to the horse your intention to make him "listen" to the leg-aid. You have to be very prompt, applying the crop within a couple of seconds of the leg-aid, otherwise the horse will not understand what you are about. Remember that the horse lives, as it were, from one stride to next. There is no reason for him to remember what he was doing two or three strides earlier. He will, however, remember vividly any situation in which he was particu-

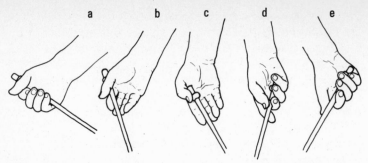

Figure 4.4
Reversing the crop. As the hand swings downward the crop is swung forward and the fingers pass the butt of the crop across the palm of the hand.

larly uncomfortable. If you are too late with your crop he will associate the chastisement with having you on his back instead of with the command to which he failed to respond. A good rule is to use the crop sparingly but to be quite definite in your intention when you do use it. Give quite a sharp blow so that the horse will feel it. There is no point in just patting him with the crop as he will not then feel any urgency to pay special attention to it.

Sometimes you may need to assert yourself when you don't happen to be carrying a crop. You can then use the spare loop in the reins to hit the horse on the front of the shoulder. With the reins in the two hands, and with the hands close together, place the slack rein from the left hand over that in the right so that the spare loop lies between right thumb and forefinger (*Figure 4.5*). Move both hands forward, close together, to avoid jerking the bit, and swing the loop of rein over the top from one side to the other by twisting the right hand at the wrist, letting

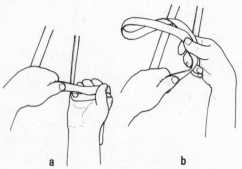

a   b

Figure 4.5
Using the spare rein as a crop, without jerking the bit.

the loop come down smartly on the side of the horse's neck at the top of the shoulder. Be very careful not to jerk the bit.

The arm and rein exercises, with and without the crop, serve to develop the rider's skill in maintaining a light contact with the horse's mouth without jerks even while the rider's body is being thrown up and down by the horse's movements. Once past this hurdle the rider can practise the stops from the trot and when these also can be achieved with confidence, then he is ready to include some gentle trotting when out hacking with more experienced riders.

Balancing exercises

The next stage is the security of the rider's seat in the saddle. For this it helps to spend a little time each day trotting round on the lunge. Tie a knot in the reins and let them lie on the horse's neck so that you can do the balancing exercises without touching them.

By this time you should no longer feel the urgent need to hang on to something with your hands. Keep the trot going by rhythmic squeezing with your calves and knees and hold both hands out sideways to their full extent, palms uppermost and level with your shoulders ("aeroplane"). Then, keeping the elbows well up, swing the hands in toward your chest and out again, either both together or one at a time. Also turn your head from side to side, looking first at one fully extended hand, then at the other. Do the exercise both at the sitting trot and at the rising trot. The aim is to develop an upright carriage, with a supple back.

To help loosen up your shoulders, try arm-circling. The arms are held straight and are swung round from the shoulder in full circles, forward, upward, backward and downward ("windmill"). First one arm at a time, then the two arms alternately, and after that the two arms rising and falling at the same time. Repeat with forward circling.

Now, with both arms out (as in "aeroplane"), circle with your head, bending the neck well forward, sideways, and backwards. Make clockwise and anticlockwise circles. Also turn your head from side to side, going as far round as you can in each direction.

Stretch one arm above your head as far as it will go while the other arm is stretched down by your side as far as it will go. Hold the position for a moment, then change over and repeat on the other side ("arm stretching").

Stretch one arm up and have the other down by your side, lean forward, and bring your raised hand down to touch first the stirrup on the same side then, after going right up overhead again, come down to touch the stirrup on the opposite side. Repeat with the other hand.

With both arms out to the side, lean forward till your seat begins to come out of the saddle. Then lean backward as far as you can, gripping with the knees and keeping the heels away from the horse all the time. Then come forward again.

After a few sessions trotting round on the lunge and doing these balancing exercises you will be surprised how relaxed and confident you become. Movements which felt very precarious when first attempted gradually come to feel quite easy and natural. As your confidence grows, you will be able to do all these exercises without stirrups. Here you should pay attention to what is happening to your feet. The lower leg should hang straight down, toes pointing forward and heels out. When you need to give a leg-aid to keep the trot going, tense your calf muscles by lifting the sole of your foot until it is above the heel. If the horse goes ahead too fast, push your heels out to the side so that your calves no longer touch the horse's side. This will emphasise the pressure of your knee against the saddle. The knee should never move from its nest in the side of the saddle.

Leg exercises

While continuing in sitting trot on the lunge, without stirrups, bring your arms up to the "aeroplane" position and practise the independence of your lower legs. Without moving the knee, push one heel away from the horse and swing the foot forward and backward without at any time touching the horse. Repeat with the other leg. Make circling movements with each foot in turn, clockwise and anticlockwise, always without touching the horse.

Now halt, take your stirrups again, and hold your hands just above the pommel in the rest position for holding the reins. With the horse standing at the halt, lean forward with your weight on your knees until your seat comes out of the saddle. Straighten up without sitting back, and balance in this position with your seat out of the saddle. Sit down again in the saddle and repeat two or three times.

Then give the leg-aids to start the trot and practise the following sequence:

Four strides sitting trot;
Four strides standing in the stirrups, that is to say, balancing
  on your knees as just described;
Four strides rising trot;
Sit, two, three, four, stand, two, three, four;
Sit, stand, sit, stand, sit, stand, sit, stand;
Sit, two, three, four, stand, two, three, four;
Sit, stand, sit, stand, sit, stand, sit, stand;
and so on.

After practising this sequence a few times without holding
the rein, take the reins in your hands and repeat the exercise
paying particular attention to the rein to make sure that the
contact with the bit remains the same all the time without ever
jerking or letting the rein go slack.

The aim in all these exercises is to learn to "sit deep" into the
saddle and to let yourself "feel tall". All the joints in your body
should become supple and well sprung, with no stiffnesses
anywhere. Each part of the body should appear to be carried
without effort so that it feels light, almost as though floating,
yet ready at any moment to react promptly to any sudden call
for action either for balance or to control the horse.

More about steering

After practising the exercises described above the rider should
feel more comfortable in the saddle and he should be better
able to control the rein. It is now time to give more thought to
the delicate and extensive topic of steering. This is a much
more subtle business than steering a car or a boat. Setting aside
telepathy and word of command, we have three ways to communicate our desires to the horse: through the reins, with our
legs, and by shifting our weight in the saddle. We use various
combinations of these kinds of "aid" to produce changes in
speed and in gait as well as changes in direction. Moreover,
there are many ways in which the horse may change direction.
He can shift the body over the feet in almost any direction
either with or without at the same time changing the direction
in which he is facing. He can also bend the body, the neck and
the head to one side or the other, the bends in each case not
necessarily being in the same direction. From time to time we
may wish to ask the horse to make particular kinds of "change
of direction" and for this we need to establish a workable code
with which to make our intention clear. The tests used in
competitive dressage are, in effect, tests of fluency in interpret-

ing the code. Specific problems are posed to determine how effectively the rider can communicate with his mount.

At first it will be sufficient to use the basic aids for turning described in the previous chapter for turns at the walk. These are: weight on the inside knee; inside leg straight down; outside leg back a little, just behind the girth; and just enough difference between the two reins to bring into view the outside corner of the horse's eye on the side to which the turn is to be made. Practise making the turns by giving with the outside hand as well as by pulling with the inside hand. If you have sufficient impulsion from your leg-aids, the horse should move his head forward to maintain the even pressure on the bit. He will thus feel the same asymmetry of the bit in his mouth when you give with one hand as he does when you pull with the other. Also practise making turns as much as possible with the legs and weight-shift alone, using the minimum of rein action.

A circle to the right is referred to as "on the right rein". When you steer out of a circle to the right and into a circle to the left, this is called "changing the rein". A figure-of-eight involves a change of rein at each crossover. Another useful practice figure is the "serpentine". This is a sequence of half-circles in alternate directions. Choose an imaginary line on the ground and change the rein every time you cross this line, making half-circles alternately on the left and right reins.

Diagonals
When circling at the rising trot, pay attention to the movements of the horse's shoulders. You will see the point of the shoulder coming back toward you on each side alternately. The shoulder moves back when the corresponding foreleg is on the ground. At this time the opposite hindleg is also on the ground and the horse is supported on a diagonal pair of legs. The two diagonals are named according to which foreleg is involved. On a circle to the right, the expression "outside diagonal" means the left diagonal, that is to say, the left foreleg and the right hindleg, and so on. You will be posting on one diagonal and sitting down on the other. Work out which diagonal is on the ground when your seat is in the saddle.

To change from one diagonal to the other you break the strict alternation of sitting and posting by sitting down for two bumps in succession, thus: sit, stand, sit, stand, sit, sit, stand, sit, stand, sit, stand, and so on. Get into the habit of always sitting on the outside diagonal. Then, every time you change the rein at the rising trot, you also change the diagonal. In the figure-of-eight you change the diagonal every time you pass the crossover point. In the serpentine you change every time you cross the line down the centre of the figure.

Practising the turns

A variation of simple circling is to make the circle gradually smaller and smaller so that you ride in a spiral. As you near the centre, change the rein and ride a gradually expanding spiral. Notice that, as the circles get smaller, the horse begins to curve his spine. He bends round your inside leg. Avoid pulling his head round because this will encourage him to bend his neck instead of his trunk. The effect of excessive bending of the neck will be to lose impulsion. Remember, to stop a runaway the rider pulls the horse's head to one side.

If your horse seems reluctant to turn in response to a slight pull on the inside rein or to a small relaxation of the outer rein, resist the temptation to pull harder with the inside rein. Instead, hold the inside rein firm and tickle the bit with the outside rein by working on the rein with a rapid curling and uncurling of the fingers as described earlier for "alerting". This draws the horse's attention to the bit. He lines up his mouth with the bit to give an equal feel on the two sides. This produces the required bend of the head into the turn.

The sharpness of the turn is indicated to the horse by the frequency and briskness of the repeated squeezes with the outside leg behind the girth and by the way you distort the saddle with your knees. You bring more of your weight onto the inside knee. The inside leg is held straight down and its calf presses on the side of the horse at the girth. When you move your outside leg back slightly to give the leg-aid for turning, you also press the knee of that leg into the side of the saddle. The combined action of the two legs tends to twist the saddle round on the horse's back in the direction of the turn, and this encourages him to bend his spine.

Drill patterns in the dressage arena

You may find that when practising turns it helps to have a track to follow. You can then judge whether or not you are making the turns as precisely as you would like. A number of useful imaginary tracks can be set up in a standard dressage arena of 40 m by 20 m. (A longer arena, 60 m by 20 m, is used in some

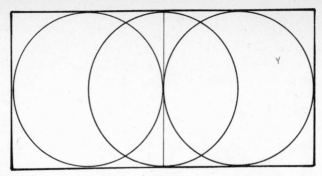

Figure 4.6
A practice arena in the form of a double square, each of about 20 m along the side. This gives three positions for a 20 m circle.

advanced dressage tests.) It is a good idea to fix in your mind some convenient landmarks in your practice area which will mark out a suitably-sized rectangle with the proportions of a double square (*Figure 4.6*). This gives three positions for a "large circle" of about 20 m diameter, one at each end and one in the middle. You can pass from one end-circle to the other by changing the rein as you ride through the centre of the arena, or you can go from one circle to another by keeping straight for the appropriate distance along one of the long sides.

If you now imagine each of the two large squares to be cut in half in each direction, this will produce eight squares in each of which you can ride a 10 m circle (*Figure 4.7*). Again you can pass from one circle to another with a change of rein where the circles touch, or you can join up parts of different circles with straight tracks along the edges of the squares (*Figure 4.8*). The

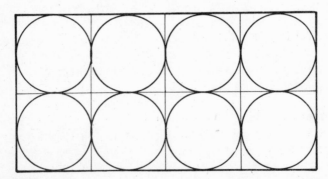

Figure 4.7
Positions, within the practice arena, of eight 10 m circles.

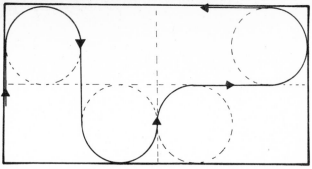

Figure 4.8
Examples of tracks made up of straight lines joining segments of 10 m circles.

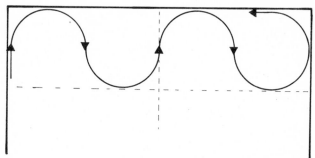

Figure 4.9
Serpentine down the long side.

pattern formed by a succession of half-circles (*Figure 4.9*) is the serpentine already referred to earlier. You can also ride a serpentine along the centre-line (*Figure 4.10*).

The 10 m circle is about as sharp a turn as the horse can negotiate safely when travelling fast. At the walk or slow trot

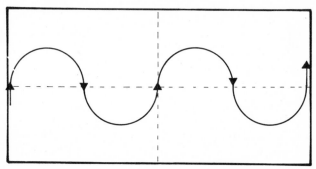

Figure 4.10
Serpentine along the centre-line.

137

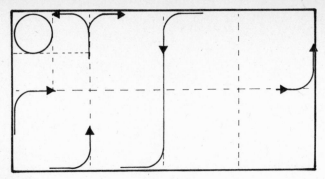

Figure 4.11
Corners formed from segments of 5 m circles.

he can manage a 5 m circle. Four of these fit into each of our eight 10 m squares (*Figure 4.11*). When you are riding a corner at a moderate pace your track should follow a quarter of one of these 5 m circles. In a regular dressage arena the "quarter markers" are placed at 6 m from the corners to correspond with the subdivisions of the 60 m arena, which has markers 12 m apart along the long sides. The dressage rules of the British Horse Society prescribe that, when riding corners, the horse should describe one quarter of a circle of approximately 6 m diameter at collected and working paces, or a quarter of a circle of approximately 10 m diameter at medium and extended paces. (The expression "working paces" implies that the horse is responding to the rider's demand for impulsion and is not just strolling along without paying much attention to the rider.

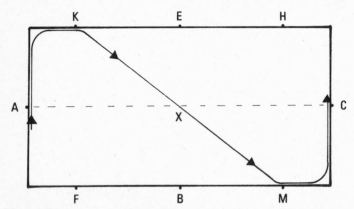

Figure 4.12
Diagonal change of hand from one quarter-marker to another in the dressage arena.

In a "medium" pace the horse is being encouraged to go forward fairly freely but he is not yet showing the full extension of which he is capable.)

Using regular corners you can build up patterns including straight-line segments in various directions. You can ride along the centre-line or across the arena along a line parallel to the short sides leaving the long side at any point. When you reach the outside track, or at any of the intersections of the rectangular grid in *Figure 4.11*, you can turn either way.

Another variation is to include diagonal lines as in *Figure 4.12*. In riding a diagonal, do not aim for the corner, but remember to allow room to make a correct arc of a 5 m circle both on rejoining the long side of the arena, and again on arriving at the corners. The track in *Figure 4.12* shows the rider as on the right rein from A to K and on the left rein from M to C. This pattern is called a "diagonal change of hand". If you are proceeding at the rising trot, remember to "change the diagonal" by sitting twice as you cross the centre-line, in order to be posting on the correct leg for the next turn. Notice that the word "diagonal" is used in two senses here:

1) The diagonal track across the arena;
2) The diagonal pair of legs used by the horse in successive strides at the trot.

A diagonal change of hand can be executed in one half of the arena either from the centre-line (*Figure 4.13*), or, in a "reversed change of hand" (*Figure 4.14*), starting from the long side near to a corner and regaining the same long side by

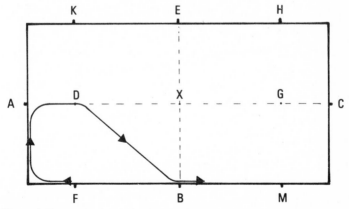

Figure 4.13
Change of hand on a diagonal moving *away from* the centre-line.

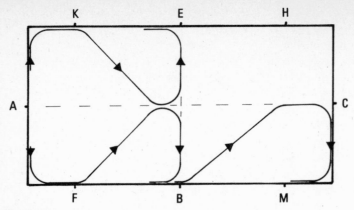

Figure 4.14
Examples of reversed change of hand, on diagonals *toward* the centre-line.

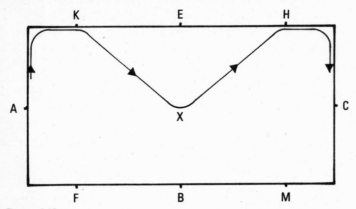

Figure 4.15
Counter change of hand. Two changes are required, one on the diagonal from K to X, the other on the diagonal from X to rejoin the long side at H.

turning in on the opposite rein from the middle of the arena.

If you ride from one diagonal track to another, changing in the middle of the arena, you will rejoin the long side on the same rein as you started. This manoeuvre (*Figure 4.15*) is called "a counter change of hand". In fact, two changes of hand are needed, one in each of the diagonal parts of the track.

Although the dressage arena is not itself very large, the repertoire of different patterns of track described above makes it possible to continue riding in a restricted space, such as an indoor riding school, for extended periods of time, and day after day, without at any stage becoming bored. You string the patterns together in whatever sequence you choose and at the same time introduce other variables, such as changes of gait and changes of speed. At all times you concentrate on keeping strictly to the chosen pattern without allowing the horse to wander from the straight lines or to cut the corners. Circles are to be performed precisely, as though drawn with a pair of compasses. Do not accept irregular patterns like the outline of an ink blot. In this way you teach yourself to watch for any indication that the horse is preparing to deviate from the pattern you have chosen.

Of course, the horse has no idea what pattern of track you have selected to ride. As he moves along, you inevitably shift about to some extent in the saddle. In consequence, each stride will feel different to the horse and he will be liable at any time to do something unexpected with his next stride. You have to be alert to feel what is happening so that you can signal back to him if what he apparently proposes is not precisely what you want. It is here that it helps to have a set pattern in mind. If you let the horse wander about just anyhow and allow him to carry you where he happens to go, the likelihood is that you will both soon become very bored as you would with a human companion if neither of you made any attempt at conversation. It is the communication that provides much of the interest.

The secret is to have a definite plan in mind so that you have some standard against which to compare the behaviour of the horse. You can then watch to see whether the horse keeps his head pointing in the direction you have chosen. He will turn his head if he is distracted. This means that he is not concentrating on what you are doing with the bit, and you will need to do something to remind him to pay attention. Alternatively he may step off the track. If he does this with a foreleg, this indicates an uncertainty of aiming. If he deviates with a hindleg, his haunches will cease to follow the forequarters, indicating that he is escaping from the control of your legs, or perhaps that one of your legs is accidentally giving a spurious signal.

Concentric circles

It is, at first, easier to spot the moments when the horse is inattentive if you are not at the same time continually changing course. You can ride for some time on the same large circle, concentrating on maintaining a steady rhythm with the horse's neck bent toward the inside of the circle just enough to bring the corner of his eye into view. From time to time alter 141 the steady pressure on the rein to produce either more collection or a more extended pace. When the horse has settled to a steady rhythm, move in onto a new circle about 2 m inside the original one. The slightly tighter curve causes the horse to make each movement a little more precisely. His action will then become more springy and he should respond more positively when you ask for more collection or more extension.

Continue on the second circle until the horse has settled to the new rhythm. Then move in another 2 m onto a yet smaller circle and repeat the process of polishing up the horse's precision. Then see if you can maintain the same lively action when you move out again onto one of the larger circles, or while riding a straight segment of track.

After you have worked for some time with fairly simple controls and when you are beginning to "get a feel for" the way the horse prepares his various movements, you can start to experiment with more sophisticated manipulation of the reins. An essential preliminary is to achieve sufficient relaxation of the arm so that the position of your hand is governed entirely by the feel of the rein against your fingers and not at all by the movements of your shoulder caused by your being bounced up and down by the horse. When the horse's head moves towards or away from the saddle, your hand should follow this movement without any change in rein tension. In particular, the rein should never be allowed to sag loosely. If it does, the rein will snap taut again and produce an unintended jab to the horse's mouth.

The thirteen positions of the hand

Up to this point we have been considering practice routines in which the hand is held always in or near a single standard position, just clear of the withers and just in front of the pommel of the saddle. When seen from the side the hand is so placed that the forearm and rein appear to form a single straight line from the bit to the rider's elbow. The upper arms hang straight down from the shoulders with the elbows just brushing against the waist, above the hips. The thumbs are uppermost and about ten to twelve centimetres apart. The wrists turn in very slightly in continual supple motion to provide the "springiness" which is needed to absorb the effects of sudden movements either of the horse's head or of the rider's shoulders.

142   We now examine some useful deviations from the standard

Figure 4.16
Vertical positions of the hand. Two alternatives to the regular position are shown, one raised, the other lowered.

position. In the first place, the hand may be raised by bending the elbow (*Figure 4.16*). In the right conditions this may help the horse to put more weight on his hindquarters and thus may make it easier for the rider to persuade an over-eager horse to drop back from the trot into the walk. If the hands are habitually held high this will encourage the horse to "poke his nose" in a "star gazing" posture which has several disadvantages. This makes it more difficult for the rider to control his horse, and it may interfere with the horse's ability to see where he is going to put his feet. An injudicious pull on the reins with the hands held high may provoke rearing.

There are some situations in which it is useful to hold the hands low down beside the horse's neck, even as far down as the point of the shoulder. This encourages the horse to bring his nose in toward his chest. The effect is very like that aimed at with draw reins. The lowered hand has a great advantage over the draw reins in that it permits a more supple action on the bit, as well as being always available and quickly dispensed with at a moment's notice.

As well as raising and lowering the hand, we may move it to one side or the other. These changes in the lateral position of

Figure 4.17
Five horizontal directions for the rein. From right to left: 1) opening rein; 2) direct rein; 3) indirect rein behind the withers (full line); 4) indirect rein in front of the withers; 5) neck rein. The horse is bent to the right and it is executing a half-pass to the right (broken arrow) in response to the rider's left leg. The right indirect rein behind the withers is being used here to check a tendency for the horse to swing his quarters to the right.

the hands alter the angle at which the rein meets the bit. Five possibilities are shown in *Figure 4.17*.

The "regular" position, which we have been using up to now, is No. 2, the "direct" rein. If the hand is moved to the side, away from the horse's neck, we have the "opening rein", No. 1. This leads the horse into a turn. Alternatively, we may apply an "indirect rein" by moving the hand across the centre-line of the neck either behind the withers, No. 3, or with the line of the rein in front of the withers, No. 4. Each of these four directions can be adopted either with the hand at the regular height or with the hand raised.

With the hand below the withers we can apply both the direct rein and the opening rein. An effect similar to that of the indirect rein may be obtained by pressing the lowered hand firmly into the side of the horse's neck.

144 The more extreme deviation across the horse's neck, No. 5 in

Figure 4.17, is used with the raised hand in the action of "neck reining" by Western-style riders, where both reins are usually held in the one hand.

The rein is also taken across the middle of the horse's neck in one of the manoeuvres for stopping a runaway. One hand, say the right, is moved well down the rein, toward the horse's mouth. Then, gripping the rein firmly, the hand is brought across the neck until the fist can be pressed strongly into the left side of the neck beside the crest. Meanwhile the other hand, held well down at the level of the horse's shoulder, pulls in the "opening rein" direction, repeatedly increasing and decreasing the pressure on the bit to insist on a turn toward that side. The "blocking" of the right rein, by thrusting the fist into the left side of the neck, ensures that the bit does not get pulled right through the horse's mouth.

Thus, each of the five rein directions shown (*Figure 4.17*) may be used with the hand at either of two heights, and there are, in addition, three rein directions available with the hand below the withers. In all, there are thirteen distinct positions of the hand.

The horse seems able to distinguish the different effects of the rein on the bit and produces appropriately different responses without special training. This is in contrast with the responses to the leg-aids, which, apart from the simple response of lifting the hindleg, will have to be carefully taught.

The indirect rein

We may convince ourselves of the naturalness of the responses to different rein actions by the following exercise. Have the horse going on steadily at a moderate pace, either at the walk or at the trot, with enough impulsion for the horse to be leaning slightly on the bit. Keep up an unchanging pressure on the rein with each hand and do not make any deliberate shift of weight. Keep the leg-aids symmetrical. Hold one hand, say the left, steady in the "direct rein" position and apply "opening rein" with the other (right) hand, still without any change in the tension on the rein. The horse will turn to the right. After a few strides, return the right hand to the direct rein position. The horse goes straight ahead. Now carry the right hand across to the left, still without altering the tension in the rein. The horse veers to the left. Also try the opening and indirect reins with the left hand, keeping the right hand always in the direct rein position. The horse will veer left and right as before.   145

The next stage is to look for differences in the responses to the indirect rein, when the line of the rein passes in front of or behind the withers. If we apply the right indirect rein in front of the withers the horse moves his head and shoulders to the left and makes a turn. If the indirect rein is applied behind the withers it affects the haunches as well as the forequarters. The whole body of the horse moves to the left in a diagonal direction, with the forelegs and hindlegs following different tracks. If your horse does not appear to understand the difference between these two rein signals, it may be that he is not yet adequately collected. You will need to give him more practice in developing impulsion.

The subtle language of the rein

There are a great many different things you can do with the rein and any particular action you make can have a different meaning to the horse according to the precise moment at which the signal is given and according to what the horse's head happens to be doing at the time. For example, the horse's head may be turned to the left, or to the right, or it may be pointing straight ahead. The mouth may be moving toward the saddle or away from it. This gives six possibilities, without considering the details of the timing in relation to the stride.

Your hand may be keeping a steady tension, or it may pull with increased tension, or give with reduced tension, or it may be imposing a fluctuating tension, as in "tickling the bit" by rapidly repeated curling and uncurling of the fingers – four possibilities for rein action in each position of the hand. Each hand can thus give fifty-two different indications – four ways of manipulating the tension in each of thirteen positions. If we suppose the two hands to be independent, and take account of the six different conditions of the horse's head, we arrive at 16,224 different ways of signalling with the rein.

Some of these logically possible combinations of independent actions of the two hands are not easily realisable in practice, nevertheless there remain several thousand usable combinations. Of these some are, of course, much more commonly used than others, and each is modified in its significance to the horse by the context of leg-aids and adjustments of the action of the weight of the rider in the saddle, as well as by the timing of the signal in relation to the horse's movements during the stride.

Another complication is that the rider may not always succeed in making a clear distinction between signals that are intended to mean different things to the horse. In consequence, the horse becomes confused and may not do precisely what the rider thinks he is asking for. As well as being confused, the horse may also be distracted or even simply inattentive.

Building up impulsion at trot

Whenever you want your horse to pay particular attention, so as to carry out a specific manoeuvre with precision, it is essential to start by getting him suitably wound up and "compressed" between your forward drive and your restraining hands. The leg-aids for maintaining the trot are a simple reinforcement of the natural sideways swing of the leg produced by the up-and-down motion of the horse. Each time the horse's feet come to the ground his legs develop a strong upthrust to catch the weight of the trunk and to throw it up again for the next stride. Part of this upward thrust is transmitted from the saddle to the rider's body, and this has the effect of bringing the rider's legs sharply against the horse's side. The rider can, at will, modify the force of this impact either by stiffening his legs momentarily to keep them away from the horse or, alternatively, by intensifying the impact, clenching the calf muscles and giving the horse a brief squeeze with his legs.

Another way of increasing impulsion is to modify the impact of the rider's weight on the saddle. In normal relaxed riding at the trot, both sitting and rising, the rider uses his thigh muscles to absorb some of the impact by putting weight on the knees. He can further modify the impact of his seat-bones against the saddle by making an active movement of the pelvis. At the crucial moment, just as his seat is approaching the saddle, the rider braces his back muscles to rotate his pelvis, thrusting his seat-bones forward under him (*Chapter 3*). At the trot the movement is repeated each time the rider's weight comes down into the saddle. It is particularly effective at the sitting trot, driving the horse forward at each stride.

As well as increasing the forward drive, by using your legs and your seat, you will also need to increase the effectiveness of your restraining hand. The aim is to get the horse to arch his neck and to carry his head more nearly vertical, with his mouth nearer to his chest than in the usual relaxed posture. Bringing his head back has the effect of putting more weight on the hindquarters. The increased drive you are asking for with the 147 legs and seat will then encourage him to bring his hocks forward under him until he is supported on a shorter base. His back becomes more rounded and his action is altogether more bouncy, like that of a stallion in his aggressive display (*Figure 1.6*).

Up to now we have been concentrating on allowing the hand to move with the horse's mouth, keeping a steady tension and never allowing the reins to flap or to be jerked taut. As the horse's mouth moves in toward the saddle and away again, we have followed in with the hand and let out again as the tension in the rein begins to rise. If we exaggerate the movement of the hand, this encourages the horse to swing his head and he steps out in a more extended stride. To produce a more collected action, we alter the timing of our changes in the pressure of the fingers on the rein. When the horse's mouth is coming back toward the saddle, instead of following it in all the way, we relax the pressure slightly, being careful never to let the rein go completely slack. Then, as the horse's mouth moves forward, we first check a little, allowing the tension to build up, then tickle the bit, and finally give again as soon as the horse responds and yields to the increased pressure on the rein. We are now working against the natural swing of the horse's head instead of encouraging it.

After a time, the horse comes to hold his mouth always at the same distance from the saddle. He continues to nod his head and neck up and down, but the rider's hand no longer moves backwards and forwards with each stride. We can now start gradually shortening the rein, stealing a little at each stride at the moment when the tension is slackening off. If the horse begins to lean heavily on the bit, let go suddenly and then immediately take up the tension again. This prevents him from getting into the habit of letting you carry the weight of his head. Meanwhile keep up the forward drive with legs and seat.

Do not insist on prolonged periods of extreme collection but do allow the horse from time to time to go forward freely in extended trot. By alternating in this way you can gradually build up the contrast between the different forms of the trot. Ideally the extended trot should have very much the same rhythm as the collected trot, but the horse should cover a great deal more ground at each stride. To help to emphasize the difference between the collected and extended trots, you can post when riding the extended trot and sit down again for the collected trot. Another variation is to introduce what is called the "jump seat".

Jump seat and drive seat

When a horse takes off for a jump his body makes a sudden surge upward and forward. If you happen to be sitting down hard in the saddle at this precise moment, you will be catapulted into the air and there is no knowing where you will land. It is much safer to have a more springy contact with the horse at the moment of take-off. Then, instead of a sudden jolt, you receive a less severe, but more prolonged, push which is much easier to cope with. It is appropriate to practise the safe posture so as to be ready for the jump when it comes.

An extreme form of the "jump seat" (*Figure 4.18*) is that adopted by professional racing jockeys who usually ride with the seat well out of the saddle. The rider carries his shoulders well forward to bring all his weight out of the saddle. The stirrup is kept on the ball of the foot with the stirrup leather vertical, as usual, but only a little of the weight is actually on the stirrups. Most of the weight is taken on the knees. This

Figure 4.18
The jump seat. Weight on the knees; seat out of the saddle; stirrup on the ball of the foot; ankle springy; heel down.

makes it easier to balance. Because the knee is several centimetres in front of the stirrup leather, a tendency to pitch forward or backward over the knees can be corrected by adjusting the push of the feet against the stirrups. It may be convenient to move the hands down the reins to bring them nearer to the horse's mouth. You can then use the pressure of your knuckles against the horse's neck as an additional aid to balance. But you should try, so far as possible, to manage without this so that you do not interfere with the independence of your hand which is so necessary for controlling the horse. A useful practise routine is to alternate collected trot in the jump seat position with extended trot in the normal sitting trot position.

If the pelvis is being used energetically at the sitting trot, this becomes the "drive seat" position. The rider's shoulders, neck and upper back are kept supple, to provide springy support, while the lower back is braced to rotate the pelvis and to drive the seat-bones forward against the saddle. The knees and thighs press firmly against the saddle, so that the driving action of the seat-bones is distributed over the whole of the saddle and urges it forward. Meanwhile the lower leg below the knee maintains its independence ready to give whatever directional leg-aids may be required.

The horse should accelerate briskly when you relax the rein and sit down into the drive seat after a period of collected trot in the jump seat position. You will need this kind of surging acceleration later for the approach to a jump. Just before the actual moment of take-off, however, you fold forward into the jump seat to cushion yourself against the sudden rise of the saddle.

In the jump seat position, the rider can no longer drive the saddle forward with his seat. He can, however, develop an additional strong leg-aid as follows. The support provided by the knees and ankles is a very springy one and the rider's lower leg accordingly slides up and down over the horse's side with each stride. The rider's weight is pressed down into the saddle at the moment when the horse is landing and thrusting off again. This winds up the spring of the muscles supporting the rider so that, as soon as the horse's thrust is over, the rider's legs tend to lift him upward away from the saddle. If the rider squeezes with his legs at this point, he can apply a sort of "lifting" pressure against the horse's side as well as the earlier squeeze associated with the moment of landing. This lifting

150

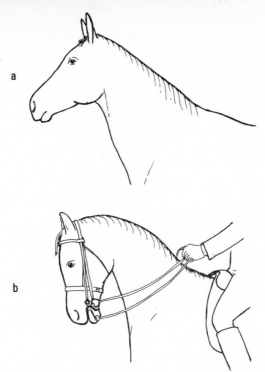

a

b

Figure 4.19
Attitudes of the horse's head. *Above*: alert but unrestrained. *Below*: nose in
and neck arched, paying close attention to the bit and ready to respond to the
rider's slightest indication. The horse in the lower figure is slightly "overbent"
and "behind the bit". Ideally his face should be vertical with the poll at the
highest point in the neck. Also, the horse should be feeling the bit and
contributing to maintaining a slight tension in the rein. The slack rein here at
least indicates that the posture is not produced by pulling with main force on
the rein.

leg-aid encourages the horse to spring higher at each step and
the increased vigour of his action is reflected in increased
impulsion.

Bringing his nose in
It may be that your attempts to build up impulsion have
succeeded in making your horse alert and responsive, but he is
still holding his head up in an attitude like that of *Figure 4.19a*,
whereas what you are aiming at is a posture more like that of
Figure 4.19b. Notice here that the line of the rein indicates a
very light tension, showing that the horse is holding his head
in for himself. His head is not being pulled in by the rein. The   151

action of the rein is much more effective here, where the pull is across the line of the mouth, than it would be in an attitude such as that in *Figure 4.19a*, where the bit would be pulled up into the corner of the mouth.

To achieve the arched neck and upright head-carriage you need first to explain to the horse what you want him to do. Paradoxically, the first step is to persuade him to stretch forward and downward. This is where the lowered hand becomes important. Ride a succession of turns either at the walk or at a slow trot. Come forward into the jump seat position and get your hands as far down the horse's shoulder as you can. Tickle the bit, first on one side then on the other and make the turns by giving with the outside hand. Keep up the impulsion with your legs. When you feel the horse reaching for the bit, reward him with your voice and by caressing his neck with the inside of your forearm.

From time to time encourage him to relax further by running your hand up and down his neck close beside the crest. You will need to be patient. After a time he will begin to lower his head into the turns, stretching his neck forward. Continue tickling the bit and gradually start stealing a little rein whenever he gives you a chance. Keep your hands very low.

The draw reins

If you find you get tired quickly in this position you can try using the draw reins. These are long reins that pass through the rings on the ends of the bit and run downward to an anchorage on the girth under the mid-line of the belly. The line of action of the force exerted by the draw rein upon the bit bisects the angle between the parts of the rein above and below the bit. This means that you can hold your hands at the normal level, just above the withers, and still pull the bit down toward the horse's shoulder, as you were previously doing with the lowered hand.

The disadvantage of the draw rein is that, because of the extra purchase of the pulley-action where the rein passes through the bit-ring, it is possible to pull the horse's head down by main force. This encourages him to pull back with the muscles that lift his head, whereas what you want him to do is to relax these same muscles and hold his head freely in the nose-in position.

You will probably need the draw reins for only a few minutes because, once your horse has grasped the idea of what you want him to do, you can go back to the regular rein. This allows a much more delicate control of the bit.

If you find that your horse is slow to learn to keep his nose in and continually fights against the rein, try working with draw reins and ordinary reins in different hands, using for each hand the modified single-handed grip (*Figure 4.42*). You can then alternate between the two reins, using the draw rein when he pokes his nose out, and changing to the ordinary rein when he starts to get a little overbent and when he puts his nose too far down in response to the draw rein. It is important to keep up the impulsion by driving with the seat. This will encourage him to keep his head up and when he eventually learns to keep his nose in it will be with an arched neck.

Some people anchor the ends of the draw reins to the girth straps instead of to the middle of the girth between the forelegs. This gives the extra purchase of the pulley-action round the rings of the bit, but the line of the pull on the bit is not lowered very much below that of the hand in the regular position. One thus achieves the disadvantages of the draw rein without the advantages.

Corners

When riding turns in the jump seat position you will notice that your weight comes naturally onto the inside knee at the beginning of the turn. This, in itself, is an effective instruction to the horse to make the turn. Do not over-emphasise the shift of weight, however, because this may encourage the horse to "fall in" on the turns, cutting the corner by stepping sideways with his forelegs. One aspect of the precision that one tries to achieve is that, unless one is deliberately asking the horse to go on two tracks, the hindquarters should follow directly behind the forequarters through all turns and corners. If your horse tends to step across the corners with his forelegs, correct him by using indirect rein instead of opening rein on the inside of the turn, asking for the turn by yielding with the outside rein. Also apply your inside leg over the girth or a little in front of it. An effective way to do this when in the jump seat is to work with the ankle of the inside foot to apply repeated brief pressures down onto the stirrup. This tenses the calf muscle against the side of the horse in a rapid sequence of nudges.

It is good practice to ask your horse to go well into each of the corners when you are riding a pattern involving right-angle turns. Do not make the mistake of allowing the horse to 153 bend too much at the neck. You need little more than just enough to bring the corner of his eye into view. He can quite easily turn his head beyond a right angle, but if you allow him to do this he may become "rubber-necked". He will then tend to respond to the rein by turning his head alone, continuing to go straight on, instead of moving into a turn when you want him to.

Bending

If all is going well, you may feel that the horse is actually bending his spine as well as his neck. He cannot, however, bend the main part of his spine very much in a sideways direction, and most of the apparent bend will be in the relative positions of the shoulders and haunches. The outer shoulder reaches forward while the inner shoulder is held back. This gives a very slight deflection of the withers as the start of a smooth curve running along the whole length of the neck up to the poll. The haunch on the inner side also reaches forward more than the outer haunch, producing a slight sideways bend of the lumbar part of the back.

This stage in the education of horse and rider is one that demands and repays prolonged practice. You should work on the development of impulsion by bracing the back, and you should keep encouraging your horse to hold his nose in without leaning heavily on the rein. Pay attention to the smoothness of the bend when riding on a circle and check that the hindquarters are correctly tracking exactly behind the forequarters. The concentric circles are an appropriate pattern to use because no change of direction is required and you can concentrate on maintaining a steady rhythm while varying the speed over the ground, periodically collecting up for a time and then encouraging full extension for a number of strides.

Stiff on one side

You should, of course, practise turns both to the right and to the left. You will probably find that there is a distinct difference between the two sides both in the smoothness with which the horse takes up the bend in his spine and in the steadiness with which he goes forward. He appears to be stiffer on one side than on the other. Make up your mind which is the stiff side and start your bending practice for the day with circles to the easy side. When the horse is warmed up, start to work on the stiff side, beginning with a number of fairly large circles and gradually reducing the diameter. After spending some minutes on this, move on to figures-of-eight. Here you should pay attention to the symmetry of the track making sure that the alternating circles to right and to left are of precisely the same size, as well as both being perfectly round.

Ask a friend to watch you carefully to see whether the asymmetry in the horse can be attributed to an asymmetry in the rider. It is very easy to get into the habit of riding with a little more weight on one side than the other without being aware of it. If you happen to have developed such a habit, you will at first feel lopsided when you move into a position that your friend says is straight. However, it will be worth while to persist. You will be rewarded by finding that your horse becomes more symmetrical in his behaviour as you cure yourself of the habit.

One way to make yourself more aware of your own asymmetry is to ride for a little with your weight deliberately more on one side than the other, and then change over to the other side. Then, after you have been riding for a time without thinking about the possibility of asymmetry, just try out the feel of momentarily putting more weight first on one side and then on the other. Ask yourself whether the two sides feel the same. If your usual position is asymmetrical, you will probably feel that the deliberate shifts of weight to the two sides do not call for the same amount of effort.

Signs of restlessness

While you are riding round and round trying to get your horse settled, watch what he is doing with his head and ears. This will tell you whether he is being distracted by things going on round about. You may also be able to tell whether he is uncertain about what you are trying to tell him by your movements of the bit. He may throw his head about and pluck at the rein.

Another common sign of restlessness, tail swishing, is not so easily seen from the saddle, though it is immediately obvious to an onlooker. In the wild, tail swishing from side to side is a sign to other horses to be on their guard. It is not a full alarm signal. It just indicates a state of unease; the horse does not feel it is safe to relax but he is not quite sure what the problem is.

When your horse has relaxed and is content to carry you steadily round the circle his actions will indicate this. His tail swishing stops, he no longer throws his head about, he works the bit gently in his mouth to maintain a light tension, and he extends his neck and lowers his head slightly without actually changing the distance between his mouth and the saddle. This neck movement is characteristic but rather subtle. You will recognise it once you have seen it.

The halt and half-halt

As well as practising the turns, to encourage the horse to bend his spine, you should also practise the halt. To produce a really smart halt you need to brace your back to drive the horse into a restraining hand. The aids are similar to those needed to increase collection but with a firmer tension in the rein. The effect is to bring the horse's hindlegs forward under his weight. If you ask for a sudden halt with the rein alone, he will tend to throw out his forelegs and will stop with his weight on the forequarters. He will probably bring his head down at the same time so that you are in danger of sliding forward over his neck.

The horse will need first to be warned of your intention to halt. You indicate this by a brief pull on the rein. You then apply a firmer resistance to those movements of the rein produced by the horse so that he knows not to go forward, and at the same time you drive the saddle forward with a braced back. The horse is, so to speak, driven up into the bit. It may be necessary to reinforce your rein signal by adding a few brief pulls to the steady tension in the rein. The process of coming to a halt is a gradual one, the horse making shorter and shorter steps. The hindfeet start to catch up with the forefeet. The horse "sits back" into the halt instead of pitching forward.

Because the full halt takes two or three strides, it is possible to ease the rein again before the horse has actually come to a standstill. This manoeuvre is called a "half-halt". The horse is brought "to attention", with increased collection. It is appropriate to ask for a half-halt as a preliminary to any manoeuvre such as a change of gait, which you want the horse to execute with some precision. When you release the rein after a half-halt the horse should surge forward with increasing extension.

Transition from trot to walk

In a dressage competition you may be required to make certain changes of gait at specified points in the arena. This calls for a certain delicacy in balancing the actions of the seat and hands, which can be achieved only with practice. Decide upon some fixed landmark in your practice area and try to make the transition from trot to walk at the precise moment that your body passes the marker. Warn the horse of your intention when you are still a few strides away from the transition point. Ask for a half-halt. Keep up a gradually increasing rein pressure and then give an extra brief pull on the rein just as you are coming up to the mark. As soon as the horse drops to the walk, ease the rein and relax your seat. Thereafter gradually build up the pattern of alternating leg-aids appropriate to the walk. If your horse is particularly lively and is reluctant to drop back into the walk, it may help if you lift your hands briefly just as you are coming up to the moment when you want him to change.

The aids for the transition from trot to walk are thus just like those for the halt, except that you ease the rein before the horse has come to a standstill. The smoothness of the transition depends on accurate timing. If you relax your tension too soon, he will continue in trot and you achieve only a half-halt. If you are too late in relaxing, he will stop completely and you will have to restart him again at the walk. To get the timing right, you have to be aware of what he is doing.

At the walk, the horse does not throw himself clear of the ground at each step in the way he does at the trot. This means that, to make the transition, he must first make a soft landing on one diagonal. You may be able to feel him getting ready for this because all the muscles of the trunk are engaged in preparing for the jolt that occurs at the trot each time the horse lands on one of the diagonals, and the preparation for a soft landing is not the same as the preparation at the trot for catching the weight on a single diagonal pair of legs and throwing it up again for the next stride.

Another difference between trot and walk is that each leg steps individually at the walk instead of being paired with its diagonal. Just after the soft landing on one diagonal, the opposite forefoot is brought to the ground early to give three-point support. Meanwhile the placing of the hindfoot of that diagonal is delayed. Then, just before this hindfoot touches down, the forefoot on the same side is lifted in the start of the walking pattern. As well as relaxing his trunk muscles to make the soft landing for the walk, the horse also relaxes his neck muscles, so that his head sinks further at the moment of the soft landing. The upward return movement of the head, while the trunk is supported on three legs, helps the horse to reach forward with the hindleg, which is still in the air at this point. If you are alert to all the small components of the horse's movement, there are several signs that you can look for as indications that the horse is about to make the change from trot to walk. In this way you teach yourself to adjust the timing of the change in your aids until the transition is achieved smoothly at the precise moment you intend.

Turn on the forehand

An exercise that helps to develop the rider's awareness of the horse's movements is the turn on the forehand. This manoeuvre is also a good introduction to lateral work, in which the horse is trained to respond to leg-aids which are different on the two sides. We have, up to this point, been dealing mainly with aids that the horse appears to understand naturally. Where the leg-aids have been different on the two sides they have been accompanied by shifts of the rider's weight in the saddle. The shift of weight is understood naturally, and the leg-aids have been used merely as reinforcement. We are now ready to try out the effects of leg-aids given in new combinations with weight-shift, rein-aid, and position of the horse's head.

The turn on the forehand is carried out from the halt, with the horse in a good state of alertness (*Figure 4.20*). He is to be asked to move his haunches sideways to pivot on a single forefoot. This pivoting foot does not remain rooted to the ground, but each time it is lifted it is put down again on the same spot. We start by tickling the bit and bracing the back to bring the horse to a state of readiness. We then warn the horse of what is coming. If the turn is to be made to the right, we ask the horse to shift his nose round slightly toward the right by being a little firmer with the right rein and giving a little with the left. We now want him to step to the left with his hindlegs. Bring the weight forward a little in the saddle, to help free the hindquarters, and work actively with the right leg, giving a series of little pats with the calf against the girth or a little behind it.

The natural response to the leg-aid is for the horse to lift his hindleg on that side. We restrain him from stepping forward by pressing more firmly with the rein just at this point. Do not press too hard or he will step backward. The right rein should be in the position for the indirect rein behind the withers, while the left hand gives indirect rein in front of the withers.

158

Figure 4.20
Turn on the forehand, to the right in this case. The horse pivots on the right forefoot, replacing it on the same spot after each step. (*See text.*) In this picture the rider has allowed his weight to slip too far to the right.

Both reins are opposing forward movement of the horse. Their lateral effects on the forequarters cancel out, leaving the influence on the hindquarters of the right indirect rein behind the withers. The effect of this is to ask the horse to move his haunches to the left. His nose is already turned to the right and a leftward movement of the haunches would tend to straighten his spine. We encourage him to step to the left by putting a little more weight on the right knee and by tapping harder with the right leg. He may cross one hindleg in front of the other or he may just bring his right foot closer to the left. In any case he will then step out to the left with his left hindfoot, make a small forward step with the left forefoot and will lift and replace the right forefoot.

When you feel the haunches starting to move across to the left, you should apply the left leg-aid, to encourage him to lift his left hindleg, and then apply steady pressure with your left leg to tell the horse to pause after making this one step in the desired direction. Relax, and reward him with your voice and by caressing his neck before asking for another step. Do not attempt too much at one time. The situation for the horse is a little unusual and he has a lot to assimilate.

Concentrate on feeling what the horse is doing. Make each step separately so that you can anticipate each stage in the movement of the horse, being ready to hold him in if he starts to move forward or to urge him on if he starts to back. Practise the turns in both directions, then take two steps round one way followed by two steps in the opposite direction. Finally, after one step, say to the left, step back again to the right.

This exercise is a first stage in teaching the horse to move away from your leg. This is not a natural reaction. Some horses will move toward your leg, particularly if you are wearing a spur. When at liberty, they will look for a tree or a post to rub themselves against to dislodge anything that is irritating the skin, so it is natural to push against the irritation of the spur. In making the turn on the forehand two signals tell the horse not to push back against your leg.

In the first place we start with the head turned to one side so that he would need to bend even further to push against the leg-aid. Secondly, we apply the indirect rein behind the withers. Even if he does not understand this at first, the intention becomes clear when it is applied on the side to which the head is already turned.

After several repetitions he comes to associate the leg-aid with the response he is making naturally to the indirect rein behind the withers. Thereafter he will give the same response to the leg even if the rein-aid is reduced. We consolidate this by asking for the turn on the forehand with less and less preliminary turning of the head, until eventually he will make the turn even when the head is first turned the opposite way. That is to say, he learns to move his haunches to the left, in response to the rider's right leg, even when his head is already turned to the left. This movement is the basis of all lateral work.

Do not overpractise the simple turn on the forehand because your horse may get into the undesirable habit of swinging his haunches whenever you ask him to bend his neck. When you set his head to the right, for example, he may move his haunches to the left, spinning round to follow his head, and keeping his body straight instead of developing a bend. In contrast, the turn on the forehand in which the haunches are moved to the same side as the head is a most valuable suppling exercise even though it is not at first easy to perform.

Haunches-in

A variation on the advanced form of the turn on the forehand is to call for a similar lateral displacement of the haunches while riding a circle. The commands for steering into the circle include a leg-aid given behind the girth by the rider's outside leg. In the normal course the rider's leg would return to the regular position over the girth as soon as the horse has settled onto the circular path. To ask the horse to displace his haunches toward the inside of the circle in the manoeuvre known as "haunches-in", the rider moves his outside leg back and applies a series of nudging leg-aids just behind the girth. The knee of the rider's inside leg presses firmly into the saddle with the lower leg straight down. Meanwhile the rider gives indirect rein behind the withers with the outside rein and uses the inside rein in the direct rein position to maintain the inward bend of the horse's neck. The horse should step across into the circle with his hindlegs and thereafter the horse's feet should make two separate tracks, the hoofprints of the hind-feet falling on a slightly smaller circle than those of the forefeet. It is important to maintain plenty of impulsion to ensure that the rein-aids have their proper effect.

Leg-yielding

Once the horse has learned to move away from the rider's leg in the context of the turn on the forehand and when turning a circle with haunches in, the rider can start to use the leg-aid on its own. We have already seen that if the horse is going straight ahead with symmetrical aids from leg, seat and reins, the effect of moving one hand across the neck to give the indirect rein behind the withers is to cause the horse to incline sideways, moving both fore- and hindquarters to the side away from the rein, while continuing to aim his head and body in the same forward direction.

Some horses respond to the indirect rein behind the withers more readily than others. Those that do not at first move readily to the side can be encouraged to do so by giving active unilateral leg-aids on the same side as the rein-aid, provided that they have first been taught not to push back against the rider's leg. After practising this for some time on a straight track, give the unilateral leg-aid without the rein-aid. Your horse should now move diagonally to the side in response to the leg-aid alone. This response is called "leg-yielding". It is convenient to practise this when hacking along quiet roads, asking the horse to move out to the middle of the road and then back to the side while all the time facing directly forward. The diagonal movement may be asked for either by the rein alone, using the indirect rein behind the withers, or by leg alone, both hands being maintained in the direct rein position.

Steering the rein-back

When your horse has learned to respond to the leg-aid applied on one side only, the other leg being inactive, and when you have made yourself familiar with the different responses you can produce with the rein, you will be in a position to improve the precision of all the manoeuvres already in your repertoire. During the rein-back, for example, you will be alert for signs that the horse is going to deviate from the straight path. When he moves his haunches to one side, you can correct, both with appropriate leg-aid and by applying indirect rein behind the withers.

Rein-back balance

You should also be able to regulate the speed with which the horse steps back. Try to persuade him to pause after each step. The pattern of leg movements during the rein-back is not the same as that for forward walking. The horse tends to step back with a diagonal pair of legs rather than with one leg at a time. With a little practice you will be able to make him pause after a single step and then, instead of stepping back further, make him go forward again for a single step. The step back and the step forward are both performed with the same diagonal pair of legs, the other diagonal remaining on the ground. The horse balances backward and forward over the stationary diagonal. Repeat on the other diagonal.

A variation in this is to go straight into a rein-back from the forward walk, without pausing in between. This manoeuvre is achieved by judiciously balancing the effect of your restraining hand against the forward impulsion of your seat and legs. You may have found your horse doing this accidentally when you were really asking for a halt, but did not relax your pull on the rein at quite the right moment.

Turn on the haunches

For a straight rein-back your hands should be in the "direct rein" position. If you move your hands to one side, the horse will step sideways with the forelegs and you can use your seat

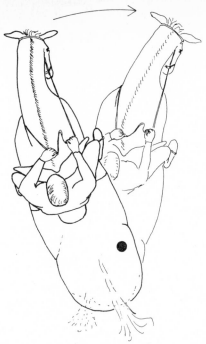

Figure 4.21
Turn on the haunches, to the right. The horse pivots on the right hindfoot, which is replaced on the same spot after each step. (*See text.*) The rider has allowed his weight to slip a little too far to the left.

to hold him from stepping back with the hindlegs. He then executes a turn on the haunches, the forelegs moving round in a circle while the horse pivots on one of the hindlegs, which is replaced on the same spot each time it is lifted (*Figure 4.21*).

To make the turn on the haunches to the right, start by bracing your back to make sure the horse is fully alert. Then give opening rein with the right hand and at the same time give indirect rein in front of the withers with the left hand in the raised position. Keep up the impulsion with your seat and press the left knee sideways into the saddle. It may help to sit back a little to relieve the weight on the forequarters. The horse should step out to the side with his forelegs. Be content at first with a single step. Apply the right leg-aid to tell the horse to halt, then relax and reward the horse.

Practise turns on the haunches in both directions, making the turn in a series of separate steps with pauses in between. It is easier to develop precision if you proceed slowly like this. Do not be in too much of a hurry.

163

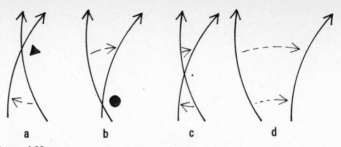

Figure 4.22
Distinctions between kinds of turn. a) Turn on the forehand, pivoting on a foreleg; b) Turn on the haunches, pivoting on a hindleg; c) Spin, or sloppy turn, with forelegs and hindlegs moving sideways in opposite directions; d) Pirouette; forelegs and hindlegs both move sideways, but in the same direction. When the spin (c) is performed deliberately it is referred to as "a turn on the centre".

The "chain"

You build up precision in your control of the horse by insisting on a proper distinction between the turn on the forehand and the turn on the haunches. In each case the horse should pivot on a single leg, which is put down again on the same spot each time it is lifted. Do not be content with a sloppy turn in which the feet just tramp all over the place (*Figure 4.22*).

An elegant exercise which helps horse and rider to understand one another is the "chain". This is a sequence of half-turns carried out alternately on the forehand and on the haunches (*Figure 4.23*). As the horse pivots first on a foreleg and then on a hindleg, the succession of half-turns results in a progression. The hindlegs walk round a foreleg and then the forelegs walk round a hindleg. It is this succession of small semi-circles that gives the manoeuvre its name. The successive turns may be made in various ways. If you turn in alternate directions, you make either all the turns on the forehand to the right and all the turns on the haunches to the left or all the forehand turns to the left and all the turns on the haunches to the right, changing the bend for each half-turn. Alternatively, all the turns may be made in the same direction either to the right or to the left, pivoting alternately on the forehand and on the haunches, and keeping the same bend throughout.

The full pass

The discipline of carrying out the pivoting turns one step at a time leads directly into the "full pass" (moving sideways without forward progression). Suppose that you make one step to

164

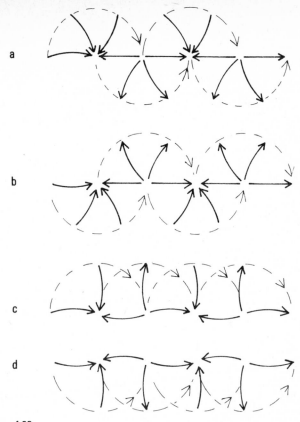

Figure 4.23
Examples of the "chain", a sequence of half-turns alternately on the forehand and on the haunches. a) Turn to the right on the forehand followed by turn to the left on the haunches, with change of bend. b) Turn to the left on the forehand followed by turn to the right on the haunches, with change of bend. c) Turn to the right on the forehand followed by turn also to the right on the haunches, the bend being to the right throughout. d) as (c) but to the left. Great care is needed to preserve precision in cases (c) and (d) and to avoid the turns degenerating into spins.

the right with the forelegs, using the aids for a turn on the haunches, pause, and then make one step to the right with the hindlegs, using the aids for the turn on the forehand. The result is that the horse has stepped out to the right with all four legs.

The next stage is to alternate smoothly between the two sets of aids in order to reduce the duration of the pause. Then, instead of pivoting at each stride, he moves steadily to the side on two tracks in a direction at right angles to the long axis of his 165 body. If the steps are large enough he should cross his legs, the left legs stepping over in front of the right legs. This exercise makes considerable demands on the horse and one should not ask for more than a few steps. The full pass should be practised to the left as well as to the right.

Gates

The rein-back balance, the pivoting turns on the forehand and on the haunches, and the full pass, all contribute to the mobility needed for opening and closing gates without dismounting. One can bring one's horse close up to the gate, and position the shoulders near the fastening. In leaning over to manipulate the fastening, be careful not to move your breastbone too far away from the horse's withers or you will lose your balance. If the horse moves, do not hold on to the gate, but let go and quickly move back into position on the saddle. Reposition the horse and start again.

After releasing the fastening you ask your horse to move in an arc to follow the movement of the gate, backing if it opens toward you or edging forward if it opens away. Pass through the opening, pivoting round the end of the gate, if possible keeping a hand on it to prevent it swinging. Then move back with the gate to close it. Get your horse to stand close to the gatepost and to stand still while you do up the fastening. Pivot, turn away, and ride on. If your horse gets excited when he is close to the gate, do not persist, but dismount to deal with the gate and try again on another day. You can get into serious difficulties if your horse charges through the narrow gap left by inadequately opening a gate that opens toward you. If anything catches on the end of the gate as you go through, the horse will be trapped against the gatepost and all his efforts to get through will just pull the gatepost harder and harder in to his side. He could injure himself, and you, very badly. However, once warned, you are less likely to allow yourself to drift into such a situation.

Lateral work on two tracks

The precision with which the horse responds to the rider's leg-aids is tested in dressage competitions by the "lateral movements" in which the horse moves in a straight line that is inclined to the long axis of his body. Forelegs and hindlegs follow two separate tracks as in leg-yielding. For competition purposes, the regulation angle with which the horse's body is

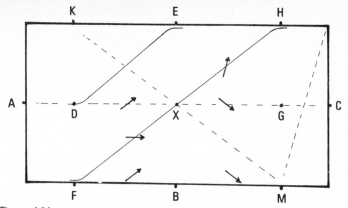

Figure 4.24
Lateral work on two tracks. Relationships between the inclination of the axis of the horse's body to the direction of progression and to the sides and diagonals of the dressage arena. (*See text*.) On the diagonal from X to H, with the nose to the left of the track, the horse's body should be parallel to the dashed line from M to the corner between H and C, rather than parallel to the short side of the arena.

inclined to the direction of progression corresponds to the diagonal between the quartermarkers in the 40 m dressage arena, for example from F to H or from D to E in *Figure 4.24*. The horse may be asked to proceed along a track parallel to the long sides of the arena while facing along a diagonal, or he may proceed along a diagonal while his body remains parallel to the long side of the arena. The head may be either to the right or to the left of the trunk. The horse's trunk may be held straight as in leg-yielding, or alternatively it may be bent either toward or away from the direction of progression. In proceeding from F to H in *Figure 4.24* with the head to the left of the track, the axis of the horse's body should be parallel to a line from the quartermarker at M to the corner of the arena between C and H, not parallel to the short side of the arena.

When riding on circles we ask the horse to bend as well as turn. In leg-yielding we ask for an inclined track without bending. The first stage in developing the other lateral movements is to teach the horse to perform the bend without change of direction.

Shoulder-forward

We start by making a small circle in a corner of the arena, entering the corner from the short side as in *Figure 4.25*. While continuing on the circle, the rider will be in what is called

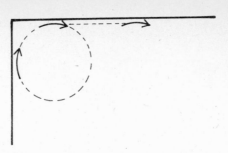

Figure 4.25
Track to prepare for "shoulder-forward". After a small circle in the corner of the arena the horse is asked to proceed along the long side without losing the bend. The heavy arrows are schematic plan views of the horse to show the bend. In "shoulder-forward" the horse's shoulders are slightly further from the wall than the hindquarters (see *Figure 4.27*) so that forefeet and hindfeet move on overlapping tracks.

"position right". That is to say, he will have asked the horse for a bend to the right and he will be maintaining the horse's head bent toward the inside of the circle using both hands in the direct rein position, with the left hand a little in front of the right (*Figure 4.26*). The rider's left shoulder is a little in advance of his right while his pelvis is turned very slightly in the opposite direction, the right hip being in advance of the left. The right leg is on the girth and the left is a little behind the girth. The legs are active only when they are needed to correct any tendency for the haunches to wander from the true circle. There is slightly more weight on the right seat-bone than on the left, though the rider continues to sit upright and does not lean inward.

The aim now is to leave the circle where it touches the long side of the arena and to continue on a straight track without losing the bend. As you pass the corner, warn the horse to pay attention, by making a half-halt with seat and reins. Then, as you come onto the track along the side of the arena, move both hands briefly to the left, giving left opening rein and right indirect rein in front of the withers, but keep up the tension in both reins so as to hold the horse's head steady in its bend to the right. The horse should step off the circle with his forelegs. As soon as he does this, return your hands to the direct rein position and use your legs to keep the haunches following straight along behind the forelegs (*Figures 4.27 and 4.29*). The horse should now proceed straight along the long side of the arena while his head remains turned to the right, with the rider continuing to sit in "position right".

Figure 4.26
"Position right." The contribution of the rider to the development by the horse of the correct bend for a turn to the right. Dotted lines show, on the right, the transverse axis of the head (looking straight ahead) and the line of the shoulders; on the left, the line of the hips. The left shoulder is a little ahead of the right. The left hip is a little behind the right. The rider is putting a little more weight on his right seat-bone and knee than on the left, but he sits upright and does not lean. The heavy arrows indicate how the bend of the horse will be represented in schematic diagrams. The displacements of the rider's shoulders and hips are only very slight; just enough for the horse to be able to feel a difference between "position right" and "position left". There should be no twist in the rider's spine because this would interfere with the bracing action that is needed to drive the saddle forward.

Because of the bend, the horse has his left shoulder ahead of his right. The manoeuvre is therefore called "shoulder-forward". Forelegs and hindlegs follow overlapping tracks.

Shoulder-in
The preparation for the manoeuvre called "shoulder-in" is similar to that for "shoulder-forward", but this time the horse leaves the circle a little later. The half-halt is given as the horse reaches the long side of the arena and the commands for the horse to leave the circle are given after the forequarters have 169

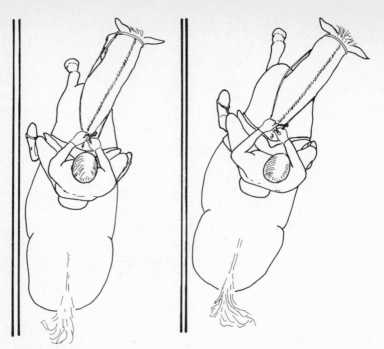

Figure 4.27 (left)
"Shoulder-forward", top view. The hindlegs follow the left foreleg on overlapping tracks. (Compare with *Figure 4.28.* See also *Figures 4.29* and *4.30.*)
Figure 4.28 (right)
"Shoulder-in", top view. Forelegs and hindlegs follow separate tracks, the track of the forelegs being nearer to the centre of the arena, i.e. the forelegs follow the "inside track" along the side of the arena. (See also *Figure 4.30.*) The rider has allowed his weight to slip too far over to the right. (Compare with *Figure 4.27.*)

moved out onto the circle but while the hindlegs are still on the side track (*Figure 4.31*).

Here again, both hands are moved briefly to the left while keeping up the tension in the rein to preserve the bend. The left hand gives opening rein and the right gives indirect rein, this time behind the withers, to encourage the hindlegs as well as the forelegs to step sideways. The right leg is strongly active on the girth to initiate the lateral progression as for the full pass. The left leg behind the girth is held ready to correct any tendency for the haunches to swing too far over to the left. The seat keeps up the impulsion, driving the horse forward into the bit to preserve the bend. As soon as the horse has stepped off the circle, the left hand returns to the direct rein position, while the right hand continues to give indirect rein behind the

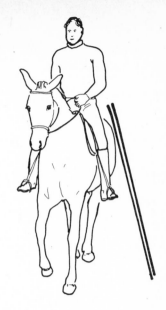

Figure 4.29 (left)
"Shoulder-forward", front view. (Compare with *Figure 4.30*.) In both of these figures the apparent difference in level between the rider's left and right feet is a consequence of perspective and the position of the camera, the rider's left foot being further forward than his right.

Figure 4.30 (right)
"Shoulder-in", front view. Forefeet and hindfeet follow distinctly separate tracks. (Compare with *Figure 4.29*. See also *Figures 4.27* and *4.28*.)

withers. Forelegs and hindlegs follow distinctly separate tracks (*Figures 4.28 and 4.30*) parallel to the long side of the arena. The horse remains bent toward the inside of the arena, so that he is facing away from the direction of progression. In *Figures 4.28 and 4.30* he is on the right rein with his right shoulder in. This movement is called "shoulder-in to the right" although the horse is actually moving to the left.

Travers

If the command to leave the circle is given before the horse has reached the long side of the arena (*Figure 4.32*), the horse will proceed on two tracks to his right instead of to his left. He is still bent toward the inside of the arena but this time his head is facing toward the direction of progression instead of away from it.

The warning half-halt is given as the horse approaches the short side and the commands to leave the circle are given as the horse reaches the corner. The right hand gives opening rein   171

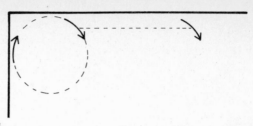

Figure 4.31
Track to prepare for "shoulder-in". After a small circle in the corner of the arena the horse is asked to move out *after* the forequarters have already left the long side but while the hindquarters are still on the outside track. The horse proceeds along the long side of the arena with forelegs and hindlegs following distinctly separate tracks. The horse is bent *away from* the direction of progression. (Compare with *Figure 4.32.*)

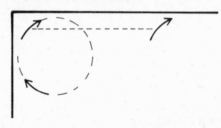

Figure 4.32
Track to prepare for "travers". The command to leave the small circle in the corner of the arena is given *before* the hindquarters have reached the long side. The horse proceeds along the long side with the forelegs and hindlegs following distinctly separate tracks. The head is toward the wall and the body is bent *toward* the direction of progression. (Compare with *Figure 4.31.*)

and the left gives indirect rein behind the withers. The outside leg is applied strongly behind the girth, as for a full pass. Instead of continuing round the circle onto the long side of the arena, the horse steps sideways, cutting across the circle with his hindlegs. The rider's right hand returns to the direct rein position as soon as the horse has started stepping to the side, while the left keeps up with the indirect rein behind the withers (*Figure 4.33*). The right leg is clear of the horse's side but it is held ready to check any tendency for the horse to swing his haunches to the right (*Figure 4.35*).

Half-pass

If all the commands just described for initiating the travers are applied later in the circle, when the horse has already reached the long side of the arena, this will make him move sideways diagonally across the arena (*Figure 4.37*). He will be bent to the right and his long axis will be parallel to the long side of the

172

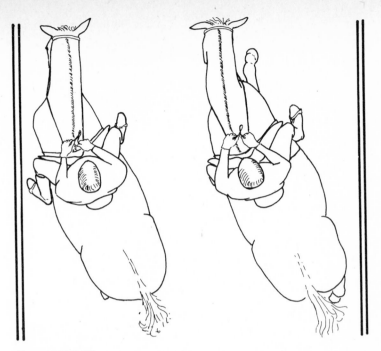

Figure 4.33 (left)
"Travers", top view. The horse proceeds on two tracks, bent *toward* the direction of progression. (Compare with *Figure 4.28.* See also *Figures 4.30* and *4.35.*)

Figure 4.34 (right)
"Renvers", top view. The horse proceeds on two tracks, bent toward the direction of progression, exactly as in "travers", except that in renvers the haunches are toward the wall while in travers it is the head that is toward the wall. If the same manoeuvre is carried out somewhere other than along a wall, it is referred to as a "half-pass" (see *Figure 4.37.*) The rider has allowed his weight to slip too far to the left and he is not sitting straight on the horse.

arena. This movement is called a "half-pass". It differs from the travers only in the direction of progression. The movement is called "travers" when the horse's head traverses along the long side of the arena or along the wall of an enclosed school. In the open, away from the wall, the movement is referred to as a half-pass. Notice that both in travers and in the half-pass the horse is bent toward the direction of progression while in shoulder-in he is bent away from the direction of progression.

Transitions in lateral work

There are three types of transition between the various movements on two tracks. In the first place one may change the inclination of the horse's body to the direction of progression   173

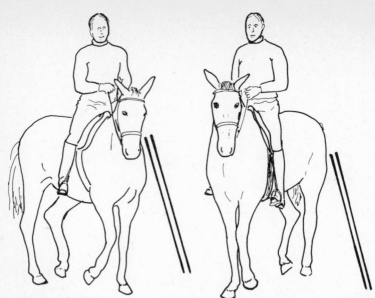

Figure 4.35 (left)
"Travers", front view. Forefeet and hindfeet follow distinctly separate tracks, with the body bent toward the direction of progression. (Compare with *Figure 4.36*.) The rider has here lifted his right leg away from the horse to an exaggerated degree. He also has his weight rather too far to his left.

Figure 4.36 (right)
"Renvers", front view. The movement is the same as for travers except that the haunches are toward the wall. (See also *Figure 4.30*, shoulder-in, where the bend is away from the direction of progression.)

while preserving the same bend throughout, passing, for example, from shoulder-in to the left through shoulder-forward to a half-pass to the left (*Figure 4.38*), or from half-pass to the right to shoulder-in to the right, and so on. Alternatively, one may keep the horse facing in the same direction and with the same bend while changing the direction of progression as in performing the counter change of hand (*Figure 4.39*), changing from a half-pass to the left through shoulder-forward to shoulder-in to the left. Yet another possibility is to change the bend while continuing on the same line of progression and without changing the inclination of the horse's body (*Figure 4.40*), changing from half-pass to the right through leg-yielding to the right and finishing with shoulder-in to the left. Or we may pass from shoulder-in through leg-yielding to the half-pass.

Thus we may start with the horse's head to one side or the other of the direction of progression and bent either to the right

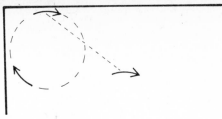

Figure 4.37
Track to prepare for a half-pass along the diagonal. (Compare with *Figure 4.31.*)

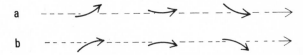

Figure 4.38
Change of inclination without change of bend, proceeding in the same direction throughout. a) shoulder-in to the left, shoulder-forward, and half-pass to the left. b) half-pass to the right, shoulder-forward, shoulder-in to the right.

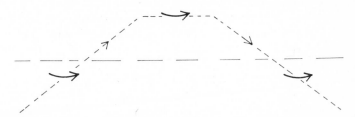

Figure 4.39
Change of direction of progression with change of inclination, but without change of bend. Half-pass along a diagonal to the left, shoulder-forward parallel to the long side of the arena, shoulder-in to the left along a diagonal to the right, as in the counter change of hand. The axis of the horse's body remains parallel to the long side of the arena and he is bent to the left throughout.

Figure 4.40
Change of bend while continuing along the same track without changing the inclination of the horse's body to the direction of progression. Half-pass to the right, leg-yielding to the right, followed by shoulder-in to the left.

or to the left. Thereafter we may change the way the horse is facing, or change the direction of progression, or change the bend. Furthermore, each of these transitions can be executed either at the walk or at the trot. Even greater variety is available if we include progression at the canter (*Chapter 5*).

175

Figure 4.41
Development of renvers from a half-turn on the haunches executed alongside the wall.

Renvers

After practising the various transitions in lateral work we may arrive at the position shown in *Figure 4.34*. Here the horse is progressing along the long side of the arena, both bent and facing in the direction of progression, and with his haunches toward the wall or to the outside of the arena. This movement is called "renvers". So far as the horse is concerned, it is a version of the half-pass, like travers, but this time with haunches to the wall instead of head to the wall (*Figure 4.36*). It differs from shoulder-in (*Figure 4.30*) in that the horse is bent toward the direction of progression rather than away from it. The renvers movement differs from all other types of lateral movement in that it cannot be developed from the circle. It is produced either by a change of bend from straight ahead along the wall, or from an incompleted turn on the haunches executed with the hindlegs on the outside track alongside the wall (*Figure 4.41*).

When working on the long side of the arena, either in travers or in renvers, the long axis of the horse's body makes only a small angle with the direction of progression. Accordingly, because of the bend, the horse's forequarters remain more or less square-on to the track and the forelegs move directly forward while the hindlegs step diagonally to one side. When performing the half-pass in the open, it is possible to increase the angle between the long axis of the horse and the direction of progession until the forelegs as well as the hindlegs are stepping diagonally out to the side. This is achieved by moving the outside rein across to act, momentarily, in front of rather than behind the withers. Then, in a fully-developed half-pass to the right, the horse may begin to cross his legs, the left feet (fore and hind) stepping across in front of the corresponding right feet.

Competitive dressage

The various movements on two tracks and the transitions between them provide excellent opportunities for developing one's skill in communicating one's wishes to the horse and for practising one's alertness to what the horse is about to do at each stage. It should be pointed out, however, that it is very difficult for a rider to appreciate on his own what kind of image he presents to an onlooker. When you enter for a competition you will be entirely in the hands of the judges. The art of marking dressage competitions is handed down by oral tradition and no amount of verbal definition can eliminate the subjective element of the personal impression made on the judge. Accordingly, if you wish to compete, it is essential to enlist the help of an experienced judge who knows what to look for and who can point out to you aspects of your performance that are visible to the onlooker but of which you yourself may be unaware. It is only after your attention has been drawn to a particular movement or habitual posture that you can start on remedial work.

It is instructive to read over the "Object and General Principles" section in the official B.H.S. dressage rules. The aim is that the horse should achieve perfect balance and extreme lightness in all his actions. He should give the impression of doing of his own accord what is required of him. Accordingly the aids given by the rider should be, so far as possible, imperceptible to the onlooker. Such perfection is achieved only after diligent practice.

The progressive series of official dressage tests do not include lateral work until a fairly advanced stage. The Preliminary, Novice, and most of the Elementary tests are concerned only with steering and with changes of gait or of speed, the emphasis being on the smoothness with which the horse performs what is asked of him.

The schooling whip
The horse has to be taught how to respond to unsymmetrical leg-aids. This is a fairly straightforward task when you are making the turns from the halt, either on the forehand or on the haunches, but problems may arise if you have taught yourself to be inconspicuous with your aids before your horse has been introduced to lateral work. He may not understand what is required of him when you use your leg-aids to produce lateral movement at the same time as you are also using the leg-aids for steering the forward progression.

One way to resolve the difficulty without having recourse to exaggerated rein-aids is to use a schooling whip. This is a very 177

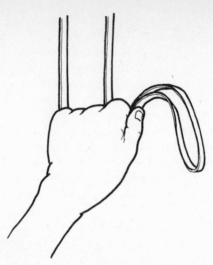

Figure 4.42
Modified single-handed grip on the rein. The two reins lie side by side, emerging over the forefinger together where they are gripped by the thumb. Separation for steering is provided by the second, third and fourth fingers. To shorten rein, the free loop of rein is pulled through by the other hand. Inequalities between the reins can be adjusted by allowing one or the other rein to slide through the fingers. (Compare with *Figure 3.21.*)

flexible whip, something over a metre long, with a very short lash. It is used discreetly to draw the horse's attention to a particular leg by gently tapping the appropriate leg as low down as possible. On no account should the whip be used with any vigour, because the horse will easily become alarmed and he will no longer be in a suitable frame of mind to absorb instruction. Once he has been introduced to the whip he will pay attention to the whistling sound of the lash moving through the air as well as to the sight of the movement itself and there will be no need for the whip actually to make any contact at all with his body. It is, of course, always very important when using a whip not to jerk the bit.

You may prefer to keep the reins in one hand, using the whip with the other hand. In which case, the modified grip (*Figure 4.42*) may be preferred to that shown in *Figure 3.21*. The spare portions of both reins lie together over the forefinger. It is a simple matter to shorten rein without disturbing the bit. One simply pulls on the loop of spare rein with the other hand. If one rein needs to be shortened more than the other, you shorten both and then allow the appropriate rein to slip a little.

178

Faster work

Most riders will wish to enjoy the canter before they have spent too much time practising lateral movements. However, although some horses will go into a canter quite freely, many others present problems to the beginner. Such problems usually disappear after the rider has started to try out the aids needed for lateral movements and it is for this reason that I have included lateral work here.

5 Canters and Jumps

Canter and gallop

The gait used by the horse when travelling at his maximum speed is the gallop. The action will be familiar to anyone who has watched horses in a race. There is a marked bending and stretching of the back, with associated up-and-down movements of the head, but the horse's body flows along very smoothly with comparatively little obvious vertical movement, allowing the jockey to remain balanced on his knees with his seat well out of the saddle.

In each cycle there is a single unsupported phase during which the horse bends his back and reaches forward with his hindlegs, lowering his head as he does so (*Figure 5.1*). He then lands on a single hindleg which makes a strong backward sweep against the ground. Similar strong sweeping movements are then made one at a time by the other three legs in turn with only brief periods when there is more than one foot on the ground. The effect is like that of a waggon-wheel, where the weight is taken successively on adjacent spokes. While the two hindlegs are making their drive, the pelvis is also rotated, like the hub of the waggon-wheel. At the same time, the horse strongly extends his back and reaches forward with his forelegs to cover as much ground as possible between footfalls. He is still bringing his head down at this point to help in delaying the footfall of the front legs. When the front legs do come to the ground, this may be in the same order as the hindlegs, transverse gallop (*Figure 5.1*) or in reverse order, rotatory gallop. While the two front legs are on the ground in turn, the horse strongly lifts his head and this helps to draw his hindlegs up under him ready for the next unsupported phase, during which he starts to lower his head again, draws his hindlegs forward, and bends his back.

From this analysis it is seen that, in the gallop, the horse takes off from the forelegs. This is in marked contrast with the gallop of many other animals, like antelopes, where the take-off is from the hindlegs in a series of leaps from each of which the animal lands on the forelegs. Sprint specialists, like the cheetah and some dogs, use a form of galloping which has two unsupported phases in each cycle, one with the body at full

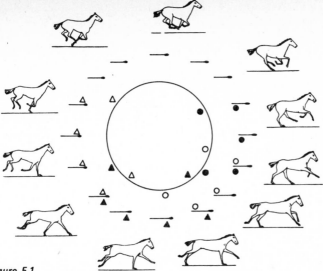

Figure 5.1
Cycle of leg movements and support patterns at the GALLOP. (Symbols as in
Figure 3.16; clockface as in *Figure 3.19*; side views from Muybridge (1893),
retouched.) The second hindleg comes to the ground before the touch-down
of the diagonally opposite foreleg.

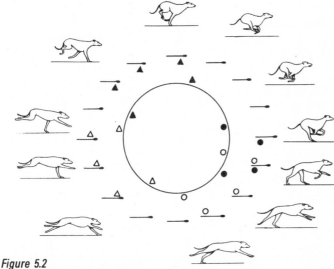

Figure 5.2
Cycle of leg movements and support patterns in the GALLOP of the DOG.
(Symbols as above.) The sequence of movements is similar to that in the gallop
of the horse (*Figure 5.1*) but there are here two principal unsupported phases,
one after the take-off by the forelegs, with the legs bunched together as in the
gallop of the horse, and the other after the take-off from the hindlegs, where
the body is at full stretch as in the gallop of the antelopes.

181

stretch as in the gallop of the antelope, and one with the legs bunched together under the body as in the gallop of the horse (*Figure 5.2*).

The canter is a less energetic mode of progression than the gallop. It involves much less extensive bending and stretching of the back. The horse lands on a single hindleg and takes off from a single foreleg, as in the gallop, but in between there are stages when he has three, or even all four, feet on the ground at once. It is convenient to think of the main support during the canter as being on a single diagonal, assisted first by the hindleg on which the horse has landed from the unsupported phase, and assisted later by the opposite foreleg, which will be the take-off leg (*Figure 5.3*).

During the unsupported phase, the horse reaches forward with the hindlegs, as in the gallop. At the same time he lowers his head and this produces a pitching motion of the trunk, the shoulders rising and the haunches falling. During the support

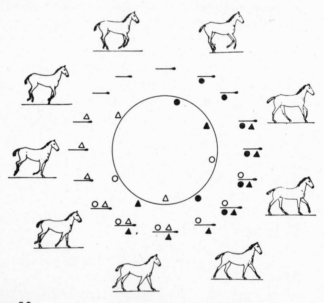

Figure 5.3
Cycle of leg movements and support patterns in the CANTER. (Symbols as in *Figure 3.16*; clockface as in *Figure 3.19*; side views from Muybridge (1893).) Note that the footfalls occur in the same order as in the walk (see *Figure 3.20*) but they are here grouped together in time, to leave a single unsupported phase. (Notice also the similarity between the action of the legs of the right diagonal pair in this diagram and in that of *Figure 4.2* for the trot.)

phase, the thrusts of the legs produce a pitching in the opposite direction because the hindlegs lift the haunches before the forelegs are available to lift the shoulders. The horse also throws his head up at this time, to be ready for the next unsupported phase.

The pitching motion of the trunk is characteristic of the canter. The motion can be quite pleasant for the rider. Indeed, this is how the gait gets its name. It is the gait preferred for rapid but comfortable long-distance travel, as for pilgrims on their way to Canterbury. "Canter" is short for "Canterbury gallop". It is also the gait usually adopted by cowboys in Western films.

When you watch a cantering horse you will see that, for most of the time, he holds one foreleg well out in front of the other. This leg is called the "leading leg". Actually this is the last of the four legs to touch down at each stride and it is also the last to leave the ground. From the saddle you can easily distinguish which is the leading leg by paying attention to the movement of the shoulders. You will see the shoulder of the leading leg lifting more prominently and moving forward during the later part of the unsupported phase. The horse seems to point his leading leg and shoulder in the forward direction. If he is about to turn to the right, he will usually lead with the right foreleg, and he will lead with the left foreleg into a left turn. We use this information to work out appropriate signals with which to indicate to the horse that we want him to canter, and on which leg.

Transition from trot to canter

In the trot, the horse springs from one diagonal pair of legs to the other, making two bounces to a stride. In the canter there is only one bounce to each stride and the single unsupported phase correspondingly lasts longer than either of the two unsupported phases of the trot. A stronger thrust is needed to launch the weight of the horse's body into this longer-lasting unsupported phase. In preparation, the horse sinks a little further onto the diagonal that is to be the main support in the canter. At the same time he brings down the opposite foreleg earlier than he would for a trot stride. This makes three legs available for the upward throw. Meanwhile he can reach forward with the other hindleg and delay putting it down till he is ready to land on it after the unsupported phase of the first canter stride.

183

Starting the canter

The horse changes naturally to the canter when he wishes to cover the ground more rapidly than at a fairly relaxed trot. He may canter on either lead. However, if we are to ask him to change into the canter, we need first to make up our mind which lead is to be used, because each lead calls for a different set of aids. To resolve the ambiguity, we make our early attempts to initiate the canter while the horse is already turning in a circle. As already mentioned, he will lead naturally with the inside leg on a circle, that is, with the right foreleg when turning to the right and with the left foreleg when turning left.

Suppose we start with a circle to the right at the sitting trot. The circle should not be too large; 10 m diameter will do very well. First make sure that the horse is trotting forward freely, with a regular rhythm. When you first turn into the circle, your left leg will be a little behind the girth, but when the turn is well established, your leg may return to the girth. Your right hip, however, remains very slightly forward of your left hip, while your left shoulder is slightly ahead of the right, in the "position right". The horse's head is turned a little to the right so that you can just see the corner of his eye. Your hands are in the direct rein position, the left having given a little more than the right.

Practise changing the speed over the ground, alternately driving forward with your seat for a few strides and then surreptitiously shortening rein for a few strides while you increase the pressure on the bit. Make sure you can produce noticeable changes in the speed over the ground. The rhythm of the footfalls should remain unchanged, but you need not worry too much about this at this stage. Now start to build up impulsion by keeping up the rein pressure instead of at once giving with the rein when you start to drive forward with the seat. The horse needs to be "wound up" between the drive of your seat and the restraint of your hands. The aim is to reach a stage where he surges forward as soon as you relax the pressure on the rein a little.

You are now ready to give the aids for the canter. Pay attention to the movements of the horse's shoulders so that you are clear in your mind which diagonal is being used for support at each bounce. Remember that it is the outside diagonal that forms the principal support at the canter. For a canter to the right, the outside diagonal consists of the left foreleg and the right hindleg. At the point of transition from the trot, you want the horse to reach forward with his left hindleg. The appropriate aid for this will be to apply your left leg behind the girth. What remains to be settled is the question of timing.

Just as in the transition from halt to walk and from walk to trot, it is necessary to proceed in stages. First build up alertness and impulsion, next give a warning of your intention, and then at the "moment of decision" apply simultaneously the appropriate aids with seat, legs, weight-change and reins. The warning for the canter is given by drawing your outside leg back, without at this stage applying any extra pressure to the horse's side. This draws the horse's attention to his outside hindleg. The "moment of decision" for a canter to the right occurs just as the horse is about to land on the outside diagonal. This is why you have to have already made up your mind which diagonal is which. Then, just as you are coming down for the bump on the outside diagonal, you brace your back to thrust the seat-bones forward against the saddle, squeeze with both legs, and at the same time momentarily relax the pressure on the rein. It helps to think of squaring your shoulders. Do not attempt to urge the horse forward by leaning forward yourself. This is likely to have the effect of moving the saddle backward instead of forward and the forward urge of the saddle produced by bracing your back is probably the most important single component in the complex of movements collectively referred to as the aids for the canter.

If it should happen that your horse strikes off with the wrong leg, that is to say leading with the left foreleg on a right hand turn, at once bring him back to the trot. Relax your legs, take up the pressure on the rein and give a few brief pulls, sitting well down into the saddle and squaring your shoulders. Remember that it is unrealistic to expect the horse to change from trot to canter on the correct leg within a single stride without previous warning. Make sure your warning indication with the outside leg is definite and early enough. If the trouble persists, use a larger circle, say 20 m diameter, for the preliminary preparation, practising the changes of speed and building up impulsion, and then turn in onto a smaller circle for the transition to canter. You will naturally use your outside leg to signal the turn. Bring it on again as a warning about halfway round the small circle and then give your main drive for the canter command just as you are coming out of the small circle 185

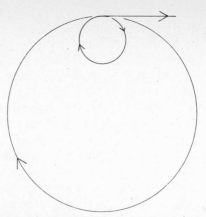

Figure 5.4
Track for starting the canter on the correct lead (here the right). Prepare by building up impulsion at the trot on a large circle. Turn into a smaller circle and give a warning to the horse with your outside leg. Drive on into canter as you rejoin the larger circle. The turn into the small circle ensures that the horse will strike off on the inside leg. Do not turn in so sharply that the horse has to slow down, and be especially careful if conditions are at all slippery.

and back onto the track of the larger circle (*Figure 5.4*). If you are working in an enclosed school where you can ride close to the wall, you can make your small circle into the corner. Apply your canter command as the horse passes the corner itself, and canter on along the side of the school.

You will find that the movements of the horse's head at the canter are very different from those made at the trot. When a horse gallops in a race the hands of the jockey execute quite extensive forward and backward movements. These movements are needed to maintain a steady contact with the horse's mouth. In the canter, just as in the gallop, the horse makes a swinging movement of his head at each stride, bringing his head down to help in reaching forward with the hindlegs and throwing his head up again when the forelegs are on the ground. You need to be very careful with your hands at the onset of the canter because, if you are not ready for it, this surging movement of the head can pull the rein taut with a snap, and this will feel to the horse like an urgent command to stop. If a horse feels a jerk on the bit every time he starts to move off in a canter, he will become more and more reluctant to canter with a rider on his back. It is this effect, in conjunction with the inherent difficulty of hitting off the timing correctly, that is responsible for most of the problems that beginners complain of in getting their horses to canter.

You should have no difficulty if you first make sure you are able to build up sufficient impulsion at the trot so that the horse accelerates with a forward surge as soon as you relax your pressure on the rein. When you are ready for the canter, you can let the horse accelerate on the inside diagonal just as you are about to give the canter command with your seat and legs. Practise starting the canter on both leads, always first turning to the appropriate side so that the horse leads with the inside leg.

Wrong lead

The reason for emphasising the correct lead is that, when the leading foreleg is on the ground, the diagonally opposite hindleg is already reaching forward. If the horse is bent toward the side of the leading leg, the hindleg will pass forward freely. But if the bend is toward the other side there is a possibility that the hindleg may trip over the foreleg, with the risk of injury, a stumble or even a fall. It is thus important that the horse should be bent toward the leading leg. He will usually do this for himself if you ask for the canter while he is turning. However, if he is going straight, you may have to look after it for him. This is only fair because he is cantering to your command. He would not get his legs mixed up if left to himself.

Disunited

There is another situation in which injudicious commands by the rider may lead the horse into difficulties. If your horse strikes off on the wrong leg, do not attempt to force him over at once onto the correct leg while he is still cantering. He may respond by changing the sequence of his forelegs while continuing with the hindleg sequence unchanged. Suppose that he has struck off, wrongly, on the right lead. The sequence of footfalls after each unsupported phase is then: left hind, left fore and right hind almost together, then right fore. You force him to change the lead and he may go: left hind, right hind and right fore together, following with left fore. This sequence works satisfactorily at the gallop – it is referred to as the "rotatory gallop" – but it leads to difficulties in the canter.

The reason is that at the canter the trunk has to pivot over the pair of legs that come to the ground together. In the correct canter, this is a diagonal pair, and the body can pitch comfortably forward. With the rotatory sequence of footfalls, the corresponding pair of supporting legs is a lateral pair. This produces lateral rolling in place of the normal fore-and-aft rocking 187 motion. The action tends to be jerky. The horse is said to be "going disunited". In the rotatory gallop, the movements of the individual legs are more spaced out in time and the same problems do not arise.

Change of lead

Accordingly, at any rate during the early stages of training, always pull back into a trot if your horse is cantering on the wrong leg. In some dressage tests you are expected to go right down to the walk before asking for a canter on the opposite leg.

Changes of speed

After practising the transition from trot to canter on a circle both to the right and to the left, you will be ready to try the transition while the horse is going straight. Make up your mind which lead you want and then go through the following stages: build up impulsion at the trot; ask for the appropriate bend with "outside" leg back and a little more weight on the "inside" knee; give with the rein as you come down on the inside diagonal; then, as he starts to accelerate, drive with your seat and both legs just as you are coming down for the next, outside, diagonal. In this description, "inside" means the side on which you want the horse to lead, because he needs to be bent to that side. After a few strides at the canter, come back to the trot and try again.

The practice routine of alternating faster and slower progression at the trot can now be extended to include periods at the canter. This provides an opportunity to become accustomed to the feel of the rein when the horse changes his gait. It is important to develop independence between hand and shoulder. Your hand should move forward and backward with the movements of the horse's head, keeping the same light tension on the rein all the time. Your shoulders will also be moving forward and backward with the rocking motion imparted to your body by the saddle. But the timing of your shoulder movements is not the same as that of the movements of the horse's head and your arm must be supple enough to absorb all the changes in relative position.

If you encourage the swinging movements of the horse's head by pulling a little while his mouth is moving toward the saddle and relaxing a little when his head is moving forward, the effect on the horse will be that he will lengthen his stride. You may see hints of this action when a racing jockey is urging his horse toward the finishing post. Do not make the mistake of overdoing it, as some beginners do, urging their horses on by flapping their elbows. All too often the effect of such exaggerated movements is just to jerk the reins and thus to unsettle the horse. If you execute your encouraging movements smoothly the horse will gradually move into gallop.

Collected canter

To get the horse to shorten his stride at the canter you apply your rhythmic pulls on the rein with a different timing. You first gently resist the forward movement of the horse's head and then you relax the tension in the rein at the moment when the horse's mouth is moving back toward the saddle. You need to be careful not to allow the rein to go completely slack. During the periods of increased rein tension you can tell the horse to pay more attention by rapidly-repeated clenching and unclenching of the fingers while keeping up the same gentle pull. This is a rather sophisticated action with the rein as the periods of increased tension do not last very long at each stride.

The effect of this rein action, working against the natural swing of the horse's head, will be to make the horse drop back from gallop to canter and even to a trot unless you actively keep the canter going, by bracing your back at each stride and driving forward with your seat-bones every time your weight comes down onto the saddle. If, at the same time, you sit up and square your shoulders you should, after a little practice, be able to develop a short, bouncy, canter for a few strides, with the horse making only a very little ground forward at each stride. You may have seen show-jumpers edging forward like this to a fence that calls for particular care in the approach. They cautiously bring their horses up toward the point they have selected beforehand as the start of their run-up.

By judiciously balancing the vigour with which you drive forward with your seat against the restraint or encouragement of your hand, you can adjust the length of stride and make the horse cover the ground either faster or more slowly while still keeping in the canter. For the apprehensive rider it is a great help in building up confidence to spend some time in practising these changes of speed at the controlled canter.

Stopping a runaway

Many horses enjoy a good canter and if they happen to be 189 feeling rather lively they may take advantage of the inexperience of the rider to accelerate forward into a full gallop. They may then easily get so excited that they forget to pay attention to the bit. If the rider pulls at the reins, the horse just puts more weight on the bit as though in an attempt to pull the reins right out of the rider's hands. The rider may even be pulled forward out of the saddle. It may be well here to recapitulate some of the advice given earlier about how to deal with a runaway.

A common reaction to being carried away faster than expected is for the beginner to try to hold on by wrapping his legs round the horse's belly. Unfortunately, this just makes matters worse, because the horse interprets the bouncing contact of the rider's heels against his side as an encouragement to gallop on even faster. The rider's best strategy is to adopt what was earlier described as the "safe position for the beginner". The first rule is "heels away from the horse, and forward rather than back". This brings the knees firmly against the saddle to give the rider lateral stability. The next rule is "fold forward at the hips to bring your elbows in front of your knees". This takes some of the weight off your seat-bones and provides a shock-absorbing mechanism to make it less likely that the rider will be bounced out of the saddle. The hands are now in a good position to take hold of the mane or of the neck strap if there is one. The feet should be held out and forward, rather than back. This helps to stiffen the knee to reinforce the lateral stability, and it also allows the rider to use the stirrups if the horse should swerve or if he should decide to stop suddenly. A relaxed or bent knee is of no use here. It just increases the chance of casually banging the horse's side with the rider's boot.

The third rule is "steer for the open spaces and gradually turn your horse into a circle". If you have enough room you can just let the horse run himself out. If he is strong and fit this may take a couple of miles and you will need to keep well clear of obstructions such as trees and gateposts. Round and round in a big field will be reasonably safe. Try very hard not to be taken onto a tarmac road as this is the worst possible place for a gallop. There is a very high risk of the horse slipping, and a fall onto such a hard surface could easily prove fatal.

After the initial shock of dismay that things are beginning to get out of hand, you should set yourself to think firmly about stopping rather than about parting company with your horse. Remember the importance of telepathy. Growing confidence in the security of your posture will help. You can also now start taking positive action with the reins.

You will already be leaning well forward with your elbows in front of your knees. You can therefore work your hands well down the reins toward the horse's mouth. Suppose you have decided to steer him to the right. Take a firm grip on the reins with your hands as far forward as you can go. Slide your left hand up the side of the horse's neck and across to the right side so that you can put your weight onto your left wrist where it lies against the horse's crest. The left rein should then be taut and firmly gripped in your left fist, which presses into the right side of the horse's neck. Now pull outwards and downwards with the right rein using a succession of brief strong pulls. Aim to bring the horse's nose right round to your knee. The simultaneous blocking action of your left hand is necessary to keep the bit from being pulled right through the horse's mouth. He will not want to dash forward so impetuously if you get his head round far enough.

If you are unlucky and the bit does manage to slip through his mouth, all is still not quite lost. You may be able to get one hand onto the cheekstraps of the bridle just below the ears, taking a firm grip on the mane with the other hand. Slide your hand down the cheekstrap of the bridle and pull his head round with the noseband. Remember to keep your breastbone over the mid-line of his neck and push your feet well forward to stop yourself being pulled out of the saddle. All this may sound rather heroic, but, after all, we are talking about an emergency situation here, and if you know in advance what to. do this will make it very much easier to cope with.

An alternative routine which works well with some horses, and which perhaps does not sound quite so alarming, is to shorten rein as before, as far as you can go, then put both reins in one hand well up by the horse's poll. Use the other hand to pull in the slack until each rein is taut. Then grip the reins very firmly so that they cannot slip through your fingers. Gradually work the fist that holds the reins little by little down the horse's neck, taking advantage of every moment when the horse relaxes, and blocking firmly when he pulls. He will finish up with his nose right in against his chest. He needs to swing his head to keep up the gallop and if you can, by this trick, manage to check the swinging movements of his head, the effect will be to check the urgency of the forward progression. You may even be able to bring him right down to the halt.

Regarding the runaway horse it should be emphasised that here prevention is much easier than cure. The more often you practise the stops, the more accustomed your horse will become to obeying your instructions and, correspondingly, the more unlikely will it be that the horse will disregard your commands even when he is excited. Do not deceive yourself with the notion that, if you let him have his head, his lust for speed will become satiated. This is very far from being likely. He will just become confirmed in his habit of making off at the slightest opportunity.

It is true that some horses have been cured of galloping off by driving them on, but plenty of space is needed for this. For example, you may need to force the horse to continue galloping for a further mile or two beyond the point where his natural enthusiasm for galloping has begun to flag. Such forcing may be necessary otherwise he will get the impression that he can do as he likes, making off when he wants to and slowing up only when he feels like it.

The reason for adopting the folded posture in the saddle, with the elbows in front of the knees and with the feet pushed well outward and forward, is that this brings your centre of gravity low down over the withers. It is here that the ride is smoothest, with the minimum of jolting from the movements of the horse's legs and from their impact with the ground. The posture is like that of the racing jockey, apart from the effect of the difference in the length of the stirrup leathers. (It is, in fact, an exaggerated version of the jump seat described in *Chapter 4*.).

Jump seat and drive seat at canter and gallop

When you first practise the transition from trot to canter, it is essential to start by building up impulsion. For this you need to be in sitting trot, bracing your back in the "drive seat position". You can continue in this position at the canter, squaring your shoulders and allowing the suppleness of your back to absorb the impact when your weight comes down into the saddle at each stride. After you have become accustomed to the motion you will find that your seat-bones no longer part company with the saddle at each stride although the pressure is very slight for a moment just after take-off.

For a prolonged canter you may prefer to move forward into the jump seat. You bring your elbows and shoulders forward and your seat-bones naturally rise out of the saddle. You will find it very easy to balance on your knees at the canter. So long as your ankles are supple and you do not let your feet get out of position, you can just float along. With a little coaxing with the rein, encouraging the horse to swing his head freely, he will change imperceptibly into the gallop, particularly on rising ground in open country. All you need do to get him to go full out is to give the occasional squeeze with your legs.

Although your horse will be obviously enjoying himself at the gallop, do not ask too much of him unless you are sure he is really fit. It is all too easy to persuade your horse to overexert himself. In former times it was not uncommon for horses to be ridden to death.

The distinction between canter and gallop is seen more readily by the bystander than by the rider. At the gallop the four legs are brought to the ground one at a time, whereas at the canter the legs of the support diagonal touch down almost simultaneously. There is, consequently, a difference in the rhythm of the footfalls and the rider may spot this if he is riding alone. Otherwise all he has to go on is the increased involvement of the horse's back as he reaches forward with hindquarters and forequarters alternately in the gallop, in contrast to the rocking motion of the whole body at the canter.

The jump seat is appropriate to relaxed conditions. When you need precise control of the horse you should move back into the drive seat so that you can give indications through the saddle by bracing your back. Normally, your horse will slow up at the gallop as soon as you sit back and start taking up the reins. If he doesn't do this you may need to treat him as a runaway.

The drive seat is essential for the half-halt with which you prepare the horse for any transition that is to be executed with precision. It is also the natural seat when riding at the canter without stirrups.

It is useful to practise changing from jump seat to drive seat at the canter and back again. You may find that, when you move back into the drive seat, the horse slows up, as though expecting a transition down to the trot. Watch for this and feel for the way he responds to the variations in the position of your weight and to changes in your pressure on the rein. Practise bracing your back quite strongly just after sitting back into the drive seat so that, instead of slowing down at this point, the horse actually accelerates forward. Also practise taking up the rein and increasing the pressure on the bit while   193 you are cantering in the jump seat. Then put these two manoeuvres together into an alternation between accelerating forward in the drive-seat position and slowing into a collected canter while staying up in the jump seat position. This alternation is fundamental to the preparation for jumping.

Transitions

At this stage in the training of horse and rider a period of consolidation is appropriate. The changes of speed should be practised at the walk, at the trot, and at the canter on both leads, together with all the possible transitions from one gait to another, including halts from each gait and starts at each gait directly from the halt. Each of the transitions involves the judicious application of forward drive of the seat-bones against the saddle, by bracing the back, carefully balanced against restraint or encouragement of the horse's head movements, by the action of the reins. At each stage the rider must be alert to feel the changes in the horse's muscles that indicate what the horse is about to do. The aim should be to produce the transitions so smoothly that the onlooker is given the impression that the horse is doing it all for himself. Be particularly on the lookout for those little jumpy movements that the horse makes when you take him by surprise, as by a too sudden or too vigorous application of the legs.

All of this work can be practised without stirrups and it is natural to combine it with exercises in steering along the various tracks in the dressage arena (*Figure 4.7*). Remember that where the track involves a change of rein, it will be necessary, at the canter, also to change the lead. This means that you have to drop back to the trot, or even to the walk, in plenty of time before the crossover point. If you need an incentive for detailed practice of this kind, there are several official dressage tests that call for not more than steering, changes of speed, and changes of gait.

The simple transitions have been described already: walk on from halt; trot from walk; canter from trot; gallop from canter; halt from walk; walk from trot; trot from canter; halt from trot; halt from gallop.

The more demanding transitions are built up from the same components as the simple transitions. The first need is to develop adequate impulsion, so that when you do give the necessarily strong indication for the transition itself, the horse does not jump right out of his skin.

194

Trot from halt

To persuade the horse to start directly at the trot from the halt, you need to hold in a little at first so that he doesn't walk on before you have built up enough impulsion. Start by calling the horse to attention by tickling the bit. Watch for his response. When he moves his ears, raises his head, and begins to play with the bit, progressively increase the pressure on the bit and start a series of brief squeezes with your legs. You will feel him tensing himself ready for moving off. Then give an extra squeeze with the legs, brace your back to drive the saddle forward, and relax the rein. You will need to practise so that the horse gets the chance to come to understand what you want and so that you can judge just how much preparatory winding-up is needed. If you overdo it before he has worked out what to do, he will just get excited and start throwing his head about and generally playing up. If this happens abandon the exercise and try again on another day, being a little more tactful the next time.

Canter from halt or from walk

The principle underlying the direct start into the canter is the same as that for the start into the trot from the halt. In this case even more preliminary winding-up is needed and during this preparatory phase you also need to tell the horse which lead you want. You do this by bringing your "outside leg" back and by adjusting the distribution of your weight into the appropriate asymmetrical position: "position right" for a right lead and "position left" for a left lead. Wait until you feel that the horse is ready before you give the "drive on" command, by bracing your back to push your seat-bones forward in the saddle.

If you are going to ask for a canter from the walk you will need to balance the increasing forward drive of your legs against an increasing restraining action of your hands so as to keep the walk going on steadily until you reach the point on the track at which you want the horse to make the transition. In a dressage test, the transitions are to be made as the rider's body passes the appropriate lettered marker.

Walk from canter

The direct transition from the canter to the walk, without any intervening trotting strides, calls for considerable alertness on the part of the rider. He has to know just when he can relax the onward drive with his seat that maintains the canter in the face of the progressively increasing restraint that he is exerting with the reins. As soon as the canter breaks, the rider must immediately start the alternating leg-aids for the walk; otherwise the horse will either go into the trot or will stop altogether. It will help the horse to slow up if you raise your hands for a moment just as you are giving the final increase in the pressure on the rein. Then, as you feel the change in the horse's action, start to give alternating pulls on left and right rein, to initiate the lateral sway of the horse's head appropriate to the walk.

You will find that precise work at the collected canter is much easier if you have already persuaded your horse to hold his nose in. You may need to spend some time consolidating this before trying more ambitious moves.

Counter canter

It has already been emphasised that the horse's body should, at the canter, always be bent toward the leading side. This bend is natural when the horse is making a turn toward the side of the leading leg. The bend has to be maintained also when the horse is going straight. Up to this point we have insisted that a change of rein, for a turn away from the leading leg, must be preceded by a change of gait. The horse is first asked to drop back from the canter to the trot and thereafter a new canter is initiated on the other lead. Sometimes it may not be convenient to go through the whole of this routine, particularly if the change of rein is to last for only a short time. The appropriate manoeuvre here is the "counter canter".

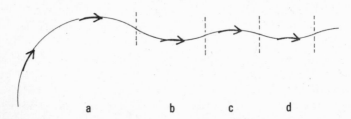

Figure 5.5
Track for introducing the horse to the counter canter. Establish the canter in a large circle, here to the right. Then occasionally veer to the left slightly for a few strides taking great care not to lose the bend. Distinguish between counter canter and "wrong lead" (in which the horse leads with the outside leg, e.g. with the right leg on a curve to the left with a left bend). In the counter canter the horse leads on the side to which he is bent, even though he is travelling along a path that is curved to the opposite side. a) Canter right; b) counter canter; c) canter right; d) counter canter.

196

It is important to distinguish between the counter canter and the canter on the wrong leg. In the counter canter, the horse continues to be bent toward the leading leg while moving on a curve toward the other side. For example, the horse may be asked to turn to the left while cantering on the right lead and remaining bent toward the right (*Figure 5.5*). If the bend is not maintained, the horse will be cantering on the wrong leg. The manoeuvre is practised with shallow serpentines, and you need plenty of space.

First, establish the canter on a fairly large circle (about 20 m diameter), say to the right, making sure that you emphasise the bend by keeping the horse's nose turned slightly to the right and sitting firmly in "position right" with left leg back, weight on the right knee, left shoulder forward, urging him on in collected canter. Now, *without changing the position of the horse's head* or altering your position in the saddle, apply opening rein with the left hand and indirect rein in front of the withers with the right. At the same time pat him on the girth with the right leg. He should swing away to the left of the circle. After a couple of strides bring your hands across to the right and discontinue the activity of the right leg, so that the horse moves back onto a curve toward the right, parallel to the original circle. Take great care that he doesn't lose his bend to the right, and at first make only small sways to the left of the straight line. Repeat on the other lead, starting from a circle on the left rein.

When you are confident that you can keep the bend the way you want it, you can gradually increase the distance covered at the counter canter and you can try turning a little more sharply. Always be on the lookout for a collapse of the bend and, if this happens, at once steer strongly toward the leading leg to avoid confirming the horse in the habit of cantering on the wrong leg.

Flying change of lead

There are some circumstances in which it is convenient to be able to change from one lead to the other at the canter without interrupting the flow by dropping back to the trot. Such occasions often arise when negotiating a sequence of jumps in a restricted area. In these conditions it is appropriate to execute what is called a "flying change".

The horse is to be persuaded to change from one lead to the other while in the air during a single stride. To develop this   197

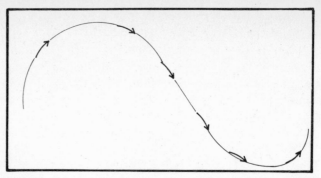

Figure 5.6
Developing the flying change of lead from the counter canter. Canter right on a large circle; straight canter along a diagonal; counter canter as you approach the long side; ask for canter left as you enter the turn for the corner. Change from "position right" to "position left" at the moment when you want the horse to change lead.

manoeuvre, start with the counter canter (*Figure 5.6*). Here the canter is first established on the right lead, circling to the right. The horse is then steered on a gentle curve to the left, maintaining the bend to the right in counter canter. Decide upon the place where you want to execute the flying change and be prepared then to do several things at the same time. The object is to ensure that the horse completes his move precisely on cue. To do this several unambiguous indications have to be given simultaneously at the beginning of the stride during which we want the horse to execute the flying change.

During the preparatory counter canter you will be sitting firmly in "position right" with a good deal of collection and with the horse bent to the right. The warning to the horse telling him that he is to do something different takes the form of a half-halt, or emphasis of the collection. Both hands are in the direct rein position at this stage and the horse's nose is turned slightly to the right, although he is moving on a gentle curve to the left. The right hand may be raised slightly as part of the indication for the half-halt. After the change of lead you are going to steer strongly into a left turn. By itself, this turn to the left is an indication that the horse should be cantering on the left lead. This will mean that you should then be sitting in "position left".

The change in your position in the saddle is the most important single indication for the change of lead. You move your weight over from right knee to left knee, bring the left leg forward onto the girth, and move the right leg back. At the same time you move the horse's nose over from right to left, by pulling the left rein a little and giving a little with the right; move your left hand to the opening rein position with the hand raised, and give indirect rein in front of the withers with the right hand at the regular height, steering firmly to the left. The horse should change his bend and strike off on the left lead.

If you build up to the flying change in this way, the horse should have no doubt about what is required of him and you should have no problems. Naturally, you both have to practise before everything gets synchronised smoothly. Thereafter you can try asking for the change of lead while cantering on a straight line. Be on the lookout for a sloppy change in which the horse alters the sequence of movements of the forelegs without changing the hindlegs. This leads to the disunited canter, which should be scrupulously avoided.

After the horse has learned to do a neat flying change when cantering on a straight line, you can ask him to change again after a few strides. Thus you can ride in succession six strides on the left lead, flying change, six strides on the right lead, another flying change, and so on. Then you can ask for the change after four strides, or after two, and finally the horse will perform for you a flying change at each stride. He skips along, leading with left and right foreleg alternately. If you can manage this without throwing your weight about too violently in the saddle, the effect can be quite spectacular. It will be a good idea to have a friend to watch while you are practising so that he can draw your attention to any untidy and unnecessary movements that you may be making without being aware of them. This helps you to avoid building up bad habits. You should also ask him to watch out for any tendency for the horse to become disunited by failing to make one of the changes with hindlegs as well as with forelegs.

Lateral work at canter

While working on counter canter and flying change, you will become accustomed to feeling for the bend in the horse, correcting and encouraging it as necessary. You can now experiment with half-pass and shoulder-in at canter. The aids for these are, in principle, the same as those you have already used for lateral work at the trot. At the canter, however, you have to be particularly careful to preserve the correct bend. It will be important to maintain a good deal of impulsion with the horse well collected. Make sure also that he keeps his head 199 well in so that he is able to appreciate what you are telling him through the reins.

After practising all the manoeuvres described up to this point you will be beginning to feel some confidence in your ability to get your horse to do what you want. However, the training of horse and rider cannot be regarded as complete until some facility has been acquired in the art of jumping.

Preparation for jumping

It is sometimes said that the horse is not a natural jumper. I do not believe this because I have observed that, when at liberty, horses will jump hedges and ditches quite freely either to obtain food or to rejoin companions from whom they have been separated. On the other hand, it is clear that the presence of a rider on his back makes the novice horse somewhat unsure of himself when he is faced with an obstacle. Novice riders also approach obstacles with some trepidation, and this feeling is inevitably communicated to their mounts. In addition, the novice rider tends to rattle about in the saddle when going over a jump and this must contribute to unsettling the horse. Accordingly it is appropriate to prepare both horse and rider before embarking on the actual jumping.

The first requirement is that the rider should be able to regulate the speed of his horse. He should be able to control the canter and keep a firm grip on the steering while riding in the jump seat position. He should also be able to produce smart acceleration from the drive seat position on the word of command. It is essential to have firm control of speed and steering both at the trot and at the canter.

Horses that have already been trained to jump will often carry novice riders over jumps successfully for a time. The problem is that, in the absence of the accustomed confirmatory indications from the rider, the horse may begin to have doubts about what is intended. He has, after all, to know whether what is in front of him is an obstacle that is to be jumped or is a gate which has to be approached gently so that it can be opened. Occasionally he will be asked to jump a gate. If he does not know what is intended he may just drift into the obstacle without actually jumping and thus bang his legs. Alternatively, he may get into the bad habit of refusing at the last moment, putting his head down and ducking out to one side while his rider sails gracefully on, to land with a crash on top of the fence. Systematic preparation avoids these hazards.

Trotting-poles

A point to remember when assembling the equipment for jumping is that the horse will not necessarily bother to lift his feet over anything that looks no thicker than his own leg. He will expect to be able to crash through, either breaking the obstacle or brushing it aside. You may have noticed that in a steeplechase the horses do not attempt to clear the brushwood fences completely but charge happily through the top fifteen centimetres or so of the obstacle. Similarly they do not expect strands of wire to present a serious obstruction. They treat wire with the contempt appropriate to brambles. They may thus easily be brought down and one must not attempt to jump gaps in a hedge where there may be a strand of wire. Poles to be used for practice jumps should be at least 8 to 10 cm thick and 3 or 4 m long.

Competition jumps are usually painted in bright colours, so you might like to paint your practice poles similarly. As well as the poles, you will need some supports. For many purposes oil drums do very well, or you can use the plastic crates made for handling bottles by the dozen. Packing cases are not suitable as they are easily broken and then present dangerously sharp pieces. You will also need one or two markers, such as half-bricks or paint cans, but remember to clear these out of the way when not in use, so that the horses do not trip over them.

Another aid that is almost indispensable is a willing assistant who can watch where your horse is putting his feet and who can move poles about or rebuild jumps when needed.

With your equipment all assembled, you are now ready to make a start. Trot steadily round and round in a fairly large circle, giving your horse a chance to get settled. The assistant now lays one pole across the track. Continue to trot round, stepping over the pole without breaking the rhythm. Meanwhile the assistant carefully watches the horse's feet as he passes over the pole and judges where he can safely put down a second pole. When your horse has learned to adjust his stride to clear a single pole smoothly, the assistant adds a second pole about 1·5 m away from the first, the distance being judged in terms of the horse's natural stride. The position of the second pole may need to be adjusted when you see where the feet come down, and this is where the aid of an assistant is so vital.

When the horse has learned to negotiate two poles, a third can be added, and then a fourth. If several horses are working together it may be necessary to arrange the poles in a fan so that each horse can be ridden on a track that crosses the poles at the distances appropriate to the stride of that particular horse.

With two or more poles, the rider should move into the jump seat position. Then, as the horse rises to clear each pole, the rider should give a little squeeze with his legs. If he has his stirrups on the ball of the foot, as he should have, his legs will be moving upward slightly over the horse's side while his body is being carried upward by the horse's movement. The leg squeeze then has a sort of lifting action. This encourages the horse to lift his feet well up as he passes over each pole in turn. At the same time the rider begins to get the feel of the horse "coming up under him".

One may be tempted to leave the poles lying, with the idea that they will then be ready to be ridden over on a later occasion. This doesn't work well in practice. The length of the horse's stride is not constant; indeed you have already seen how you can adjust the stride by varying the balance between the forward drive of your seat and the restraint of your hands. It turns out, however, to be much more difficult to adjust the horse's stride to suit the poles than it is to set the poles to suit the horse while he is being maintained in a steady rhythm. It is for this reason that it is so difficult to set the poles satisfactorily if one is on one's own and has to dismount to make each adjustment. If the horse is forced to make an alteration to his stride because the poles are not quite at the natural spacing for the pace he happens to be using, the effect is to disturb his rhythm, and much of the benefit of the exercise is lost. The aim is to get the horse used to passing freely over the poles with no disturbance, and to encourage him to respond to the presence of the poles by making his action more springy, throwing his weight up higher at each stride. Continue for some time with this exercise, riding most of your circle in sitting trot and moving forward into the jump seat as you come to the poles, ready to give your lifting aid with the legs.

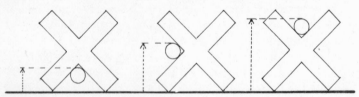

Figure 5.7
Cavalletti rolled over to provide obstacles of different heights.

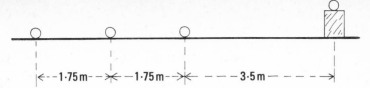

Figure 5.8
Arrangement of three trotting-poles followed by a small jump. Suggested distances: 1·75 m, 1·75 m and 3·5 m. Adjust the distances to suit the stride of the horse.

Cavalletti

For the next stage it is convenient, though not indispensable, to have a few poles fitted with wooden crosses at their ends to hold them a little way above the ground. The actual height can then be varied by rolling the crosses over (*Figure 5.7*).

When the horse has settled down and passes smoothly over three or four trotting-poles without changing his rhythm, have the assistant place a small jump (say 50 cm, or one of the cavalletti at its full height) at a distance from the last pole about twice that between adjacent trotting-poles (*Figure 5.8*). Now that the horse has learned to pay attention to the poles, he will probably accept the small jump without hesitation. He should, however, notice that the last pole presents a different kind of obstacle from the poles on the ground. To make sure of this you need to make the jump high enough. If it is too low, the horse may attempt to treat it as another trotting-pole, and he may stumble over it instead of making a definite jump.

Transition from trot to jump

The rhythm of the horse's movement over a jump is quite different from the rhythm at the trot, but the rider should at this stage not make any deliberate adjustments in his own posture. Just ride straight through in the jump seat position as though the jump were, in fact, just another trotting-pole. Pay attention, however, to the feel of the horse's movement and make sure that your hold on the reins is sufficiently springy so that, if he stretches his neck suddenly, the rein will not jerk the bit in his mouth.

The horse has to make several alterations to his stride when negotiating a jump. Instead of tossing his weight from one diagonal pair of legs to the other in the trot, he has to reach forward over the jump with both forefeet together, holding them curled up under his chest, and he has to use both hind- 203 feet together to propel his body upward and forward over the jump. Just as it is an advantage to a golfer, when he wants to drive his ball as far as possible, to take his club back in a preparatory back-swing, so also is it an advantage to the horse, in preparing to take off in a jump, to lower his quarters and bend his hindlegs. In this way he not only develops a stronger push against the ground, but he also gives himself more time for the thrust to act on the body before the feet leave the ground. These two factors together ensure that the horse's body is projected up and over the jump with the greatest possible momentum for the amount of effort put out by the muscles. As well as lowering his haunches, the horse also raises his forequarters so that the trunk is tipped back like a javelin ready for launching.

In making these various adjustments the horse uses the momentum of his head in a sequence of strong up-and-down movements. The head is relatively heavy so that, when the neck muscles pull the head upwards, they also have an important effect upon the trunk, tending to lift the hindquarters. This action has already been described in relation to the nodding of the head that occurs in brisk walking. When the head is pulled upwards, the body tends to pivot forward over the support of the forelegs. Thereafter the forequarters can be lifted in their turn, by pulling down on the head to transfer its upward momentum to the body.

The sequence of events in the transition from trot to jump is illustrated in *Figure 5.9*. In this case the obstacle to be jumped is so placed that, if it were merely another trotting-pole, it would be straddled by the horse's right diagonal. The horse has to have made up his mind to jump while this same right diagonal pair of legs is coming down to the ground in the previous stride.

The first stage of the horse's preparation for the jump is a slight exaggeration of the normal tossing movement of the head associated with the rhythmic tossing of the body from one diagonal pair of legs to the other during the trot. He allows his head to sink a little more than usual at the moment when the legs of the right diagonal are beginning to take the weight, and then he throws his head up a little more forcibly than usual. In this way the head develops extra upward momentum that is used during the succeeding unsupported phase to modify the step performed by the left diagonal pair of legs.

204   By pulling down on the head in this unsupported phase the

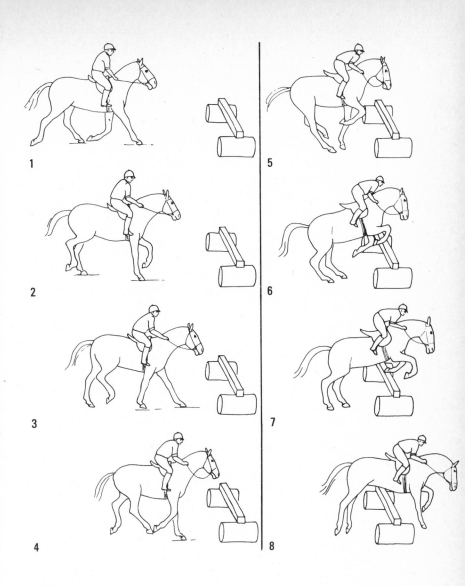

Figure 5.9
Stages in the approach to a jump from the trot. The right hindleg reaches forward to be set down close behind the left foreleg. The horse takes off from the two hindlegs. Here the rider, a novice, has his stirrup too far back under his foot. He also allows his foot to go back so that, when the horse rises, he is propelled forward out of the saddle. In consequence, the rein comes tight suddenly when the saddle catches up with the rider a little later on. The sequence is continued in *Figure 5.13*. (The interval between frames is one-eighth of a second.)

horse can reach forward with his right hindleg so that it will land just behind the left forefoot. Instead of moving in time with the left foreleg, the right hindleg now doesn't touch down until its diagonal foreleg has almost completed its support phase. The delay in the support to the hindquarters has the effect that the foreleg upthrust on landing at this stride tends to tip the trunk backwards.

While the left foreleg is on the ground, the head is thrown up again very strongly. The effect on the trunk of the action of the neck muscles to lift the head enables the horse to bring his left hindfoot forward so that he can set it down close beside the right hindfoot, in the position needed for take-off. The extra upward momentum of the head is then used to lift the fore-quarters, both forelegs being folded up under the chest ready to clear the obstacle. The trunk is thus positioned ready to be launched upward and forward over the jump by the combined thrust of the two hindlegs.

The rider can observe the exaggerated up-and-down movement of the head and he can also feel the haunches sinking under him just before take-off. Because the body is also moving up and down, the head-movements are not so noticeable from the side as they are from the saddle. Indeed, from the side one gets the impression that the head remains at almost the same height above the ground while the horse's withers move up and down. One can, however, deduce the relative movement of the head from the attitude of the neck as seen in side view.

As well as getting the horse used to negotiating small obstacles without fuss, this exercise with a few trotting-poles followed by a jump gives the rider an opportunity to accustom himself to the feel of the various stages in the jump itself. After some practice he will be able to anticipate the horse's move-ments and he can then start to work on the timing of his command to jump. As explained above, if the horse is to jump an obstacle which he would meet on the right diagonal, he needs to start his preparations while the same right diagonal is coming down to the ground in the previous stride. This means that the command to jump must be given a little before this.

One virtue of the use of trotting-poles in front of a small jump is that there is some control over the relationship between the footfalls and the take-off point for the jump. The horse arrives at the jump either on the left diagonal or on the right diagonal according to which diagonal is used for the first trotting-pole. There is no occasion for the horse to put in an additional short stride or to make any other kind of adjustment to his rhythm. With three trotting-poles (*Figure 5.8*), the diagonal on which the jump will be met is the same as the diagonal that straddles the first pole. The horse comes down on the same diagonal again when the rider's body is over the third pole. The appropriate moment at which to give the command to jump has to be just a little earlier than this, that is to say, during the upward spring after crossing the second pole. This gives the horse a chance to start his preparatory head-movement during the half-stride over the third pole.

When practising with trotting-poles alone, the rider gives an encouraging squeeze with the legs during each upward spring of the horse when he is tossing his weight from one diagonal to the other. The timing for the command to jump is the same as the timing of one of these "lifting" squeezes. To make a distinction that the horse will recognise, use a double squeeze and apply it during the spring between the second and third poles.

Seeing a stride

One of the main problems with jumping is for the rider to choose the correct moment for his command to jump. With the trotting-poles in place, the position of the footfalls is determined, and the rider is left only with the decision as to which is the right stride during which to give his command. In the more usual situation the rider also has to position the horse, and to adjust his stride length, so that he enters the "preparatory zone" in front of the jump with his feet in the right places. Otherwise, when the horse actually arrives at the jump, he will not be at the correct distance from it. He will take off either too late or too early, or he will try to put in an extra stride. In any such case, the rhythm of his preparation for the jump will be upset. This may not matter for small simple jumps because the horse can make many adjustments in the course of a single stride. In a competition, where the nature of each obstacle has been adjusted by the course-builder to present particular difficulties in order to sort out the better performers from the less good, every departure from precision carries the penalty of an increased risk of failure.

The exercise with three trotting-poles and a small jump may be used to help the rider to develop the ability to "see a stride", as it is called. A rider is said to have this ability when he can present his horse to a jump in such a way that the horse approaches and takes off smoothly with no occasion to make any last moment adjustments in his stride. The crucial task here is to pick a spot on the ground directly in front of the jump and three strides away from it, and then to adjust the horse's approach so that, when the rider is directly over this spot, the horse is landing and taking off for one of the bounces in a steady stride pattern.

Three strides are needed for horse and rider to work together in harmony in tackling the obstacle. In the first stride, the rider consolidates his aiming of the horse at the centre of the obstacle and indicates his intention to jump by a number of subtle adjustments of weight distribution, posture, and feel on the rein which are the unconscious consequences of "making up his mind to it". During the second stride the rider urges the horse forward, to confirm that this is an obstacle to be jumped and not a gate at which to pause while the fastening is manipulated, and this is when he gives the actual command to jump. The third stride is needed by the horse so that he can make his own preparations, without interference from the rider. He can then get his feet organised and wind up his muscles ready for take-off.

It is not a very straightforward matter to measure off three strides in front of the jump because the stride-length is not a fixed distance. Each horse has his own preferred stride-length for a particular gait. To some extent this depends on the conformation, temperament, and training of the horse, but there is also an important element that depends on the mood of the moment and on the degree of collection, so that part of the skill in seeing a stride lies in the rider's ability to gauge the way his horse is reacting to the situation at the crucial moment in question. In the exercise with the trotting-poles as described above, the spacing of the poles has been selected by the assistant to suit a steady rate of striding which is being maintained by the rider as he trots calmly round and round on his circle.

If you are going to practise with a jump that has separate supporting uprights, start your trotting-pole exercise with one pole on the ground between the uprights just under the place where you will later put up a pole for jumping. Have your assistant put down the second and third trotting-poles in front of the pole that is lying between the uprights, adjusting the spacing to suit the horse. Now have your assistant move the first pole to be one stride in front of the other two, and then

move the second pole back also, to finish in the pattern of

Figure 5.10
Experienced rider just after take-off.

Figure 5.8. This procedure ensures that all the distances will be correctly adjusted to suit the horse.

After the rider has got used to giving his double squeeze for the command to jump at the moment when he is passing over the second pole in *Figure 5.8*, both this pole and the third pole can be removed, leaving only the first in position. When he comes round again the rider now continues his sitting trot over this remaining pole, gives his jump command at the place where the second pole used to be, and then goes forward into jump seat position for the actual take-off. The horse's rhythm for the trotting circle should remain unchanged throughout.

Jump seat over a jump

It is important to be in the jump seat position when the horse gives his main thrust with the hindlegs at take-off. If the rider's seat-bones are in contact with the saddle at this point, he is liable to be thrown strongly upwards and it will be difficult to predict where he will land. For any but a very small jump the rider should fold right forward at the hips and reach out with his hands beside the horse's neck and with his elbows in front of his knees. Keep the head slightly to one side to avoid being hit in the face by the horse's neck (*Figure 5.10*). You may notice, when watching top-level show-jumpers coming in at the end of a round, that the front of the rider's jacket often shows signs of having been in contact with the horse's neck.

The importance of moving the hands forward briskly cannot be too strongly emphasised. As the horse passes over the 209

Figure 5.11
Experienced rider at the top of the jump.

obstacle he throws his head well forward as part of the effort to
lift his forequarters (*Figures 5.11 and 5.12*). If the rider does not
give with his hands at this point, it is inevitable that the horse
will feel a jab in the mouth. If this happens repeatedly, it is only
to be expected that the horse will become less eager to jump.
Moving the hands forward doesn't necessarily mean letting
the rein go slack, as you can see in *Figure 5.11*, where the rider's
hands have moved well up the horse's neck. A light contact
will be needed for steering out of the jump on landing.

Figure 5.12
Experienced rider preparing to land after a jump.

There is an advantage in allowing the feet to come forward a little as you are coming down to land (*Figure 5.12*). With the stirrup on the ball of the foot to take advantage of the springiness of the ankle-joint, this provides additional shock-absorbing for the impact of landing. Most of the rider's weight on landing should, however, be taken on the knees and one should not allow oneself to become dependent upon the stirrups. It is very easy for one foot to come out of its stirrup during the preparation for a jump and then it is sometimes advisable to quit the other stirrup also because, if the rider's weight were to come down on one stirrup alone, this would almost certainly tip him sideways and he might be thrown off. Another hazard of depending upon the stirrup is that, if the stirrup slips back under the arch of the foot, the cushioning action of the ankle is lost. The weight then comes down on the stirrup with a severe jolt which may break either the stirrup or the leather and, again, the rider risks being thrown off to one side.

If the rider's feet are allowed to move back when he is over the jump, he is in danger of losing contact with the horse during the descent. It is then possible that when he lands he will not be over the mid-line of the saddle, and if this happens he is liable to be thrown to one side. Do not be tempted to excuse yourself for letting your feet go back on the grounds that many successful show-jumpers also do this. Remind yourself that many prominent show-jumpers have been competing successfully from a very early age. They owe their success partly to natural balance and acrobatic flair. They may never have thought it necessary to pay much attention to style. Lesser mortals get on better with more orthodox techniques. It is noticeable that horse-trial competitors, who have to contend with dressage tests and cross-country obstacles as well as with show-jumping, often ride in a more orthodox style, as may be seen from the world-class riders illustrated in *Figures 5.10, 5.11 and 5.12*.

Landing after a jump

After taking off from the hindlegs the horse lands on the forelegs. During the descent the horse's body acquires a great deal of momentum and substantial forces are needed to absorb this momentum on landing. The horse solves this problem in dynamics by using the springiness of his muscles to make a very soft landing in which the work of arresting the downward   211

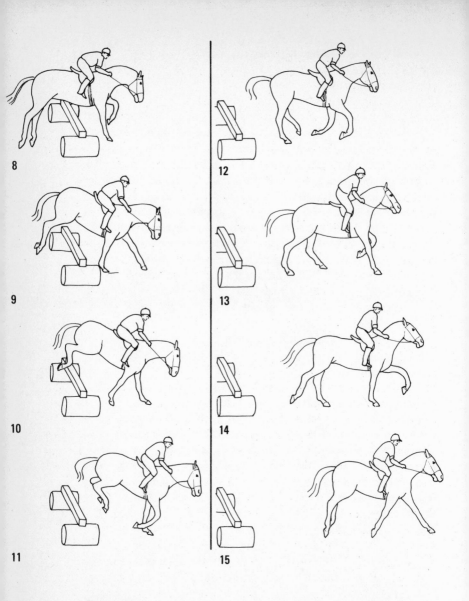

8

9

10

11

12

13

14

15

Figure 5.13
Stages in the landing after a jump (continuation of the sequence shown in
Figure 5.9). The forelegs are used one at a time to absorb the impact. The
hindlegs come down later in the rhythm of a canter stride (see *Figure 5.3*).
(Interval between frames: one-eighth of a second.)

movement of the trunk is spread out over a comparatively long time. The forelegs are used one at a time, the footfalls being well separated as they are in the gallop (*Figure 5.13*). The hindlegs come down later, sometimes after the forelegs have already left the ground. The forelegs then come down again to form with the hindlegs a support phase like that of a canter stride. It is, accordingly, natural for the horse to continue in canter after a jump.

The forelegs contain several special shock-absorbing mechanisms that are important in landing from a jump. In the first place the pastern is set at an angle to the cannon bone, so that it is only the foot itself that has to be stopped suddenly. When the foot strikes the ground the leg bends at the fetlock, pulling on the springy tendons at the back of the leg. Sometimes a horse may land awkwardly with the fetlock straight so that the jolt of landing is transmitted up the whole leg. The pastern bone may be broken in such an incident. Laboratory tests show that the pastern bone of a steeplechaser can support a compression of nearly seven tons before giving way. This gives some idea of the stresses involved in catching the weight of the horse as it comes down after a jump.

Another shock-absorbing mechanism is found in the zig-zag arrangement of the bones at the shoulder and elbow joints. Here again the joints fold up during the impact, stretching the muscles that work over these joints. Lastly, the horse's shoulderblade is not firmly attached to the skeleton of the trunk. There is no collarbone, and the weight of the trunk is slung from the shoulderblades by long bands of muscle which can stretch like springs.

The rider's contribution to the jump
At this point it will be convenient to review all the various tasks that the rider should set himself to perform during a jump. An important component is the rider's determination to pass cleanly over the obstacle without striking it. If the horse senses that the rider is uncertain or that he is not secure in the saddle, this will lead to uncertainty in the mind of the horse and this will inevitably affect his performance. A crash against the poles will undermine the horse's confidence and it may take a great deal of patient training to get him back to form. The moral here is: do not put your horse to a jump unless you are sure not only that you really mean it but also that the horse is being given a reasonable chance to clear the obstacle. Drifting casu-

ally into jumps has a very unsettling effect on the horse and he is unjustly punished when he bangs his legs on the poles after the rider has not played his part properly. Always do your best to prepare the horse for the jump and be quite unambiguous in your commands.

Your first task after deciding to attempt a particular obstacle is to select the point at which you are going to start your three-stride run-in. Adjust the approach so as to be facing the middle of the jump and to be exactly at the bounce of a stride as you arrive at the selected spot. Then steer straight for the jump and make sure the horse feels your determination to get over it. Once you have presented the horse to the jump correctly, and once he has made his own decision to jump in response to your "asking" command, your most important task is to avoid interfering with his execution of the jump itself.

You no longer need to look at this particular obstacle. Indeed if you continue to gaze too intently at it during the later part of the approach, the horse will sense that perhaps there is some nasty concealed hazard that he has not yet seen for himself and he will start to worry about it. It is preferable to look straight ahead over your horse's ears at something on the far side of the jump so that he comes to regard the immediate obstacle as merely a minor triviality on the way to a desirable and eagerly sought goal a little further off. With this mental attitude he will sail easily over the obstacle as though jumping at liberty.

To get used to picking the right spot for the run-in, have your assistant set down a marker for you to aim at and ask him to watch and tell you whether you are arriving early or late. A good time to start this exercise is as a continuation of the work with three poles and a jump. After the second and third poles have been taken away, the remaining pole continues to control the placing of the horse's feet in relation to the approach to the jump. The assistant puts down the marker one stride ahead of this pole. Thus, if the poles were 1·5 m apart, with the jump 3 m from the third pole, the marker will be 3 m before the first pole, or 9 m from the jump. The exact distances will, of course, be dependent upon the length of stride that the horse has chosen for the steady trot round the circle that keeps bringing him back to the jump.

When the assistant is satisfied that he has the marker in the right place in relation to the remaining pole, that pole can then be removed. The whole of the approach to the jump is now in the hands of the rider. Because the exact track round the circle will naturally vary a little each time, the horse will not always arrive with a bounce at precisely the same place. The rider has to adjust the horse's stride, by reining in or urging on, during the few strides before he reaches the marker, in such a way that the bounce occurs exactly as the rider's body passes the marker. Thereafter all he needs to do is to steer, urge, ask, and fold. The horse does the rest.

Indications by the horse

During the run-in, the rider should be alert for the rhythm of the horse's movements. He should watch for the up-and-down movement of the horse's head and he should feel for the moment when the horse lowers his haunches to reach forward with the hindlegs. He will also be able to feel the change in the horse's muscles as he braces himself for the extra effort required for the jump. If these indications are present, the rider knows that the horse has decided to jump, and all will be well. If the indications, or some of them, are absent, there is the chance that the horse has not yet made up his mind. If the rider is quick enough, an extra squeeze may save the day.

Refusals

The rider should be particularly wary if he feels the horse is not surging forward into the jump. Instead of increasing the up-and-down swing of his head, the horse may be inclined to lower his head and keep it there. He may throw his head forward to try to pull the reins out of the rider's hands. The next thing the rider knows is that, instead of the horse lifting his forequarters and reaching under himself with his hindlegs, he suddenly puts both forelegs straight out in front of him and comes to a dead stop with his head right down. The horse then swings briskly away to one side, leaving the rider with nothing to hold on to.

It is important to avoid giving the horse a chance to practise the technique of refusing a jump. If he stops a second time, try a different jump, or have someone give you a lead over the jump and follow closely behind, leaving about two horse's lengths clear. Horses usually jump freely in company and follow one another without hesitation. If your horse refuses this also, get someone else who is a stronger rider to take him over a couple of times for you. Then go back to the beginning again. Make sure you can control the speed, getting him to go faster or slower at will. Repeat the work with the trotting-poles and re-introduce the jump only after the horse has accepted the trotting-poles without any disturbance of the rhythm of the trot.

Horses at liberty usually approach a jump at the canter rather than at the trot and, so long as they do not get jabbed in the mouth, they will often canter over small jumps quite freely even when ridden by a novice. This may give the misleading impression that the novice rider is already reasonably competent. Care is needed in deciding whether the rider has passed the stage of needing instruction. Problems will arise as soon as the horse finds himself slightly out of position for a smooth take-off. The horse will then make his own adjustments, but the change in his rhythm may unsettle the rider. In the course of regaining his balance the rider makes involuntary movements which the horse takes as commands, particularly if there is a jerk on the reins. The rider then complains that his horse has suddenly developed the habit of making mistakes. He will be tempted to chastise the horse, whereas the proper remedy is for the rider to discipline himself to accept further instruction. Although to approach a jump at the trot is a more demanding exercise for the horse, because he has to pay attention to what he is doing, it is a more instructive exercise for the rider than the uncontrolled approach at the canter, and there is less chance of unintentional jabs on the horse's mouth.

During the run-in to the jump build up a fairly firm pressure on the rein and maintain the impulsion by driving forward with your seat. Do not on any account allow the reins to jerk. Very often the cause of the trouble is that the rider's hands are not sufficiently springy. It is not that the rider is deliberately jerking the reins, just that because the rider's shoulders don't move in quite the same way as the horse's mouth, the rein occasionally goes slack and then snaps taut again. Be on your guard against any tendency for the horse's nose to deviate to one side or the other. Correct this at once so that the horse knows you are not going to tolerate any attempt to run out to one side.

If the horse succeeds in ducking out to one side, immediately bring him to a halt and turn him back toward the jump. If he has run out to the left, turn him to the right, and so on. Do not let him get the idea that you will allow him to turn whichever way he pleases. Remember that the problem is most likely to be one of the horse misunderstanding your commands, or not being certain what you want him to do.

Accordingly there is little point in chastising him. This only serves to make him more reluctant to submit to the ordeal of being put to a fence. He comes to associate the nearby presence of the poles and uprights with the unpleasant experience of being beaten.

When you do succeed in getting him over the jump, be sure that you let him have the rein completely free while he is in the air and reward him at once with effusive praise and caresses. He will be happy to have discovered the solution to his problem.

Arm exercises over the jump

It does not require very much effort for a horse to pop over a small jump from the trot. All the problems arise in the timing and from unintended jerks on the rein. For the rider to learn about the timing he needs to practise jumping. Meanwhile the horse must be protected from having the bit jerked about in his mouth. A routine that helps here is to jump without reins. You will need an alternative means of steering.

Some horses will jump any obstacle that is offered, but it usually helps if there are larger obstacles on either side to define just where the horse is intended to go. In the show-jumping arena the uprights supporting the poles are extended sideways in short fences called wings, often with the top rail sloping up toward the jump. What is needed for the present exercise is an extension of the wings to form a lane about two or three strides long on the approach side of the jump. It is often convenient to use the wall of an enclosed arena as one side of the lane. Poles and drums, or a couple of spare cavalletti, can form the other side of the lane. The rider steers into the start of the lane and then drops the reins before reaching the jump itself. Tie a knot in the rein so that, when you let go, there are no long loops of rein dangling down for the horse to catch his foot in.

Start without any obstacle in the lane. Get used to riding through at sitting trot, dropping the rein as you enter the lane and taking it up again as you emerge. Make sure you have plenty of impulsion, driving the seat forward each time until the horse gets the idea that he is to accelerate through the lane. Have your assistant put down a single pole at the far end of the lane where the jump will be eventually. Ride through two or three times, moving into jump seat as you pass over the pole. Then have the assistant raise the pole about 60 cm, or replace it 217 with one of the cavalletti, and continue round as before. Approach at the sitting trot, then, as you enter the lane, drop the reins and urge the seat forward. Ask for the jump by giving your double squeeze with the legs at least one full stride ahead of the jump. Then move into jump seat position and fold forward from the hip when you feel the horse gathering himself for the take-off. This will happen when his nose is almost at the pole.

The arm exercise described below is intended to confirm the distinction between the drive seat for the approach and the jump seat for the take-off. As soon as you are ready to drop the reins at the opening of the lane, bring your arms up to shoulder height. Have your upper arms straight out to the sides, level with your shoulders, elbows bent forward, hands in front of your shoulders just below your face. This posture helps you to square your shoulders and straighten your back while you are driving your seat forward into the saddle during the "urge" phase of the approach. Just after the "ask" command, move forward into jump seat position and throw your fists and shoulders as far forward as they will go, alongside the horse's neck, folding forward from the hips as you do so and also bringing your feet forward a little. This forward thrust of the fists should coincide with the take-off so that, as you feel the horse rising under your knees, your shoulders should come forward to meet them. The effect of this is to make your body feel very springy to the horse. Your body gives as the horse pushes the saddle up under you. He feels that he doesn't have so much weight to lift. In consequence he jumps more freely and easily. This is a very good exercise for training horse and rider to move in harmony over the jump.

Jump from canter

When you are confident that you can keep your balance in the saddle over small jumps approached at the trot, and can be reasonably certain that you will not jerk the bit in the horse's mouth, it will be time to get used to approaching the jump at the canter. The jumping lane is very useful here. Again start with no obstacle in the lane. Ride through the lane at the canter, sitting well down in the drive seat for the approach and moving forward into jump seat as you near the end of the lane. Practise altering the horse's speed over the ground, holding back while in jump seat going round your circle, and urging forward when in drive seat as you come toward the lane. Make sure you can get a definite acceleration just as you enter the lane.

You are now ready for your assistant to put up the small jump, or one of the cavalletti, at the end of the lane. If you are accelerating into the lane, the horse will almost certainly take the jump in his stride, apparently without any change in the movement as you feel it in the saddle. In these conditions he jumps without needing any definite action on your part. Move into jump seat position as you approach the pole and fold briskly forward when you see the pole about to pass under the horse's nose. You can see this without actually looking directly at the pole. Indeed, as mentioned earlier, it is better to look straight out ahead of you between the horse's ears and not to look down at all. If the horse shows any reluctance, or slows down in the lane instead of accelerating, take the obstacle away and go back to practising the changes of speed until you can rely on the horse surging forward as he comes to the lane.

Transition from canter to jump

Although it feels to the rider that the horse will take a small jump at the canter without changing the rhythm of his action, there are, in fact, some adjustments necessary in the movements of the individual limbs. The ordinary take-off in the canter is from the forelegs and the horse lands on his hindlegs after the unsupported phase. For the jump he has to take off from the hindlegs and land on the forelegs.

To make the transition, the movements of the support diagonal are spread out in time (*Figure 5.14*). Instead of these two legs landing almost simultaneously, as they do in the canter, the hindleg lands early and the foreleg is held up and stretched forward over the jump. The two hindlegs thus land close together in time, and provide some of the thrust for take-off. As well as reaching forward with the foreleg of the support diagonal, the horse also reaches over the jump with the leading foreleg, ready to make a landing, after the jump, on the two forelegs just as in the jump from the trot. These adjustments are sufficient for a small jump. For a larger jump the two hindlegs may put in an additional short stride, coming to the ground before the haunches have begun to rise so as to be able to develop a long strong thrust to accelerate the body upward for take-off.

To make these adjustments at the right time, the horse must be warned, during the take-off for the previous stride, that the 219

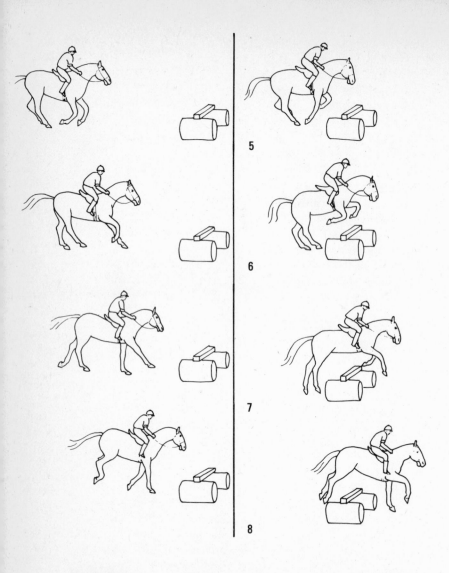

Figure 5.14
Stages in the approach to a jump from the canter. Instead of taking off from the forelegs as in a normal canter stride (see *Figure 5.3*), the take-off is from the hindlegs. To achieve this, the forequarters are first thrown up at the end of the last full canter stride before the jump, and the hindlegs are then drawn well forward to give an extra thrust for the actual take-off. (Compare frames 4 to 7 in this sequence with frames 11 to 15 in *Figure 5.13*.) (Interval between frames: one-eighth of a second.)

rider wishes him to make a jump. It is also necessary for the rider to take care to adjust the horse's stride during the approach, so that the last three strides before the jump may be taken at an accelerating pace without interference from the rider. The same rules apply as for a jump from the trot. Select the start point for the run-in and adjust the stride so that the bounce occurs as your body passes the selected start point. Then aim, urge, ask, and fold, just as for a jump from the trot.

Casual jumps

Horses usually enjoy jumping, provided they are not repeatedly and unjustly punished by being hit in the mouth by improper movements of the rider's hands, or by getting tangled up in the poles and banged on the legs because they have been ridden into the jump with inadequate impulsion or without sufficiently unambiguous commands. Once the rider has been introduced to jumping by careful systematic preliminary work over small jumps, his later development is largely a matter of practice.

A problem with many eager youngsters is that they are keen to jump everything in sight without having the patience to spend adequate time on the early stages of training. Because their ponies are at first clever enough to take them over the jumps whatever the rider does, they get the impression that they "know everything" and they become resistant to advice. Meanwhile they gradually undermine the earlier training of the pony and assiduously practise whatever bad habits they happen to have acquired. Instead of improving steadily and continuing to enjoy their riding, they are liable to run into a phase of refusals and knockdowns unless they are very lucky. They tend to put the blame on the pony and start to beat him unmercifully. This only upsets the pony and leads to a further deterioration in performance, until eventually the rider gives up and the pony is sold at a loss.

A parent who buys a pony for his child will avoid many disappointments and greatly enhance the value of his gift if he is firm enough to insist upon laying a proper foundation for his child's training as a rider. It is not sufficient just to pack the child off to a riding-school for a few lessons. Riding-school ponies behave very differently from family pets. Because they work daily with an instructor, riding-school ponies come to respond to the instructor's voice rather than to the rider's signals, so that one may get the impression from his performance at the riding-school that the child is reasonably expert. When he gets home, however, the situation is suddenly very different. The exercises set out in this book have been specifically designed for the novice who has only the casual support of friends or relatives, who are none of them particularly expert.

When horse and rider have developed mutual understanding by practising in a jumping lane, the next stage is to set out several small jumps in the practice area at various positions so chosen that they can be jumped independently. Cavalletti do very well here. For each jump the rider should select a suitable start point. He then rides round at trot or canter, turning this way and that, and every so often takes in one of the jumps. In each case, he rides carefully over the selected start point so as to be directly in line with the jump for the approach, and he then urges forward with determination and unambiguous commands. This is usually a most enjoyable stage both for horse and rider.

The opportunity can now be taken of jumping any suitable obstacle, such as a fallen tree-trunk or a ditch, that may happen to present itself during a cross-country hack. One may even venture out with the hunt. Remember that "the hunt" is a society with a long tradition of strict ceremonial, and you will not be welcome unless you are prepared to adhere to all the rules, written and unwritten. You will need to pay close attention to all the guidance given you by the friend who introduces you. Horses tend to get very excited when galloping along in company and it is as well to confirm from time to time that your horse still remembers how to stop. Most hunting accidents arise from riders being carried over-enthusiastically into awkward situations that are beyond the competence of that particular combination of horse and rider. Look ahead, be on your guard, take care – and enjoy yourself.

When riding through woodland remember that your horse may not bother to leave enough room for you. He will pass without hesitation under a low branch that just clears his withers and he will leave less than a couple of centimetres between his shoulder and a tree-trunk. The low branches you must steer round. Sometimes you can get through by lying forward over the withers with your head right down beside your horse's neck, but you may still be in trouble if the hood of your anorak catches in the tree; so go through very slowly.

Steering will also help to save your knees, and you can use

your leg-aids to increase the clearance, provided you have trained your horse in leg-yielding.

Crossing water

Horses differ a good deal in their reaction to ditches and streams. This is largely a matter of what they have become accustomed to. Some horses enjoy splashing about and will paw the water with enthusiasm. Some like to roll in water and the rider must be on his guard and urge the horse on strongly as soon as he shows the slightest inclination to bend his knees with his head down. The preparation for a roll is not quite the same as just putting his head down to drink. Usually, before actually bending his legs to go down for the roll, the horse will shuffle his feet to bring the hindfeet closer than usual behind the forefeet. To prevent the roll, pick his head up with a few brief strong pulls on the reins, urge the saddle forward with your seat, and drive on strongly with both legs and the crop.

Other horses are very reluctant to put a foot into water. It may be necessary to dismount and lead them in. Wade in yourself to show the horse that the footing is sound. Splash about a bit and get him used to the feel of the water splashing against his legs. You may need to talk to him and reassure him with caresses until he realises there is no danger. Finally you turn away and lead him on across the water while a friend urges him on from behind by throwing small pebbles aimed at his rump just beside the tail. Pebbles are better than a stick here as they are less likely to provoke kicking.

To get the horse used to ditches, you need to start with small dry ditches with good firm banks. Bring him to the edge and urge on with your legs. Resist any attempt he may make to turn his head to one side. It may be helpful to be given a lead over the ditch by a friend on another horse. Alternatively you can use the pebble trick mentioned above. The normal "startle reaction" to the impact of the pebbles is a sudden bending of the hindlegs. This is just what you need in the preparation for take-off. The startle reaction may have the effect of overbalancing the horse into the ditch and his natural response will be to jump it. The jump from a standing start is a very sudden movement. It is essential that you should let his head go forward freely without the reins jerking tight. You will need to be careful, as no doubt before the jump you will be holding the reins pretty firmly to prevent him from turning out to one side. It helps to have a neck strap to hang on to.

223

Types of obstacle

As confidence begins to be built up, the severity of the obstacles can be gradually increased. The cavalletti may be arranged in pairs instead of singly. The distances should be chosen carefully. With about 4 m between cavalletti, the horse will bounce once without taking a stride. The assistant should watch to see that the second obstacle is placed as near as possible halfway between take-off and landing for the second jump.

To leave room for one stride between the cavalletti they need to be about 7·5 m apart. For two strides, leave about 10·5 m. With these distances in mind, you can build up sequences of cavalletti, and you can then use such a sequence to lead up to a slightly higher jump. In the early stages watch carefully to see that the distances suit the horse so that he does not become unsettled through meeting one of the obstacles awkwardly. You can then go on to individual obstacles of different shapes and sizes, but there is no point in going much over 1 m in height except for competition purposes. If your horse jumps 1 m smoothly, he will not need to adjust his technique much even for the biggest obstacles that he can manage.

In the show-jumping arena you will be faced with jumps of many different kinds. Course-builders employ much ingenuity in providing variety in the appearance of obstacles, but basically there are two main types: uprights, in which the emphasis is on the height, as in a wall or a gate, and spreads, where the horse has to jump for distance as well as height. An example of a spread fence is the "oxer" which consists of a hedge with poles in front and behind. Often two poles are set up on separate supports, one behind the other, with no hedge in between. Or there may be a group of three or four poles, each with its own supports, set at progressively increasing heights one behind the other, like a staircase.

The space below the top poles in some of these jumps may be filled by other poles, either parallel or sloping to form a cross, or by planks or stout wooden boxes painted with bold geometric patterns or made to look like brickwork, stone arches, or the like. The individual jumps may be grouped into combinations such as a spread followed by an upright, or an upright followed by a spread, and there may be three obstacles in a combination. Where obstacles are not more than 12 m apart they together rank as a single obstacle.

224   The art of the course-builder consists partly in the selection

of the sequence and heights of the obstacles, but perhaps more importantly, in the placing of the obstacles in relation to one another and to the boundaries of the arena, particularly where the distances between obstacles are less than about 25 m, so that the landing from the first influences the stride with which the horse meets the second. Obstacles that interact in this way are said to be "at related distances".

All the obstacles in a show-jumping competition must be capable of being knocked down. In contrast, the obstacles in a cross-country course are solid and immovable. The fences are often combined with banks, ditches, and water. In some horse-trial courses, the competitors are offered a choice of route over a complex obstacle, such as a pair of long post-and-rail fences meeting at a narrow angle. Where there is some variation in the spacing of the elements along their length, as in this example, one may elect either to aim for a place where the fences are close together so as to jump two elements as one spread, or by taking a different track, one may take the two elements separately with a stride in between.

Competitive jumping

In order to perform well in any jumping competition it is essential to be able to select the best possible track between the obstacles. The competitor's defence against the wiles of the course-builder is to plan carefully while walking the course before the start of the competition. Here one has the opportunity to measure the distances between obstacles by pacing them out, and one can also work out where to make any necessary turns in order to leave a just adequate distance for the run-in to the next obstacle.

One can turn quickly after a jump, but it is a mistake to attempt a sharp turn during a run-in. On the other hand, many jumps can be negotiated safely when approached at an angle. Where the time to complete the course is important, as in a jump-off against the clock, it is usually better to ride carefully over the shortest possible track than to rush on madly and consequently be forced out into wide turns.

In preparation for competitive jumping one should set up practice obstacles of different kinds to accustom your horse to those you expect to meet in the next competition. Thus you will need spreads as well as uprights, and you should arrange some of them as combinations. Also, when you have worked out the distances your horse prefers, get used to measuring these distances in terms of your own paces. It is this kind of measurement you will have to rely on in competition. Remember that your horse uses different stride-lengths for different types of jump. You approach an upright with short bouncy strides, while a spread calls for longer strides and more speed over the ground. When dealing with combinations, the natural distance for a spread followed by an upright will be longer than that for an upright followed by a spread. The distances between the obstacles you meet in a competition will almost certainly be slightly different from the distances that are ''natural'' for your horse. You should be on the lookout for this when walking the course so that you will know beforehand where you need to lengthen the stride and where to hold back.

To get used to adjusting the stride between jumps, start with obstacles set up, say, 14, 17, and 20 m apart, or whatever distances near these values suit your horse. Work on these for a while, then move one of the obstacles a metre or so one way or the other and ride the combination again with the appropriate aids to adjust the stride. Again, pace out the new distances so that you will be able to anticipate the kinds of adjustment that are effective for the various distances.

Rushing fences

Some horses get so excited when they see a set of jumps that it is hard to hold them back. In this excited state they often do not judge the approaches to the jumps correctly and they will make many mistakes. To persuade them to take things more calmly, keep them down to a walk. Move in and out among the obstacles without jumping them. Occasionally walk right up to a jump and halt, as though it were a gate. When your horse has begun to settle, take him quietly into one of the jumps at the trot and at once bring him back to a walk and continue moving among the jumps as before. Eventually he will come to realise that, when he sees one of these contraptions with painted poles and so on, he is not necessarily expected to jump it right away, and he will be content to wait for your command.

It is also important to train him not to go rushing on like mad after landing from a jump. In a competition it may be vital to be able to slow up promptly in order to turn toward the next obstacle. It will help your horse considerably if you yourself start looking toward the next fence as soon as you are over the last one. He will feel the change in the distribution of your weight and this will tell him which way to turn even while he is still in the air. He can then adjust his landing to suit the direction of the next turn.

One effect of over-enthusiasm on the part of the horse is that he may tend to get too close to the jump before taking off, particularly if he is comparatively inexperienced. To help him to learn the proper distance for take-off you can put a pole on the ground in front of the jump. The distance between this pole and the jump should be about equal to the height of the jump.

Further development

It is not appropriate in a book of this kind to go into too much detail about the finer points of advanced competitive work. Once you are launched into competitions you will find yourself learning rapidly by experience, provided you have taught yourself the fundamentals correctly and do not have too many bad habits to handicap your development. You will also inevitably come into contact with other competitors, with their coaches, and with judges. You will not lack for advice. Your problem is more likely to be that of selecting which advice is relevant to your own case. Do not change just because someone else has a different technique from yours. By all means try out other people's ideas, but make up your own mind. Decide what suits you and what suits your own horse. Once you have established an understanding with your horse, it would be a shame to disturb it for a casual remark by a stranger not familiar with your own special problems.

6 Special Movements

Preparation

A rider who has mastered the movements described in earlier chapters will be well prepared to start competitive work in any of the equestrian arts that he may choose, from Pony Club games and gymkhanas to show-jumping, dressage, and horse-trials for combined training (eventing). There are, however, certain interesting additional movements that are called for only in the more advanced dressage tests and which can be regarded as "display items", rather than as part of the basic training of the horse and rider. These movements – the pirouette, the passage, and the piaffer – present a particular challenge to the rider's skill. Even if one never intends actually to offer these movements in competition, one can still derive a good deal of entertainment and pleasure from attempting them.

An essential preliminary to these special movements is that the horse should have been trained to keep his nose well in without being "overbent" and without leaning on the bit (*Figure 6.4*). The rider should have practised urging his horse on by the action of his seat-bones, preferably without at the same time squeezing with the legs. The combined effect of this preparatory work is that the rider can obtain substantial impulsion without using his legs and with only a very light touch on the rein. The horse is ready to respond enthusiastically to the least indication by the rider's hand or leg.

The reason for practising the independence of seat and legs is that the legs will be needed for control of the horse's hindquarters. It is an advantage to be able to maintain the impulsion without confusing the horse by using the legs for forward drive at the same time as you are trying to give delicate indications for lateral movement. Practise bracing your back and driving forward with your seat-bones while at the same time holding your lower legs away from the horse's sides. As a further refinement, try reducing the pressure of your knees against the saddle while urging on with your seat, the lower legs still being held away from the horse's sides. The aim is to drive the horse forward into the bit. He does not actually accelerate forward because you are continuing to restrain him with your pressure on the rein. You should feel him ready to

228

surge forward instantly the moment you give a little with the rein.

Also practise lateral work (*Chapter 4*), particularly the turn on the haunches and the half-pass. It is an advantage to be able to perform both the half-pass and the shoulder-in at the collected canter as well as at the trot.

Spurs and double bridle

The B.H.S. Dressage Rules prescribe that spurs are obligatory for all tests of Medium standard and above, while they are permitted for other tests. The double bridle is forbidden at Preliminary and Novice standard, optional for Elementary and Medium and obligatory for tests at Advanced standard and above, such as Prix St Georges, Intermédaire I and II, Olympic, and Grand Prix Special. It should be clear from these provisions that the spurs and double bridle are instruments for fine control such as are needed for producing movements of extreme precision. They are definitely not weapons for violent coercion, despite the rather terrifying appearance of some of the specimens that have come down to us from the Middle Ages.

Before attempting to use spurs, the rider must be absolutely certain that he can keep his heels well away from the horse. Accidental application of the spurs can produce sudden violent reactions and may even cause injury to the horse. In preparation, the rider should get used to riding with rather long stirrup leathers. He should still be able to have his heel below the line of the sole of his foot and his knee can be nearly straight. This is the natural leg-position when riding without stirrups; it is not an appropriate leg-position for jumping. With this attitude of the legs it is possible to use the spur very gently, just stirring the hairs of the coat. There are now several places where your leg can act against the horse: seat-bones, knee, inside calf, and spur. Each gives a different kind of message.

The spur is used to add emphasis to the leg-aids, particularly when these are used with the "lifting" action like that used when riding over trotting-poles. The effect is to encourage the horse to lift his hindleg higher on the side indicated by the spur. It is sometimes necessary to judge the timing of the application of the spur rather carefully to produce the best effect.

When you first start to use the double bridle, it will be sensible to leave off the curb chain. This gives the horse a 229

Figure 6.1

Fillis system for managing the reins to a double bridle. "The reins should occupy the same respective positions in the hand, as the snaffle and curb do in the mouth, namely, the snaffle reins should be above the curb reins." Fillis himself advocated using all four fingers to separate the reins (as in *Figure 3.21*). Here the rider is using the modified grip (of *Figure 4.42*), the curb rein below the little finger and the snaffle rein between second and third fingers.

chance to get used to the feel of the extra bit in his mouth and it gives the rider the opportunity to get used to handling two pairs of reins without any risk of overdoing the action of the curb.

There are two systems for holding the two sets of reins.

The "Fillis" system is based on the idea that a tilt of the hand, thumb forward or back, will produce a corresponding tilt of the cheekpiece of the bit. The curb rein is accordingly passed under the little finger while the snaffle rein lies over the forefinger and is gripped by the thumb (*Figure 6.1*). Thus the free parts of the two reins cross the palm of the hand in opposite directions.

In the "English" system the curb rein is held above the snaffle rein, being gripped with first and second fingers only, while the snaffle rein is in the normal position below the third finger. The two reins are separated by the ring finger, or by the ring finger and little finger together (*Figure 6.2*) if not too much force is going to be needed on the rein. The free parts of both reins run forward together over the forefinger where they are gripped by the pressure of the thumb.

If the curb rein is held above the snaffle rein, the finger movements that the rider has learned when using the snaffle alone will still work as before. When additional curb action is needed, this can be produced by turning the hand in the horizontal plane to bring the fingernails nearer to the rider's chest. This is a fairly natural movement to make in response to a situation calling for firmer control of the horse's head. In the Fillis system, by contrast, a completely new set of finger movements has to be learned for the management of the double bridle because those fingers that formerly played upon the snaffle rein now bear against the curb rein instead.

When the reins are to be taken together into one hand, the forefinger of that hand is used to separate the curb and snaffle reins received from the other side. The two curb reins are now adjacent, separated only by the middle finger, the two snaffle reins being to the outside, one on each side, separated by the whole width of the hand. The rider can steer with the snaffle rein by moving his hand so that the thumb is carried either further forward or further back, and he can bring on both curb reins together by rolling his hand to bring the fingernails nearer to the chest.

By this stage in the rider's development he will have become quite used to adjusting the relative position of his hands on the rein, allowing the rein to slide a little through the fingers, or

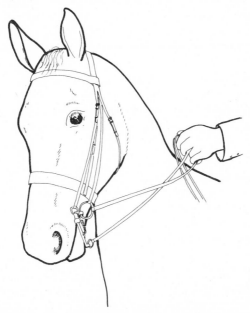

Figure 6.2
"English" system for managing the reins to a double bridle. The curb rein is above the snaffle rein. The finger movements for controlling the snaffle bit are thus the same as when using a snaffle alone.

231

taking up rein, as required. It should not take him long to get used to the extra rein and to adjust the two reins in his fingers to give more purchase on the snaffle or more on the curb, according to the needs of the moment. The curb chain can now be fitted. Be sure that the chain is correctly twisted so that all the links lie flat against the horse's chin, and adjust the length so that the chain is drawn tight when the cheekpieces of the bit are at about 45° to the line of the horse's mouth.

Most of the control of the horse by the rider's hands is produced with the snaffle rein. The curb rein is used occasionally to remind the horse to keep his nose well in so that the snaffle rein can work at the most effective angle, across the line of the horse's jaw. The curb can also be used to ask the horse to pay attention when he is day-dreaming. It should not be used with excessive force because this will just stimulate the horse to resist and his mouth may be bruised in the ensuing battle.

Pirouette at walk

The track of the footfalls in the pirouette is the same as for the turn on the haunches. The horse pivots on one of the hindlegs and the forelegs move laterally, the outside foreleg crossing in front of the inside foreleg. The turn on the haunches is performed from the halt, one step at a time. In contrast, the pirouette is performed in the course of a forward progression without interruption of the cadence of the footfalls. It can be performed at walk, trot, canter, or piaffer. It is permissible for the hindfeet to move slightly to the side, instead of pivoting precisely, but if they do, they must move on a very small circle in the same direction as the forefeet (*Figure 4.22*).

Because of the marked change in the speed over the ground at the start of the turn, it is essential to have plenty of impulsion in order to preserve the rhythm of the footfalls. For this reason it is not appropriate to check the forward motion simply by pulling on the reins. What is needed is an increased drive with braced back, as in the half-halt. The horse is driven into the restraining hand so that his weight is thrown more onto the haunches. The rider assists this shift of weight by moving his shoulders back slightly and raising his hands.

As soon as the horse shortens his stride, the rider carries both hands over toward the side to which the horse is to turn. Thus, if the horse is being asked to pirouette to the right, the rider gives opening rein with the right hand and indirect rein in front of the withers with the left hand. The horse's nose is moved slightly to the right and the rider applies his left leg over the girth to encourage the lateral movement of the forelegs. The rider's right leg is held in readiness to check any inclination for the horse to step sideways with the inside hindleg.

If the horse shows signs of stepping back, both legs are brought on and the seat-bones urge the saddle forward, while the tension in the reins is relaxed for a moment and then taken up again. Throughout the whole manoeuvre the rider has to be supremely alert to gauge at what moment, and in which direction, the horse is beginning to shift his weight over his feet, and to judge just when he is about to move each of his legs. The indications that the rider makes with his hands and with his legs are brief and very precisely timed so as to influence each stage of the horse's movement individually.

The first attempts at the pirouette can be made at the walk. Ride a 10 m circle in collected walk, urging the horse forward with seat and knees rather than with the lower leg. Bring a little of your weight onto each knee in turn to emphasise the natural swing of the shoulders. With the rein you work against the forward and backward swing of the head but encourage the lateral swing. This should produce short steps with the feet lifted well up at each step. Draw the outside leg back and give indirect rein behind the withers with the outer hand, the left if the turn is to the right. These aids should produce the "haunches-in" position with the hindlegs tracking on a smaller circle than the forelegs.

Eventually, of course, you will be asking the horse to make a larger movement to the side with his forelegs than with his hindlegs. The object of starting with the inward movement of the haunches is to ensure that the horse is not tempted to step outward with the hindfeet; this would lead to a spin instead of to the pirouette aimed at. Once he gets used to the manoeuvre, the emphasis on the initial haunches-in can be reduced until the pirouette is finally performed by moving the forehand alone.

After establishing the haunches-in, bring the left hand over a little further to give indirect rein in front of the withers, give opening rein with the right hand, and bring the left leg forward again onto the girth. The horse should now be stepping into the circle slightly with his forelegs, making a half-pass but continuing round the circle. The rein-aids to move his forequarters to the right should be given just as he is lifting his right foreleg and again just as he is lifting his left foreleg. The action of the rider's left leg is to ask the horse to step diagonally toward the right with his left hindleg. The rider may need to keep readjusting the point where he applies this leg-aid, moving his leg forward or back according to the response he feels in the horse.

Moving inward in half-pass gradually reduces the size of the circle. Do not attempt too much all at once because this is a difficult exercise for the horse. With patience and much practice you will eventually be able to bring the circle right in until the horse is pivoting on the inside hindleg, the hoof being replaced on the same spot after each step. When both rider and horse are familiar with what is required you can start to ask for the pirouette from a straight progression at the walk. For this stage it helps to have a high solid fence or a wall to work against, like the wall of an indoor riding-school. Walk a straight track parallel to the wall (*Figure 6.3*) and move into the renvers position, that is to say, a half-pass with the haunches toward the wall, at about one horse's length away from the wall. Then give a half-halt and turn in toward the wall in a half-pirouette, coming out into travers along the wall.

When the half-pirouette against the wall is being executed smoothly either to the right or to the left, you can ask for a full pirouette during a straight walk without the support of the wall. The point of using the wall in the early trials is that it prevents the horse from moving forward after you have started the turn, and this gives you a chance to concentrate on the indications for the lateral components of the manoeuvre.

In particular you need to be very tactful in your management of the hindquarters. If you are too energetic with your left leg and not quite quick enough with your right, the horse will move his hindlegs to the side, producing a full pass instead of a pirouette. If, on the other hand, you are too energetic with your right leg, the horse will spin, the hindquarters moving to the left while the forequarters move to the right. The horse finds it much easier to spin than to perform the pirouette correctly. If you once allow him to make a habit of it, you may later find this habit extremely hard to eradicate.

In practising difficult manoeuvres like the pirouette it is essential to avoid confusing the horse. This means that you should not spend too much time repeating the same thing over and over again in the same session. If you do so there is the risk that the horse may be learning the wrong things, practising his mistakes as well as the moves you want him to make. Reward

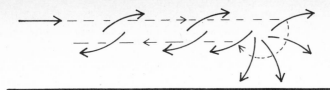

Figure 6.3
Developing the half-pirouette against the wall. Renvers on the left rein about one horse's length from the wall. Half-halt and turn in toward the wall. Emerge into travers on the right rein.

him with caresses and by making much of him whenever he does any part of the manoeuvre correctly. Then go on to do something quite different, leaving the horse time to forget those wrong moves of his which you did not reward.

Your own technique for influencing the movements of the individual limbs of the horse can be developed by further practice of the step-by-step turn on the haunches and of the rein-back balance. Both of these contain elements that are used in the pirouette. Also use these manoeuvres to practise "tuning in", so to speak, to the feel of the movements of the horse's muscles as he shifts his weight and prepares to lift one leg or another.

Pirouette at trot

The preparation for the pirouette at the trot is essentially similar to that for the pirouette at the walk except that even more impulsion is required to keep the trot going when the circles are getting smaller and smaller. The rein-aids for the lateral movement of the forequarters are applied as the horse is rising on the right diagonal (for a turn to the right). The horse then moves his right foreleg out sideways while it is in the air, and the consequent shift of weight has the effect that the next thrust of the left foreleg will push the forequarters to the right. At the same time the rein gives a slight check to the forward movement to make sure that the right foreleg goes out to the side rather than forward. Meanwhile a leg-aid on the left encourages the horse to reach forward with the left hindleg.

When the horse is rising on the left diagonal, you relax the rein pressure slightly as well as giving the indication to move the forequarters to the right. This asks the horse to reach over with the left foreleg to cross in front of the right foreleg. The pressure of the rider's left knee and leg encourages the lateral movement of the forequarters so that after the right hindleg has been lifted it will be set down again on the same spot.   235

Care has to be taken here again to balance the vigour of the leg-aids on the two sides so as to avoid letting the horse go into a spin. It will be preferable to accept a small amount of forward progression with the inside hindleg rather than to permit any lateral movement away from the point on which the horse is supposed to be pivoting.

As before, start with the half-pass in decreasing circles, then try the half-pirouette toward the wall, and finally the full pirouette during a straight-line progression without the aid of a wall. The pirouette at the trot presents a considerable challenge to the rider's skill, particularly as he may need to use "lifting" leg-aids to maintain the trot while at the same time using his legs to control the lateral movement of the hindquarters. For competitive dressage purposes all the aids have to be given very discreetly so as to be barely visible to the onlooker. It is also required that the same cadence of the footfalls shall continue throughout the manoeuvre without any interruption or hesitation in the rhythm.

Pirouette at canter

The canter pirouette is the most spectacular as well as the most satisfying manoeuvre that can be performed by the ordinary rider without recourse to the highly-specialised training routines needed for Haute École or for the circus repertoire. The first requirement is a very active collected canter. This is obtained by the combination of a strongly braced back with a carefully-adjusted rhythmic action on the reins.

The rider should "sit deep" into the saddle, driving on with his seat rather than with his legs. The rider's back has to be kept supple to absorb the impact as his weight comes down into the saddle at each stride. The seat-bones are thrust forward just as you begin to feel the increasing pressure against your seat. The legs are relaxed with the knees gently touching the saddle. The shoulders are squared back to open the chest and the head is held erect. The rein action is quite subtle. In the first stages of collection, the hands are working against the swing of the horse's head, without at any time allowing the rein to go slack. As the horse responds and brings his nose in, the rider increases the pressure on the reins and begins to encourage the head swing again, this time lifting his hands a little at each stride and putting particular emphasis on the phase where the horse's nose is moving toward the saddle. The aim of this action of the rein is to ask the horse to arch his neck and to lift his head without at the same time poking his nose out. This movement of the horse's head alters the horse's balance to throw more weight on the hindquarters and to lighten the forehand. The continued urge of the rider's seat also encourages the horse to reach forward with his hindlegs so that he rounds his back and bounces higher and higher at each stride while making less and less ground forward.

When you have achieved a really bouncy collected canter, turn in to ride a 10 m circle. With your outside leg ask the horse to bring his haunches in and then move your hands over to get him to make a half-pass round the circle. It may help to lift the outside hand a little higher than the inside hand. With the half-pass you gradually decrease the size of the circle. Do not be in too much of a hurry or the horse will get excited and begin to resist.

In the early stages, before he has worked out what it is you want him to do, the horse is liable to try something he has done before, like a full pass, a spin, or even a rear. You must be careful to give him no opportunity to learn that one of these unwanted movements is rewarded by a relaxation in the vigour of your commands. It is better for you to stop short before he has completed his manoeuvre, and to allow him to relax at a moment of your own choosing, rather than to persist until he breaks away and then to let him get away with it.

Another disadvantage of attempting too tight a turn too early at the canter is that the horse may not have learned to lift his feet neatly. He can strike one leg against another and cut himself. This will be an irrelevant punishment which will interfere with the smooth progress of his training. Uncertainty leads to excitement, particularly if the rider is obviously trying to say something emphatic and the horse doesn't understand what it is that is being asked of him. Horses do not learn quickly when they are excited. They keep trying moves that have been appropriate in previous moments of excitement and they do not pay too much attention to the rider's commands; they just try frantically to escape from the tense situation by one means or another. Naturally any move that allows them to break free and relax will be tried again on future occasions when the rider is trying to teach something new.

After the decreasing circles, try the half-pirouette toward the wall, first on one hand and then on the other. You should then be able to produce a full pirouette at the canter on a straight line without the help of the wall. Ask a friend to watch the horse's hindlegs carefully and to tell you if the horse is not pivoting accurately. Steer the lateral movement as necessary by adjusting the position at which you apply your outside leg. Bring the leg forward to encourage the sideways movement of the forelegs and move the leg back behind the girth to regulate the movement of the hindquarters. Use the inside leg to restrain the horse from stepping into the turn with his inside hindleg.

Passage and piaffer

After you have succeeded in keeping the trot and canter going while the speed of forward progression is gradually being reduced for the start of the pirouette, you will have taught yourself most of the commands needed for the passage and piaffer. These movements are closely related to the collected trot. The horse tosses his weight from one diagonal pair of legs to the other, just as in the trot. The difference from the trot lies in the height of the spring at each step. At passage and piaffer the horse springs so high, and consequently spends so long in the air at each step, that he has time to make elegant display movements with his feet. When the feet are first lifted, the

Figure 6.4
Piaffer. An elevated, springy trot, without forward progression. The raised feet perform elegant display movements.

hooves are tucked right up, with strongly bent fetlocks and pasterns (*Figure 6.4*). Then, before the descent proper, the hooves are pointed at the ground with a sort of hesitation. The horse appears to be hanging in the air at each step before the legs are extended in the preparation for landing.

The expression "piaffer" is used for this specially elevated and collected trot, with the characteristic display movements of the feet, when it is performed on the spot, without forward progression. If the horse moves over the ground, with the same elevated gait, the movement is referred to as a "passage". This very elevated springy trot, with arched neck and head tucked in, is part of the natural display behaviour of the horse. Often one will see high-spirited horses displaying to one another in this way when they are first let out from stable to paddock on a bright spring morning. They appear to be proudly showing off their vigour and their feeling of well-being. From time to time they hoist their tails like pennants, make snaking movements with head and neck, and suddenly take off in short high-speed sprints and chasing games. It is a most exhilarating sight. They are so obviously enjoying themselves.

To produce the elevated action of passage and piaffer the rider must sit deep in the saddle with a supple back so that he can urge the saddle forward at each step to keep up the impulsion. His hands are very still, but with some encouragement to the lateral sway of the horse's head by curling and uncurling the fingers on the two sides alternately, tightening one rein a little while relaxing the other, and then changing over at each stride in time with the horse's natural head-movement. The rider's legs hang at their full length, either with long stirrup leathers or without stirrups altogether. Spurs may help. The springy action of the trot is encouraged by using "lifting" leg-aids. In addition, an extra tickle is given with the spur on each side in turn just as the hindleg of that side is beginning to develop its thrust. The tickle tells the horse to push a bit harder with that hindleg so as to have time to lift the leg higher, this being the natural response to any leg-aid. The timing is rather crucial and the rider may need to experiment a little before he gets it right. He will feel the difference when the horse lifts his feet properly because of the play of the muscles when the horse is making the additional pointing movement with his feet that distinguishes the passage from the ordinary collected trot.

The various lateral movements described earlier (*Chapter 4*), such as the shoulder-in and half-pass, can all be performed at the passage, as can the rein-back. Indeed the piaffer can be regarded as a balance between forward progression and rein-back. Turns on the spot can be executed at piaffer – turn on the forehand, turn on the haunches, and finally the pirouette.

When the rider has taught himself, and his horse, all these various manoeuvres, he will have the great satisfaction of knowing that he can feel what the horse is telling him through the muscular adjustments that precede every movement, and that he can also indicate to the horse just what movements to make at any given moment. Both horse and rider will derive long-continued pleasure from the intimate relationship that develops through such an interchange of messages, which is truly a conversation between friends.